Shell
Education

D1628531

Promote READING Gains

with Differentiated Instruction

Laura Robb, M.S.Ed.

David L. Harrison, M.S.

Timothy Rasinski, Ph.D.

Consultant

Leslie Reichert, M.A.T.

Publishing Credits

Corinne Burton, M.A.Ed., *President* and *Publisher*
Aubrie Nielsen, M.S.Ed., *EVP of Content Development*
Kyra Ostendorf, M.Ed., *Publisher, professional books*
Véronique Bos, *VP of Creative*
Cathy Hernandez, *Senior Content Manager*
Laureen Gleason, *Editor*
David Slayton, *Assistant Editor*
Fabiola Sepulveda, *Junior Art Director*

Image Credits: photos courtesy Laura Robb; all other images from iStock and/or Shutterstock

A division of Teacher Created Materials

5482 Argosy Avenue
Huntington Beach, CA 92649
www.tcmpub.com/shell-education
ISBN 978-8-7659-0342-1
© 2024 Shell Educational Publishing, Inc.

With love to my grandchildren, Lucas and Helena, and to
my great-grandchildren, Amelia and Liam.

—Laura Robb

To Jennifer Jackson Harrison, more than a master teacher,
more than a beloved daughter-in-law, one of the bravest
people I've ever known.

With love forever,
—David L. Harrison

For all teachers who strive to make teaching reading an art
as well as a science.

—Tim Rasinski

Table of Contents

List of Lessons

Foreword

Whenever I open a book aimed at improving instructional practice, I judge it on how useful it will be for teachers who will ask:

- Will this book help me reach and teach my students?
- Do the authors have real-life experiences that will shine a light on my own practice?
- Are they talking about the science, or research, that supports their work?
- But are they also talking about the art, or heart, of teaching?

You hold in your hands the answers to all these questions (yes, yes, yes, and YES!).

As educators, it is our collective responsibility to ensure that every student is equipped with the necessary tools to navigate the world of words and harness the power of reading. Reading is not a one-size-fits-all process; it is a deeply personal and individualized experience. The methods and techniques employed to engage and inspire students to become readers must be adaptable, inclusive, and responsive to diverse learning needs. We recognize that every student comes to us with unique backgrounds, strengths, and challenges. By embracing this diversity and celebrating the richness it brings to our classrooms, we can create an inclusive reading environment where every child feels valued and empowered.

Laura Robb, David L. Harrison, and Timothy Rasinski embark on a transformative journey, exploring the vast landscape of literacy and revealing innovative strategies to help all students become readers. Drawing from extensive research, practical experiences, and the collective wisdom of educators and experts in the field, they present a comprehensive guide that empowers educators to enhance skills while nurturing a love for reading. You will delve into various aspects of reading instruction, from the foundational building blocks to fostering critical thinking and analytical skills. You will explore the importance of word study, vocabulary development, fluency, and comprehension strategies, through practical tips and evidence-based approaches that help students navigate the complex world of words. And you will have at hand a toolbelt of ideas for nudging along every learner you encounter.

Laura, David, and Tim's thoughtfully crafted book provides an exciting opportunity to make real change in the classroom. With excellent guidance, the authors provide the framework needed to plan work driven by the students, thus keeping them engaged while providing a window into their thinking and skills. Anchored with David's thought-provoking poems and short texts, students are provided a variety of ways to enter "into" the text. Vocabulary, comprehension, word work, and fluency all play a part. Tim's well-known word ladders follow, making vocabulary work fun and memorable. This research-based activity that Tim uses in his university reading clinic is a favorite among teachers and students alike. Laura's work with students struggling to keep pace with their peers is the groundwork that supports the many well-defined and easily accomplished lessons. Rubrics and assessment guides provide opportunities to see growth in students' abilities and engagement.

In today's debates of "best ways" to teach reading we often see a narrow picture of what students should be spending time doing. Laura, David, and Tim open the lens, addressing the many skills a reader needs to be confident and independent, and give each student the chance to unlock the doors to knowledge, imagination, and endless possibilities through the gift of reading.

You will also find the collegial nature of teaching front and center. The authors suggest ways to engage with colleagues and help create a professional conversation from which both teachers and students benefit. How powerful it will be for teachers to sit together to discuss, analyze, and plan. This supportive structure emphasizes the importance of collaboration and community in creating a culture of readers. When teachers engage in reflective practice, individually and collectively, they continuously improve their teaching. They reflect on their lessons, share insights, and seek feedback from colleagues to refine their instructional approaches and enhance student learning. Each chapter of this book develops these collegial relationships that will create a supportive and nurturing atmosphere.

We stand at a critical juncture, where the power to shape the future lies within our hands. Let us seize this opportunity to build a world where all students can make reading gains through instruction aimed at their specific needs. Let us embark on this journey with Laura, David, and Tim as we step toward a future where every student is empowered as a reader.

—Mary Jo Fresch, Ph.D.
Academy Professor and Professor Emeritus
College of Education and Human Ecology
The Ohio State University

Preface: The Science and Art of Teaching Reading

Over the past several years, an emphasis on reading instruction has emerged called *the Science of Reading* (SOR). The Science of Reading refers to scientific knowledge about how people learn to read and argues that reading instruction should be guided by this science. The genesis for this approach can be traced back to the National Reading Panel (2000), a group of literacy experts who were assigned the task of identifying the science-verified components of reading that are necessary for children to become proficient readers. Nearly every teacher of reading has since become familiar with those components—phonemic awareness, phonics or word decoding, fluency, vocabulary, and comprehension. The Science of Reading is based, to a large extent, on scientific research into the competencies that must be mastered to achieve proficiency in reading. However, like a lot of research, SOR does not provide much direction into how those competencies should be taught to students (Shanahan 2021). Very often, the implication for instruction is that the SOR competencies be taught using approaches that are direct, systematic, and, for students who are struggling, intensive. How instruction actually plays out in classrooms depends, in large part, on school districts' background knowledge and philosophy of teaching reading as well as that of the teachers who present reading lessons to their students.

Moving Toward the Art and Science of Reading Instruction

We would take Shanahan's argument a bit further to suggest that we also need scientifically verified approaches to instruction that are authentic, aesthetic, and that give teachers freedom to respond to each student's unique needs by combining their creativity and educational knowledge to design such instruction. Although it may be easier to define a *science* of reading instruction than it is to define an *art* of reading instruction, there are three characteristics or principles that make reading instruction artful: authenticity, aesthetics, and creativity (Young, Paige, and Rasinski 2022).

Principle 1, Authenticity: Reading instruction should look like reading-related activities that are done in real life—outside the classroom. We want students to make the connections between what they are doing in their classroom with what they see happening beyond the classroom walls. When teachers help students understand that the goal of phonemic awareness, phonics, and fluency practice is to read expressively with automaticity and understanding, then practicing these skills is authentic because they lead to reading well, an experience people young and old do in real life.

Principle 2, Aesthetics: By *aesthetics*, we refer to the work of Louise Rosenblatt (1978) who argued that reading should be both efferent and aesthetic. At the risk of oversimplifying, efferent reading is essentially reading to learn or to educate the mind. Aesthetic reading, on the other hand, is reading for beauty and/or to touch the heart. It seems that reading instruction in many schools has become increasingly focused on the retention of facts and information from the reading. While we acknowledge the importance of recalling facts and information from reading, we also see the need for reading to be aesthetic, touching our hearts and minds.

In this book, the poems and short texts by David L. Harrison can stir powerful feelings in the hearts of your students, raising their awareness of the wonders in the natural world and how people go about creating change in their communities. Harrison's texts can inspire students to be more aware of the environment and develop a keen understanding of why some species have become endangered as well as why some people need food, clothing, shelter, and friendship.

Principle 3, Creativity: While the science of reading provides guidance for the overall aims and approaches to reading instruction, artfulness allows teachers the freedom to use their creativity and knowledge of students' reading skill to deliver instruction in ways that meet the individual needs of students. Moreover, artful instruction should also allow students freedom to express themselves in creative ways.

How This Book Aligns with the Science and Art of Teaching Reading

This book features differentiated lessons that are based on original poems or short texts by David L. Harrison. These lessons integrate the science of reading by including word work that's appropriate for students in grades 3, 4, and 5—word work that grows out of the poems and short texts. This word work offers students tools for reading with expression, fluency, and depth of comprehension. In addition, you'll find that with artful instruction, the differentiated lessons can help students improve their comprehension using four higher-order reading strategies: *visualize, infer, draw conclusions*, and *compare/contrast*.

Word Study in the Lessons

The differentiated lessons offer students practice with word study that can boost their reading, thinking, discussing, and vocabulary. Students will use word families to develop analogous thinking, the ability to transfer word knowledge by being able to pronounce new words using known words. Additional phonics and word meaning practice occurs with the word ladders students complete in their lessons and during teacher-led focus lessons. Here's a menu of some of the word work students complete in the context of the poems and short texts in the differentiated lessons:

- **Synonym and antonym** study is an excellent way to build students' vocabulary.

- **Multiple forms of words** enable students to understand a set of related words and how each form works.

- **Word families** offer opportunities to develop analogous thinking and improve decoding.

- **Figurative language** shows students how writers' tools such as simile and metaphor can enhance visualization and comprehension.

If you have students who have difficulty decoding or have gaps in their knowledge of phonics, word families, and word patterns, then continue with the phonics or word study program you're presently using by setting aside time in your reading block or adjusting the lessons to gain additional time.

- **Connotations**, the associations students have with a specific word or phrase, can improve comprehension, visualization, and build their vocabulary.

- **Context clues** practice helps learners use clues in a text to figure out the meaning of an unfamiliar word.

- **Word ladders** are not only engaging and motivating but they invite students to think about phonics and the meanings of words.

The Art of Comprehension in the Lessons

Even when decoding and fluency are strong, there's no guarantee that reading comprehension automatically follows (Duke, Ward, Pearson 2021). To comprehend texts, children need background knowledge, vocabulary, an understanding of text features and structures, and the ability to apply strategies such as making inferences, drawing conclusions, comparing/contrasting, and visualizing. When readers reflect upon and critically analyze the facts in a text, comprehension becomes artful, moving readers beyond recall of information to using facts and details to create new understandings, think critically, learn about the experiences of others, and consider their own roles as responsible contributors to society.

How the Lessons Are Organized

The differentiated lessons are presented in chapters 8 through 11. Each chapter features one of the following reading strategies: visualizing, inferring, drawing conclusions, and comparing and contrasting. The chapters begin with focus lessons presented by the teacher. The focus lessons are followed by the differentiated lessons.

Teacher-led Focus Lessons

There are two parts to each focus lesson. The first part asks the teacher to model artful comprehension and application of reading strategies, while the second part focuses on word work. After teachers model and think aloud, they invite students to practice using the focus lesson's short text.

Differentiated Student Lessons

After the focus lessons, students will partner with classmates for the differentiated lessons. Each lesson includes a new poem or text, and students will experience several comprehension-building strategies.

- **Students practice expressive reading** with their partners using poems and short texts.
- **Rereading** is built into the differentiated lessons, supporting and improving students' understanding, recall, and fluency with multiple readings of all or parts of a text.
- **Conversations about reading** occur when students use prompts and questions about a poem or short text.
- **Notebook writing** invites students to write to show their understanding of a reading strategy, to demonstrate their ability to think critically, and to complete the word work.

The texts in the lessons are different for readers who are below grade level, near and at grade level, and above grade level. When students can read and recall information from texts, they can improve their comprehension through discussions and critical thinking as well as successfully complete word work. Text readability, developed by using the Flesch-Kincaid readability measures, ensures that students, with support from their partners, can read and recall details in the short texts and the directions for discussion, word work, and writing in notebooks.

Formative Assessment and Intervention

Formative assessment includes observations while students work and during conferences with students, listening to partner discussions, and reading students' notebook writing. The purpose of formative assessment is to collect information that informs teachers' instructional decisions.

Intervention decisions occur after students complete a set of lessons and the teacher has gathered and reviewed information from multiple formative assessments. Chapter 6 details how to plan, schedule, and implement interventions for *all* students.

The thoughtfully developed texts and lessons provided in this book combine the science and art of reading with the goal of improving students' depth of comprehension and enlarging their reading, writing, thinking, and discussing vocabularies.

Overview of the Book

This resource is organized into two parts: Part I (chapters 1–6) provides information that supports the differentiated lessons in Part II (chapters 7–11).

Chapter 1, Promoting and Nurturing Reading Gains, introduces the structure of the differentiated lessons and explains how they align with a four-part reading framework: daily teacher read-alouds, instructional reading, writing about reading, and independent reading. This chapter also explores three types of instructional reading, the importance of volume in reading, creating culturally relevant classroom libraries, the benefits of teaching with short texts, and conferring.

Chapter 2, The Differentiated Lessons: Getting Started, presents suggestions for effectively using the lessons. You'll explore why working with one or a small group of colleagues is helpful, preplanning and then working together on lessons for the same reading strategy. In addition, you'll review how to organize students into three groups: developing readers and students who are at- and above-grade-level readers. You'll find tips for presenting teacher-led focus lessons and using formative assessments to inform instructional decisions, and suggestions for moving forward after completing the first set of differentiated lessons.

Chapter 3, Reader's Notebooks, discusses the benefits of notebooks for students' reading progress and offers suggestions for inviting students to respond to read-alouds, focus lessons, and short texts. You'll see how students' notebook writing informs your understanding of their reading growth. You'll also explore how your cold writing helps students develop their mental model of specific kinds of notebook writing.

Chapter 4, Practice and Performance, discusses routines for organizing the practice and performance of texts such as poems and reader's theater scripts. This chapter incorporates Tim Rasinski's research on practice and performance, which shows how students can improve their fluency, expressive reading, comprehension, and vocabulary. The chapter includes five poems by David L. Harrison that can be used for practice and performance in your classroom.

Chapter 5, Student-Led Discussions, provides a road map of the elements of successful student-led discussions and explains how to use the fishbowl technique to build students' mental models of these types of discussions. The chapter includes guidelines to follow when students discuss poems or short texts from the lessons in this book.

Chapter 6, Assessment-Driven Interventions, discusses the kinds of formative assessment suggested by the differentiated lessons and how to use the information gathered to organize students into three groups for additional practice and support: (1) students who require scaffolding and/or reteaching, (2) those in need of some extra practice, and (3) an enrichment group. Sample schedules for 60-minute and 90-minute daily literacy blocks demonstrate how you can work with each group within the course of a week.

Chapters 1 through 6 each end with a section called "Take Time for Reflective Conversations," which includes reflection questions you can use on your own or with your colleagues about the content in the chapter.

Chapter 7, Using the Differentiated Lessons, provides an overview of the lessons, including information about how to introduce and use the lesson components.

Chapters 8–11 present the differentiated lessons for grades 3, 4, and 5. The chapters begin with information and teaching tips about a reading strategy (visualize, infer, draw conclusions, or compare-and-contrast) and include two focus lessons presented by the teacher. The focus lessons are followed by the differentiated lessons, which invite students to analyze and think critically by interpreting what they've learned, to write about their learning in their notebooks, and to complete word work.

Acknowledgments

This book sits on the shoulders of all the students I've learned with and the teachers I've coached, and I thank them, for they've taught me so much! Special thanks to the educators who presented a set of lessons to different grades and provided me with valuable feedback, students' notebook writing, and photographs: Lee Slavin, third-grade teacher at Powhatan School in Boyce, Virginia; Logan Fisher, literacy coach at Glens Falls Public Schools, for her work with fourth graders in Brandie Breault's class; and Wanda Waters, fifth-grade teacher in Maryland. Sincere thanks to my coauthor Tim Rasinski, who read all my drafts and offered excellent edits and revisions, and to poet David L. Harrison, who composed engaging and motivating poems and short texts for the teachers' focus lessons and the differentiated lessons in chapters 8 through 11. It's been so rewarding and delightful to work with Tim and David on a book that we believe can move readers at diverse instructional levels forward. To our editor, Cathy Hernandez, I offer huge thanks for meeting with the three of us and for answering myriad questions about the manuscript. I appreciate your prompt replies to my questions and your encouragement throughout the process of tweaking the proposal and editing the manuscript!

—Laura Robb

I have many people to thank for the opportunity to create poems and short texts for this book, beginning with my good friends, esteemed colleagues, and co-authors Laura Robb and Tim Rasinski. Working with them was a joy that kept me eager to get to work each morning to add my share to the growing manuscript. I owe thanks to many other gifted professors and teachers, too, starting with Bernice (Bee) Cullinan, with whom I cowrote my first book for the classroom—how to write poetry—twenty-five years ago. I didn't anticipate, then, how that initial effort would shape the rest of my career. At the time of my "Bee book," I was unfamiliar with the names of such stars as Mary Jo Fresch, Tim Rasinski, and Laura Robb. I was a trade book author and poet with no prior experience in collaboration or in writing for educational publishers. My degrees are in science. I had spent thirty years writing for children. I knew my audience. But starting with the partnership with Cullinan, I began a long process of learning on the job about this vast new field I'd voluntarily entered. What wonderful teachers I've had! I start with the professors and teachers already mentioned, but I've also done quite a bit of reading on my own, which is why I have so many to thank. My reference library, which once boasted mainly science books on snakes, insects, mammals, mountains, rivers, caves, and such, is now well stocked with books by Douglas Fisher,

Lesley Mandel Morrow, Lori Oczkus, Linda Gambrell, Ralph Fletcher, Michael Opitz, Regie Routman, Donald Graves, Richard Allington, Ruth Culham, Ray Coutu, and, of course, Bernice Cullinan, Tim Rasinski, Mary Jo Fresch, and Laura Robb. I'm grateful to these great thinkers and leaders. Each has taught me something about early literacy learning. Too many classroom teachers to count have added to my education. Thank you, Su Hutchens, Jennifer Jackson Harrison, Dawn Licata, Ken Slesarik, and so many others over the years. I should put at the top of the list my wife, Sandy. She looks up and there I am with another page of some manuscript in my hands and the pitiful, begging expression she knows so well. And she always reads it and she always improves it. Thanks, everybody.

—David L. Harrison

The last tip offered in Peggy Rathman's classic *Officer Buckle and Gloria* (1995) is one that has meant a lot to me throughout my career: "Always stick with your buddy." I have had many buddies and mentors throughout my career and would like to acknowledge just a few—Jerry Zutell, Diane DeFord, and Mary Jo Fresch from The Ohio State University; Dave Reinking from the University of Georgia; Nancy Padak, Rich Vacca, and Rick Newton from Kent State University, Evangeline Newton from the University of Akron; Bill Rupley from Texas A & M; Camille Blachowicz from National Louis University; Chase Young from Sam Houston State University; David Paige from Northern Illinois University; and especially my buddies on this particular project—Laura Robb and David L. Harrison. A sincere thank you to all of you for your friendship, knowledge, and inspiration.

—Tim Rasinski

Part I

Improving Comprehension and Fluency

Chapter 1

Promoting and Nurturing Reading Gains

More than 40 years ago, Richard Allington wrote a groundbreaking article: "If They Don't Read Much, How They Ever Gonna Get Good?" His words ring true today:

> Too often the procedures commonly employed in remedial and corrective reading instruction seem to mitigate against developing reading ability by focusing more on the mastery of isolated skills with relatively little emphasis on or instructional time devoted to reading in context. To become a proficient reader, one needs the opportunity to read. (1977, 60)

Most adults understand that students need to practice sports such as soccer, basketball, tennis, and football to become proficient enough to compete with other schools. Practice develops automaticity and self-confidence, and it can lead to enjoying a sport. The same is true of learning to read well. Students practice reading to develop decoding automaticity, fluency, and vocabulary so that they can read and comprehend grade-level texts. When students have a history of not reading, they don't develop the skills needed to enjoy reading.

Recently, Laura Robb has been supporting students who entered fifth grade reading four years below grade level. Teachers' accommodations included reading books aloud or having students listen to audiobooks. Perhaps listening capacity was improving; reading wasn't.

In looking back on the instruction these students received in previous years, a pattern emerged. Students completed activity sheets designed to teach skills for reading, but they lacked opportunities to read books. By third grade, many of these students had practiced reading on a computer with a program that promised great progress. However, students read selections with only five or six short paragraphs, and they had to answer factual, right-there-in-the-text questions. Authentic reading builds stamina—the ability to concentrate on reading for 30 minutes or longer—but this program's steady diet of only very short texts gave students no opportunity to build stamina. The teachers' role consisted of reviewing computer-graded quizzes and letting the computer program decide what students should do next.

By fifth grade, many students were unable to name a book they had read on their own. The reading comprehension data reviewed by Robb and the fifth-grade teachers revealed that students had made little to no progress while using the computer reading program as the children's instruction wasn't targeted to their specific needs. The absence of differentiated reading instruction, combined with the elimination of daily read-alouds and independent reading of self-selected books in favor of isolated skills practice, resulted in students with limited reading vocabularies, weak decoding skills, and no experience discussing books or writing about reading. The work the children had been doing wasn't giving them what they needed to improve and grow as readers.

Literacy Snapshot: Developing Readers

The first time Laura began working in classrooms with groups of fifth and sixth graders reading at kindergarten to grade 2 instructional levels, her belief in her ability to work with these students wavered. Laura shares:

> Questions bombarded my mind: *Did my desire to help outweigh my ability? Did I have the tools, the skillset to bring these children into the reading life?* Sure, I'd worked with students reading a year or so below grade level. *Was my more than 40 years' experience applicable?* I mention this because I know from experience that I'm not alone in feeling this kind of doubt: I have worked with many dedicated teachers who have asked themselves questions like these. Over the course of my career—especially in recent years—I have seen how self doubts can be a good thing because they push us to be better observers, to work to understand students' feelings and behaviors, and to accept students' attitudes toward reading without blaming them or others. Elementary and middle school students frequently have difficulty finding the words to say, "Help me! I can't read!"
>
> For two years, I worked one hour a day with four girls and two boys who arrived in fifth grade reading at a first-grade instructional level. They felt little to no connection to books, and reading was such hard work for them that they tired easily and often gave up trying.
>
> I don't have one sure way of working with them to offer you. In fact, it was the students who taught me what they needed. Reading and even listening to long texts tired them, so I began with poems—short, accessible texts they began to enjoy reading aloud and rereading. Poetry increased their background knowledge, enlarged their vocabularies, and strengthened their self-confidence. The students discussed poems; they checked out collections of poems from the school's library and shared favorites with me and their group.
>
> The students' listening capacities increased through daily teacher read-alouds: poems, fairy and folk tales, myths, short stories, and short informational texts from magazines such as *Zoobook*. Their curriculum also included phonics, word sorts, and vocabulary-building work (Bear et al. 2011), independent reading of self-selected books, writing about reading in notebooks, and practicing and performing poems.
>
> The first book the group completed that totally engaged them was *The True Story of Balto*. After discussing the ending, one student wrote in her

notebook: *I am a reader.* During a conference with her, she elaborated on her entry. "This was the first time I read a whole book and wanted to reread it," she said. "I can't wait to read about Malala next."

By the end of fifth grade, four students were reading on a third-grade instructional level and two were at a mid-second-grade level. Each student received eight books to read over the summer, and two read all eight while four read five or six. At the end of sixth grade, the students were reading books at a fourth- or early fifth-grade instructional level. Not only did all six complete twenty minutes a day of independent reading at school but they were also taking books home to read and rereading favorites. Increased volume in reading offered the practice that improved their decoding and comprehension.

As Laura and the fifth-grade teachers worked with students, one question continually replayed in their minds: *How can we best serve these students?* By observing students, holding frequent and brief conferences, and discussing formative assessments, they created a safe environment where students could ask questions and see mistakes as an important part of learning. Laura and the teachers did this by listening to and accepting students' fears and hopes about reading and enlisting their help to find ways to support them. Laura continues:

> We recognized that a one-size-for-all curriculum wouldn't work and developed a differentiated reading curriculum so students read texts that enabled them to grow as readers, thinkers, and writers. Much of what we learned influenced the content of this book. We developed an asset-based model and made instructional decisions on students' strengths, interests, and desires to learn. In addition to differentiating reading instruction and inviting students to write about reading in their notebooks, we identified six areas that supported students' growth in reading.
>
> - Start class every day with 15 to 20 minutes of independent reading.
> - Build trusting relationships all year long.
> - Enlarge students' background knowledge and vocabulary about a topic through teacher read-alouds and short videos.
> - Improve comprehension and move from recall questions to higher-order thinking questions.
> - Reserve time for students to have literary conversations with partners and in small groups.
> - Use formative assessments that include teacher observations, students' notebook writing, and short conferences that allow students to discuss texts and reflect on their evolving attitudes toward reading.

With these practices in mind, we developed differentiated reading lessons that provide targeted practice for below-grade-level, at-grade-level, and above-grade-level students in grades 3, 4, and 5. We also include strategies that can help you improve students' comprehension, build their vocabulary and background knowledge, increase their knowledge of phonics, and write about reading in notebooks.

Differentiated Lessons Support All Learners

The differentiated lessons in this book are based on poems or short texts (included) and engage students in using four important reading strategies—visualizing, inferring, drawing conclusions, and comparing and contrasting.

Students reading below grade level, near or at grade level, and above grade level read different texts that meet them where they are so they can successfully read and comprehend (Afflerbach 2022). The lessons students complete always connect to the focus lessons. Using a poem or short text, students:

- Build background knowledge and apply the reading strategy the teacher modeled.
- Practice literary conversations.
- Write about their reading in notebooks.
- Expand their vocabulary through word work and word ladders.
- Figure out the meanings of unfamiliar words by using context clues in the text.

You'll find more information on literary conversations in chapter 5. Appendix B provides a student resource on using context clues.

The set of lessons for each strategy begins with two teacher-led lessons that use a common poem or text by David L. Harrison. The first lesson focuses on applying the reading strategy and building background knowledge. The second presents the word work, supporting students so they can complete similar word work. During these focus lessons, you are showing students how to think about their own reading in terms of strategies, word work, enlarging their vocabularies, and writing about reading. These lessons are the glue that connects students' practice with short texts to their application of what they've learned to longer texts.

> Each set of lessons can be used as part of your instructional reading block. Depending on students' needs, lessons will take 20 to 30 minutes per day over four or five days.

The purpose of the lessons is to offer all students opportunities to develop critical and analytical thinking skills and to increase their fluency and vocabulary at the same time. However, these differentiated lessons are only one powerful element of a four-part reading framework:

1. **Daily teacher read-alouds** can develop a joy of reading in listeners. They also serve as a teaching tool for teachers to think aloud and show students how to interpret texts, as well as how texts affect emotions.

2. **Instructional reading** is in students' learning zone (Vygotsky 1978) because students read texts that they can access and learn from with the support of their teacher and/or a peer partner. Instructional reading can improve students' understanding of concepts (such as endangered species), enlarge their vocabularies and background knowledge

of a topic, and deepen comprehension and critical thinking through the application of reading strategies. The **differentiated lessons** in this book are part of instructional reading time. Depending on the length of your reading block, the differentiated lessons will be part of, or the focus of, your instructional reading curriculum.

3. **Writing about reading** in reader's notebooks represents students' reading journeys as they develop hunches, analyze texts, enlarge their vocabulary, and complete word work.

4. **Independent reading** provides the reading volume and practice needed to increase students' reading skills and develop them into lifelong readers.

The four-part reading framework can also allow students to step into the shoes of characters and real-world figures (Bishop 1990). For independent reading, you'll want a well-stocked classroom library so that books for a wide range of reading abilities and interests are at students' fingertips.

Developing Readers

It's difficult to find a term with positive connotations that refers to students who read two or more years below grade level. The term *developing readers* actually describes each one of us at diverse points in our learning, and this is what's important to keep in mind. Any time you read a book with little background knowledge of the topic, you might have to build your understanding prior to reading, by watching videos or reading a short text, as well as reread sections to recall details and comprehend. Reading at your frustration level is humbling, and it creates an understanding of what it's like for students who lack the vocabulary and background knowledge to read texts above their instructional reading level.

The term *developing readers* offers hope that with choice, practice, and teacher support, all students can improve enough to read and learn from materials at and above grade level. We have designed the lessons in this book to boost students' comprehension and critical thinking. However, the lessons themselves aren't enough. To make significant progress, students need to read, read, read!

Creating Culturally Relevant Classroom Libraries

Book collections in classroom libraries, resources in the school's media center, and texts used for teacher read-alouds and instruction should mirror the diverse cultures and lifestyles in the community, the nation, and the larger world. Readers' imaginations link them to the experiences of a character or another person, enlarge their knowledge of the human condition, and allow them to see themselves in texts they are reading. Moreover, culturally relevant texts prepare students to better understand differences and find similarities among people, equipping them with tools to be the productive citizens and problem solvers the world needs them to be.

Independent Reading Increases Reading Volume

Volume in Reading is a strategy that helps developing readers increase their reading skills and desire to read through daily practice (Allington and McGill Frazen 2021; Harvey et al. 2021; Krashen 2004; Robb 2022; Samuels and Wu 2004). Proficient and advanced readers also benefit from volume in reading because the more they read, the more they boost their vocabulary and background knowledge, and the more they develop the skill to read challenging, long texts. In 1988, Richard C. Anderson, Paul T. Wilson, and Linda G. Fielding published a landmark study and wrote:

> In sum, the principle conclusion of this study is that the amount of time a child spends reading books is related to the child's reading level in the fifth grade and growth in reading proficiency from the second to the fifth grade. The case can be made that reading books is a cause, not merely a reflection, of reading proficiency (302).

A rigorous scientific study conducted by S. Jay Samuels and Yi-Chen Wu (2004) also found the more time students read, the higher their achievement compared to a control group, corroborating what earlier studies had shown. Thus, research shows a correlation between the time students devote to daily independent reading and their reading proficiency and comprehension.

Students in grades 3, 4, and 5, the grades targeted in this book, who complete 20 minutes per day of independent reading at school, read 1.8 million words per year (Allington and McGill-Franzen 2021; Anderson, Wilson, and Fielding 1988; Samuels and Wu 2004). Those who read an additional 20 minutes at home double the number of words they read. The benefit for learners is that they continually grow their vocabulary as they repeatedly meet words in different contexts and increase the mileage registered on their reading odometers (Beck et al. 2013; Robb 2014, 2022).

Volume in reading also builds students' understanding of literary genres, nurtures their desire to read self-selected books, increases their fluency, and develops their literary tastes and personal reading lives (Allington 2012, 2014; Allington and McGill-Frazen 2021; Krashen 2004; Miller 2009; Miller and Sharp, 2018; Robb and Robb 2020). We agree that for students to become confident, fluent, analytical readers, they need to read self-selected books daily at school and at home—and this is especially the case for developing readers.

> You'll find tips on helping students choose good-fit books in appendix A.

Instructional Reading

The purpose of instructional reading is to increase students' capacity to comprehend a variety of literary texts and to apply strategies that develop analytical and critical thinking. Often in grades 3 to 5, a class will have students reading one or more years below grade level, several at grade level, and some above grade level. Having five or more different instructional reading levels in a class poses challenges that can be resolved by using two practices:

1. **Strategic reading groups:** Groups of five or six students meet for about 15 minutes, at least three times per week, to read a common text that is at, or close to, their instructional reading levels. While you work with one group, the other students are focused on reading; their choices can include independent reading or writing about reading in notebooks. With your support and scaffolding, students you're working with practice applying strategies, figuring out the meaning of unfamiliar words by using context clues, identifying themes, and studying how plot, settings, and interactions can change characters and people as they live through events from the beginning to the end. When you organize and teach small groups, you can identify areas in which group members will benefit from extra support and offer the practice needed to help them succeed. Sometimes, you'll decide to confer with one or two students who need more time working closely with you. Either way, the goal is to enable all students to improve their reading skills.

2. **A genre-based approach:** You can organize genre-based units that represent students' instructional reading levels, using books from your classroom and school libraries. Place selected books into three color-coded plastic tubs or crates: The first crate (say, a green one) contains books—all two or more years below grade level for developing readers. Another crate of a different color (say, purple) has books one year below grade level and at grade level. And a third crate of another color (say, orange) houses books above grade level. Each crate includes a range of reading levels, and you can guide students in selecting books from specific crates.

When using a genre-based approach, it's important to select a text to use as your teaching tool. Called an anchor text because it anchors your teaching and students' learning, this text should be short and the same genre and/or theme that students are studying. The anchor text can be a picture book, a very short story, a fairy or folk tale, a myth, a short article, or an excerpt from a longer text. Here's what you can model with an anchor text:

- The structure of a specific genre
- The application of a reading strategy such as inferring or visualizing
- How context clues help readers figure out the meaning of unfamiliar words
- Emotional reactions to events and characters
- Changes in characters from the beginning to the end and causes of these changes
- Literary elements and how each applies to a text
- Themes and big ideas found in the text
- How to write diverse responses to the anchor text

What you model for students is what they will practice using their own texts and what you assess when observing them and reading their notebook entries.

Organize students into reading partnerships and invite them to discuss their different texts after completing a few chapters. Partners should be no more than one year apart in instructional reading levels so that both students can contribute to discussions that open with sharing a quick summary of the section they've completed. Then, the pair can focus on what you've modeled with the anchor text.

Consider alternating genre-based instructional units with strategic reading groups to improve students' reading skills and stamina. Remember that as you support students during conferences, and as they increase their independent reading of self-selected books, they will make progress, the composition of strategic reading groups will change, and students will have more choices of books to read.

The **differentiated lessons** in this book are part of instructional reading time. These lessons use short texts to prepare students for the demands of longer books with complex text structures, subplots, multiple characters, and layers of information. The goal is to use the short texts in the lessons to develop students' reading skills and abilities to concentrate so they can transfer these skills to enjoying and comprehending the longer texts they'll read in ELA and content classes and during independent reading.

Research on Reading Long Texts

A study by William G. Brozo, Gerry Shiel, and Keith Topping (2007), using three Program of International Assessment (PISA) countries, concluded that student engagement in reading, the reading of long texts, and a rich leisure or independent reading life contributed to high reading scores on the PISA test, with student engagement having the highest correlation with reading achievement.

The Long and Short of Texts for Reading

The short texts in the differentiated lessons help students improve their comprehension, vocabulary, and fluency, increase their background knowledge, and strengthen their abilities to discuss and write about a text. Teaching reading with short texts enables you to quickly know whether students' understanding of a concept or reading strategy is developed enough to be successfully applied to longer texts. You can identify which students are experiencing confusion and provide needed support and scaffolds before confusion becomes a roadblock to progress. At this stage, you can repeat all or part of a focus lesson to those students who need to re-experience your think-alouds and modeling. Reteaching provides students with immediate support that can move them out of their frustration zone and into their learning zone (Vygotsky 1978).

Reading longer texts offers students practice with recalling information occurring early in a book as they access it during their later reading to identify changes in characters, people, and central themes. In addition to increasing stamina, reading longer texts can foster a positive reading identity, which in turn contributes to students becoming lifelong readers.

> Teaching reading with short texts enables you to quickly know whether students' understanding of a concept or reading strategy is developed enough to be successfully applied to longer texts.

Think of each student's reading identity as a work in progress, and know that learners develop reading identities when they have daily opportunities to self-select books they can and want to read. Students who have strong, positive reading identities see themselves as readers and choose to read at home and during free time at school. They think about characters, people, events, and settings and are able to analyze details and make inter-text connections. Some students may enter our classes telling us that they hate reading. We can support these students by creating conditions in our classrooms that offer them multiple opportunities to develop the skills and expertise needed to become engaged, fluent readers.

Three Practices Develop Progress in Reading

Whether students are reading short or long texts, three practices will nurture their reading identities and strengthen trusting, positive relationships with you and their classmates: in-the-moment conferring, responsive teaching, and reflection.

In-the-moment conferring with students is a strategy you'll use during instructional and independent reading. The two or three minutes of conferring enables you to understand where students are with reading and can increase their self-confidence when you notice and share every increment of progress. As students read, discuss a text, or write about reading, circulate among them and be a dedicated kid-watcher: observe, listen, ask questions, and pause to have a brief conversation (Owocki and Goodman 2002). Use objective "I notice" statements such as "I notice that you're flipping through the book's pages," "I notice that you've chosen and returned three books since class started," or "I notice how much you enjoyed reading an excerpt from your book to Ali." Then, stop and give the student time to respond.

Be intentional about knowing students, and respect where they are with reading. When a student honestly says, "Give it up. You'll never get me to like reading," put yourself in their shoes, be empathetic, and tell them that you understand their feelings toward reading. Changeover to the reading life won't happen immediately. Students will benefit from the gift of time and your support.

If you're unsure about starting conversations with students, you can use the reflective questions in figure 1.1 or simply ask, "How's the reading going?" In appendix C, you'll find guidelines for mini-conferences that include suggestions for responding to negative statements and abandoning a book.

Carry a pencil and a clipboard with dated sticky notes and jot key points that can act as reminders for students and support them as they work with partners and at times independently (see figure 1.2). Place these sticky notes in students' notebooks, and ask them to keep each note on the page they've discussed with you. When you return to read students' work, the sticky note helps you recall your brief conference and assess students' revisions.

Responsive teaching asks you to be totally tuned in to students as they read, discuss a text with a partner or small group, write in their notebooks, and confer with you.

Figure 1.1—Reflective Questions for Thinking about a Text

Questions about feelings:

- What emotions or feelings did the main character or person show?
  Give an example from the text, and explain what caused these feelings.

- Do you have feelings that are like the feelings of the main character or person? Name those feelings you have in common.

- What did you learn about people, animals, or friendships from your book?

- Did this text change your feelings about people, animals, or friendships? What information or what part of the story changed your feelings? Share an example from the book with your partner.

Questions about fiction and nonfiction:

- How do you get ideas for what books to read?

- Why did you choose to read this book?

- Do you want to read more books by this author? Explain why.

- What was the main character's or person's big problem? If they solved the problem, explain how.

- What was your favorite setting? Explain why this setting was your favorite.

- How have you improved as a reader?

Responsive teachers know that their students inform instructional decisions and practices. Each day, students show you what they understand, what they can do independently, and when they require scaffolding. As you support students, gradually release responsibility to them when you notice that they're ready to complete a task independently (Pearson and Gallagher 1983).

Reflection, or pausing to think about a poem, short text, or book while reading and after completing a text, can focus students on the emotions and ideas raised by the text. Reflective thinking can also highlight students' attitudes toward reading as well as to the text's content (Crowder 2020). Most students in grades 3, 4, and 5 aren't naturally reflective readers. Provide students with a mental model of what reflective readers do by sharing your reflections at the end of focus lessons and daily read-alouds. For example, you might share the emotions an event or character raised, a connection to an event or information in a different text and what you learned, how the text affected your attitude toward reading, how the text changed you as a reader, or why you didn't want the book to end. You can post reflective questions (see figure 1.1) and invite students to select one or two.

Figure 1.2—Reminders support students while they work on their own.

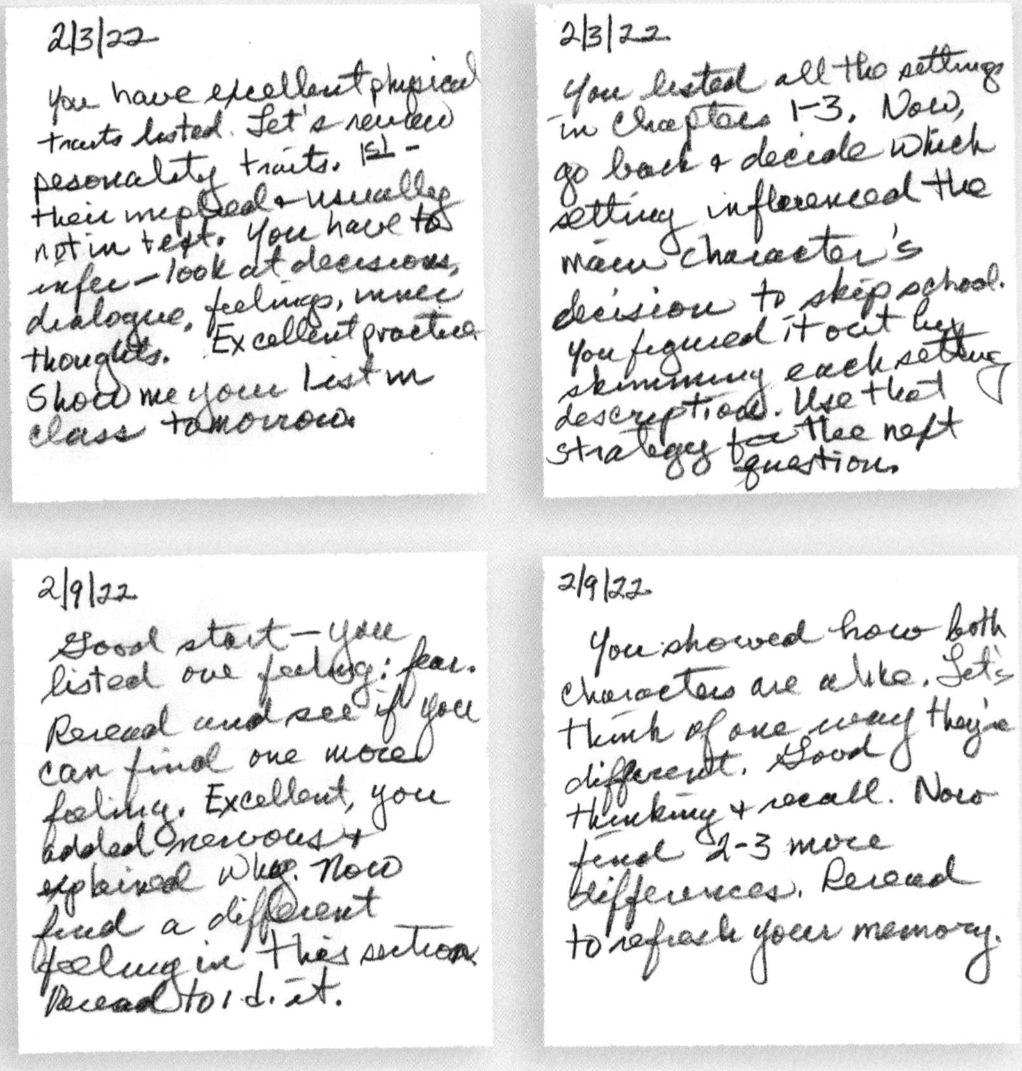

2/3/22

You have excellent physical traits listed. Let's review personality traits. [They] are implied & usually not in text. You have to infer — look at decisions, dialogue, feelings, inner thoughts. Excellent practice. Show me your list in class tomorrow.

2/3/22

You listed all the settings in Chapters 1-3. Now, go back & decide which setting influenced the main character's decision to skip school. You figured it out by skimming each setting description. Use that strategy for the next question.

2/9/22

Good start — you listed one feeling: fear. Reread and see if you can find one more feeling. Excellent, you added nervous & explained why. Now find a different feeling in this section. Reread to i.d. it.

2/9/22

You showed how both characters are alike. Let's think of one way they're different. Good thinking & recall. Now find 2-3 more differences. Reread to refresh your memory.

Provide quiet time so that students can think about a short text, a specific book, or their feelings toward reading. You can also have them share ideas with partners. Then, invite them to jot their thoughts on dated pages in their notebooks (see figure 1.3). Having a dated record of reflections enables students to review changes in their thinking. The more students practice reflecting on their reading, the sooner they'll internalize some of the questions and automatically think reflectively during and after reading.

Figure 1.3—Sylvie Rose understands that choice and reading at school every day improves her reading.

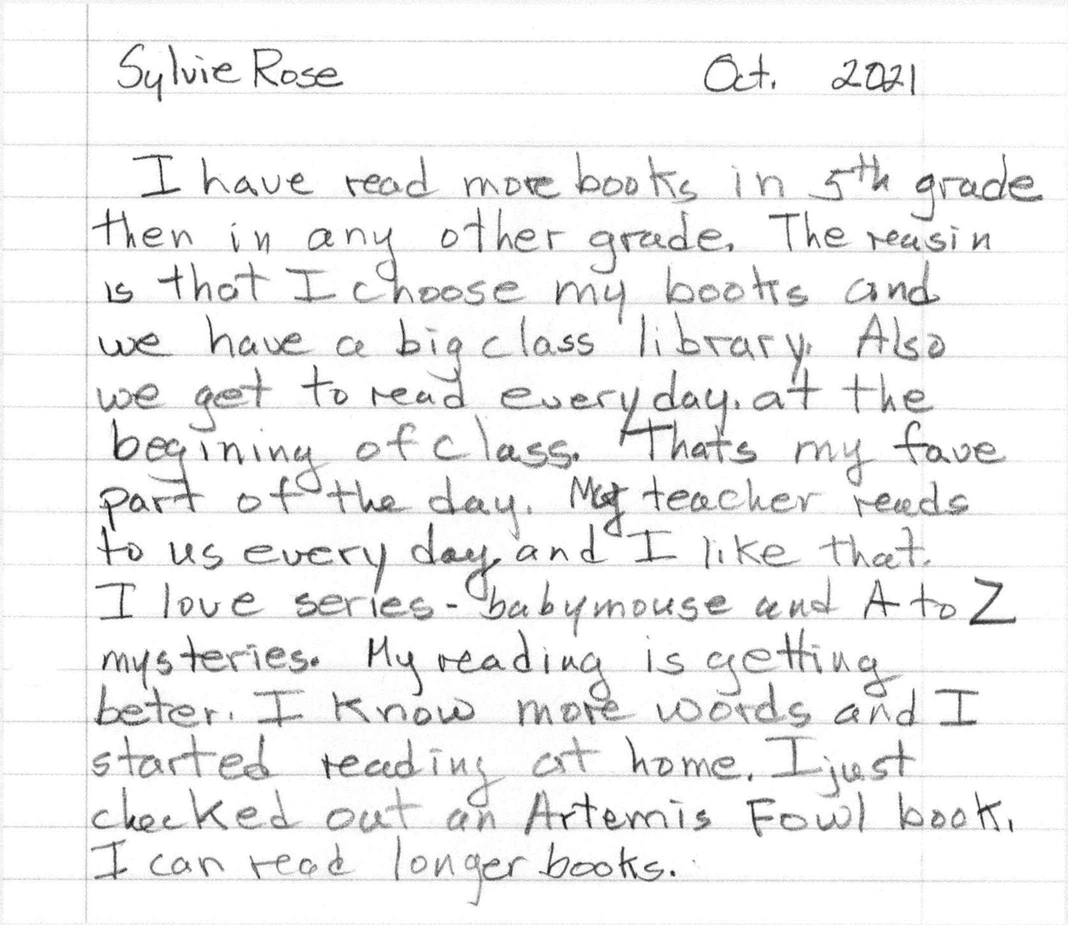

> Sylvie Rose   Oct. 2021
>
> I have read more books in 5th grade
> then in any other grade. The reasin
> is that I choose my books and
> we have a big class library. Also
> we get to read every day. at the
> begining of class. Thats my fave
> part of the day. My teacher reeds
> to us every day and I like that.
> I love series - babymouse and A to Z
> mysteries. My reading is getting
> beter. I know more words and I
> started reading at home. I just
> checked out an Artemis Fowl book.
> I can read longer books.

Take Time for Reflective Conversations

Reflect on these questions independently and then discuss them with colleagues:

- How do the differentiated lessons in this book support all students?
- Why is a combination of short and long texts for instruction helpful to students and teachers?
- Why should teachers nurture students' reading identities? How can teachers do this?
- How does volume in reading support students' progress and benefit all readers?

Chapter 2

The Differentiated Lessons: Getting Started and Moving Forward

I don't know where to begin!

I feel overwhelmed when I think of starting.

I need support, but there isn't a coach in my school to help me.

These words reflect the honest feelings of teachers as they consider taking the plunge to implement new instructional practices. We understand these feelings because we have had them ourselves and have shared them with colleagues. If you feel this way, you're not alone; most teachers experience these feelings when change and new practices are on their teaching menu. However, these feelings can diminish when you collaborate with others to expand your background knowledge of new instructional practices. We suggest that you find a colleague to partner with and take positive steps forward.

Learning with a Partner or Small Group

Even if your school has a literacy coach or reading resource teacher, it's best to have one or a few colleagues with whom you can share positives and challenges about instruction and have conversations that enable you to work through questions. You can form a partnership with a member of your team or with a colleague from another grade. If more than one teacher in grades 3 to 5 plans to implement the differentiated lessons in this book, form a small group. There are several benefits to setting up weekly or bimonthly meetings during common planning times or before school starts. At these meetings, you can do the following:

- Have conversations about what's working and what needs adjusting.
- Discuss ways to measure success.
- Share literacy stories about students and gather feedback for next moves from one another.
- Plan together and work through any questions you have.
- Set times to observe another group member to learn from how they implement the lessons and/or provide helpful feedback.

- Vent when you feel frustrated, and support one another.
- Celebrate successes and set reasonable goals for moving forward.
- Discuss how to share what you are doing with the larger school community.

The first item on your agenda should be building your background knowledge about the lessons in this book. Having conversations with colleagues about parts of this book (or any book you're studying) makes the learning more enjoyable and also enhances your recall and connections to your present teaching practices.

Enhancing Your Prior Knowledge

To build your background knowledge, we suggest dividing the learning into two parts:

1. Before you present a set of lessons, read (or reread) chapters 1 through 3 and discuss them with your learning group. These chapters are short and shine a spotlight on information you'll use while presenting lessons. You'll explore ways to promote reading gains and you'll experience the benefits of writing about reading as you use your teacher's notebook to illustrate how to respond to a text. Your notebook will offer students a prototype when it's time for them to respond to their differentiated texts.

2. After completing one set of lessons, read chapters 4 through 6. Chapter 4 discusses how practicing and performing poetry and other texts can improve students' fluency, expressive reading, and comprehension, and enlarge their vocabularies. Chapter 5 offers suggestions for organizing student-led conversations about reading. Chapter 6 discusses how to assess students' progress and provide additional practice and support.

Once you've completed a study of the first three chapters, set aside time to prethink and preplan, as doing this will help you present engaging and motivating lessons.

Prethinking Matters

Because the lessons in this book include texts for students reading below, at, and above grade level, you'll need to know your students' reading levels. Review students' results from end-of-year tests by looking at two or three years of scores to see if the pattern of their reading and vocabulary test results continually increases, decreases, or increases and decreases. Since results from these tests are not always released in time to use them at the start of the school year, here are other measures to consider:

- Gather information from students' previous teachers to collect their ideas on students' needs and instructional reading levels. Some students may be new to your school; review the records and information sent from their previous school.
- Ask students to write the title and author of the last book they worked on with their teacher last year. You can find the Lexile reading level of that book by entering "Lexile level of," the title, and the author into a browser search window.
- Ask students to write the title and author of the last book they read and enjoyed for independent reading.
- If you're unsure of how to place certain students or the entire class into groups,

administer a short reading comprehension check. We recommend using *3-Minute Reading Assessments: Word Recognition, Fluency, and Comprehension, Grades 1–4* and *3-Minute Reading Assessments: Word Recognition, Fluency, and Comprehension, Grades 5-8* (Rasinski and Padak 2005).

It's helpful to use more than one measure to determine students' groups. Let students know they should tell you whether the poems and/or short texts are too easy or too difficult as they work with the materials for their group. Also, observe students carefully as they read, discuss with partners, and write in their notebooks. Note whether they're recalling details, discussing the details, and using information to think critically about the text. This type of observation should occur frequently and can help you adjust placements in specific groups.

Keep in mind that student groups are flexible. As students practice reading and responding to their differentiated texts and completing word work in their notebooks, monitor their progress and collect information that enables you to decide whether they should move to a different group. During one-to-one conferences, assess students' fluency, vocabulary, ability to apply a specific reading strategy, recall, and depth of comprehension revealed in notebook writing to decide whether students have progressed enough to be successful in a higher group. In addition, if a student struggles with the elements previously listed, confer with them to determine whether the text is too challenging and whether they should be moved into a group where they can experience success and improve.

Preplanning Matters

After you've identified students' reading levels, do some preplanning. First, consider the materials that each student will need:

- A file folder with the student's name printed on the tab to hold the activity sheets for their lessons. (If you have a self-contained class, place the file folders in a plastic crate or on a shelf near your desk. If you teach two or three sections of ELA, place each section's folders in a separate crate or on a shelf near you. Label the shelf to quickly identify each section's materials.)
- A reader's notebook to record their responses to the texts they read and to complete word work that relates to their text.

Each student will also need a partner from the same reading-level group to work with and discuss texts with. (We suggest that you choose partners so that no student feels left out. If the number of students in a group isn't even, have a group of three learn together.) After you've planned for students' materials, prepare these items:

- Set up a notebook for yourself. You will write and think aloud to show students what a response to a specific text looks like and offer models for the word work students will complete. Your notebook will become a resource for students, as they can refresh their memories of concepts and strategies by rereading parts of your notebook as they work on the differentiated lessons.

- Use a document camera or your computer to display texts from the focus lesson on the board as you demonstrate how to complete reading responses and word work.

When you've completed these planning steps, you'll be ready to dig into the differentiated lessons.

Getting Started with the Differentiated Lessons

Once you've completed preplanning and are ready to begin presenting the differentiated lessons, preview the appendixes and familiarize yourself with their contents so you can access supportive suggestions. In addition, we suggest that you and your colleagues complete the set of lessons on a specific reading strategy before using them the first time to maximize the support you can provide one another. Here are some tips to consider:

- Read chapter 7 (Using the Differentiated Lessons), which includes information that applies to all the lessons and a student resource titled *Reading and Enjoying Poems*. Discuss the content of this chapter with your colleagues.
- With your colleagues, read and review the contents of the first focus lesson you'll present. Explore and discuss the guidelines and raise questions.
- Skim the work for each group of students, and print enough activity pages for each group.

Now, you'll be ready to start the focus lesson.

Moving Forward

Meet with colleagues frequently as you teach the first set of lessons; you can meet less frequently as you move on to other sets of lessons. Most likely, you and your partner or colleagues will be working on different strategies as you progress, but because the process of presenting the lessons is the same, you can still meet to support one another.

Through differentiation, students will be able to read the poems and short texts selected for their groups, and through practice, they will develop their ability to discuss texts, improve their comprehension and fluency, and enlarge their vocabulary. The differentiated lessons and subsequent assessment-driven interventions, combined with 20 minutes of daily independent reading of self-selected books, will enable students to make the reading gains needed to develop their reading skills, which in turn will lead them to find joy in all reading and learning!

Take Time for Reflective Conversations

Reflect on these questions independently, then discuss them with colleagues:

- Why is it helpful to work with one or more colleagues when preplanning lessons?
- Why is it important to build background knowledge before presenting a set of lessons?
- How do your responses to a poem or short text in your teacher's notebook support students' notebook writing about their reading?
- What needs to be done to move a student to a different group? Why is gathering this data important?

Chapter 3

Reader's Notebooks

When my teacher writes about the read-aloud, I can watch and listen to how she thinks. It helps me see what it [writing about reading] looks like.

Teachers engaging in "cold writing"—composing notebook entries without preparation—in front of students dramatically changes students' outlooks on writing about reading! And that makes so much sense. Watching teachers compose notebook entries, and listening to them think aloud and make their processes visible, reduces the anxiety that many students develop when asked to write. When students have a mental model of diverse ways to write about reading, they can respond with more confidence. Research spotlights a correlation between writing about reading and increased comprehension of texts.

The Compelling Research

In 2010, the Carnegie Corporation of New York published a research report by Steve Graham and Michael Hebert called *Writing to Read: Evidence for How Writing Can Improve Reading.* This extensive study demonstrates that when students analyze and then reflect on texts they can read, they gain insights into the reading—insights that are revealed in the written pieces they compose. As students write about reading, they can improve their comprehension of texts written by others. Graham and Hebert's meta-analysis of the research demonstrates the importance of teaching students skills and processes that are part of creating a text as well as increasing the amount of writing students do at school. As students practice the craft of writing, they are better equipped to deepen their comprehension by writing about a text. Graham and Hebert recommend that students write to do the following:

- Record their personal reactions to texts, as well as their analysis and interpretation of the decisions and actions of characters and people
- Summarize part or all of a text, which requires selecting key information and setting aside less essential details (see appendix D for more on writing summaries)
- Generate questions a text raises, discuss them, and summarize the discussion
- Take notes on some of the material they've read
- Create concept maps showing the connections between concepts in a text
- Develop lists of words and short phrases that describe the emotions a passage or section raised for them while reading, a character's or person's personality traits, the impact of settings on characters' decisions, the text's theme, and so forth

In 2015, Steve Graham, Katherine Harris, and Tonya Santangelo published groundbreaking research on writing about reading for elementary students. They concluded that when students write about a text they are reading, their comprehension of the text significantly outperforms other students who reread and study the text. These data make a strong case for integrating writing about reading across the curriculum. We have seen this firsthand as well. Laura Robb coached two fifth-grade inclusion teachers on reading and writing for three years, and they began using teacher's notebooks. Both reported that modeling and using cold writing improved the quality of students' responses to their instructional reading books.

A Deep Dive into Teacher's Notebooks

To support students in writing about their reading with clarity and depth of thought, think aloud as you model your process of writing in a teacher's notebook; this not only is an effective strategy but your notebook becomes a valuable student resource.

Modeling Cold Writing with the Focus Lesson Text

The focus lesson in each set of differentiated lessons is an ideal opportunity for modeling writing about reading. You'll find specific suggestions for cold writing in each lesson. As mentioned previously, it's beneficial for students to write about their reading because it improves their comprehension of a text. Moreover, when students respond to questions about texts and complete the word work in their reader's notebooks, they have multiple opportunities to practice writing with clarity and specific examples. The research is clear: students can only write about what they understand, and writing enables them to leap beyond recall to deeper learning (Graham and Hebert, 2010; O'Brien Mackey 2005).

Though cold writing in front of students might seem challenging, the more you do it, the easier it will become. Cold writing shows students what the writing process looks like in the planning and drafting stages as well as during revising and editing. You can respond to prompts or questions such as "List the emotions the protagonist felt during this event" or "What personality traits helped the character/person cope with their loss?"

Your adjustments of word choices and organization show students that writing can be messy when moving from in-the-head-thinking to writing on paper. Feel free to model that as you draft: cross out and replace words, adjust sentence openings, and change the order of sentences by numbering them. Follow these guidelines to make your process and thinking visible to students:

- As you cold write, display your teacher's notebook using a document camera (see figures 3.1 and 3.2). Think aloud so students observe and gain insights into your process. Encourage students to ask questions.
- Place your teacher's notebook under the document camera and leave it there as students write, allowing them to review your responses while crafting their own writing.
- Store your teacher's notebook in a place that's accessible to students. Let them know that they can reread notebook pages to refresh their memory of specific examples.

By keeping a teacher's notebook, modeling cold writing, and sharing how you respond to different texts, you provide mental models to students. Your cold writes serve as road maps for students to craft clear and thoughtful written responses to texts.

Notebooks have the following benefits:

- They build students' mental models of writing about reading.
- They provide a resource for students to revisit and reflect on before they write.
- They demonstrate to students diverse types of responding, such as lists, related words, diagrams, connections, summaries, applying strategies, and writing paragraphs.
- They show students how to organize their thinking in a notebook.
- They dispel the mystery of writing about reading as students observe the teacher writing and thinking aloud.
- They allow teachers to establish expectations, such as required headings and content, before students compose their own notebook entries.

Notebooks support students' growth in these ways:

- They make visible the thinking done before, during, and after writing.
- They encourage reflection about reading.
- They enable students to self-evaluate their progress by reviewing a set of notebook entries.
- They improve students' comprehension of texts they have read.
- They offer students opportunities to experience how writing about reading can increase their vocabulary and use context to figure out unfamiliar words.
- They present guidelines or criteria that can guide students' responses.
- They provide practice for applying reading strategies to texts.
- They develop the habit of reflecting on texts in their notebooks, which carries over to students' minds as they read and complete in-the-head responses and questions.

Suggestions for Cold Writing Responses to Reading

Use this list of suggestions to determine what types of responses might work for students in your class:

- **Lists** can identify settings, problems, decisions, personality traits, obstacles, and conflicts.
- **Summaries** can be created for part of a long text or an entire short text. Appendix D presents frameworks for summarizing different types of texts.
- **Using reading strategies** such as visualizing, inferring, drawing conclusions, and comparing and contrasting invites students to think deeply about texts.
- **Using context clues** in texts helps students understand the meaning of unfamiliar words (see page 210 in chapter 10 and appendix B for more about context clues).
- **Written conversations** invite students to have a brief discussion with a peer partner or with you in their notebooks. Students or you can provide the prompt, but make

sure that it can't be answered with a simple yes or no (Daniels and Daniels 2013). The prompt should stimulate several exchanges and can raise more questions. (See appendix E for more on written conversations.)

- **Emotional reactions** such as fear, anger, joy, happiness, sadness, worry, anxiety, surprise, dislike, disgust, and so on are common responses to texts. Show students your emotional reactions, and point out the text details that evoked these feelings.

- **Four Words** is an excellent strategy to use after reading a powerful text. Immediately after reading, show students how you write four words that the text brought to mind. Then, select one of the words and show the connection between the word and details in the text.

- **Drawing responses** improves students' recall of concepts and information as well as their understanding (Terada 2019). Readers can draw, draw and add a caption or explanatory notes, or create a cartoon with writing inside speech bubbles.

- **Make notes** of specific words and phrases from a text, such as those that create settings, reveal personality traits, show emotions, identify inner thoughts, or use figurative language (such as metaphor and simile).

- **Sketchnoting** uses words and doodles to organize ideas visually and can improve students' recall and understanding. Model this technique as an option for students, as not everyone will be comfortable with it. Explain to students that they don't have to be artistic to create sketchnotes. Point out that integrating doodles, drawings, and words is fun and makes what you're learning easier to remember because combining drawing and writing integrates the visual, kinesthetic, and linguistic areas of the brain (Terada 2019). (See appendix F for more on sketchnoting.)

- **Questions** arise as readers engage with a text. Think aloud and note the questions a text raises in your mind, and explain that readers who pose questions and read on to search for answers develop the motivation to continue to read.

- **Connections** can be made to ideas, settings, and details in the text or to the reader's existing knowledge and prior experiences. Model making connections to show how this deepens your understanding of a text.

- **An analytical paragraph** starts with developing a plan and using the plan to write the paragraph (see appendix H for details).

- **Word work** is an integral part of the differentiated lessons. Modeling the word work during the focus lessons provides students with the concrete examples they require to complete similar word work independently.

After you have modeled and students have practiced several different kinds of responses, invite them to suggest ways to respond to texts in their notebooks.

The think-alouds and cold-writes you present and document in your teacher's notebook offer students beneficial insights that they can then apply when crafting responses in their reader's notebooks. Moreover, by frequently responding to reading in notebooks, students can develop the habit of creating in-the-head responses and reactions to texts while reading.

Figure 3.1—Fifth-grade teacher Stacey Yost models cause/effect and problem/solution

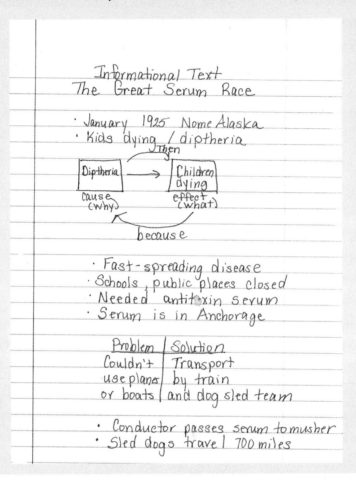

Informational Text
The Great Serum Race

· January 1925 Nome Alaska
· Kids dying / diptheria

Diptheria → Children dying
cause (why)   effect (what)
Then
because

· Fast-spreading disease
· Schools, public places closed
· Needed antitoxin serum
· Serum is in Anchorage

Problem	Solution
Couldn't use planes or boats	Transport by train and dog sled team

· Conductor passes serum to musher
· Sled dogs travel 700 miles

Figure 3.2—Laura Robb's cold write for grade 3 using the poem from the Drawing Conclusions focus lesson

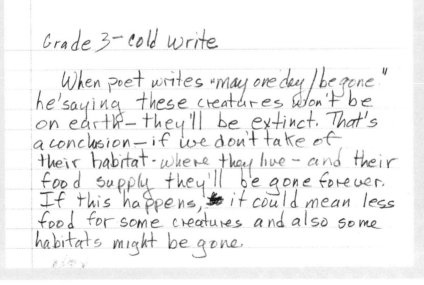

Grade 3 - cold write

When poet writes "may one day / be gone" he's saying these creatures won't be on earth—they'll be extinct. That's a conclusion—if we don't take of their habitat—where they live—and their food supply they'll be gone forever. If this happens, it could mean less food for some creatures and also some habitats might be gone.

Reader's Notebooks for Students

When students write in their notebooks, they embark on a journey of reflecting on their reading as well as on texts you read aloud. Students' notebooks are records of their hunches, wonderings, ideas (and adjustments), notes, and conversations with peers that enable them to monitor and observe their growth as readers and thinkers throughout the year. Notebooks permit students to not only play with ideas and words but also to adjust thoughts and positions after discussions and reflection. When you allow students to try on ideas and disagree with peers' interpretations as long as they support their ideas with text details, you encourage risk-taking and diverse thinking about texts.

Keep students' notebooks at school, stored in a plastic crate or cardboard box, or on a bookshelf. Before the lesson starts, ask three or four students to distribute notebooks quickly. It's helpful to have notebooks ready for writing about reading when the lesson starts, freeing you to invite students to turn-and-talk and write at different points. At the end of the lesson, ask students to return their notebooks to the appropriate place. Avoid sending notebooks home, because you'll find that many don't come back the next day. Instead, have students complete any writing-about-reading homework on separate paper. After you read their work and provide feedback, ask students to paste or tape the homework entries into their notebooks.

Always have students write headings in their notebooks when the lesson begins. Write the heading on the board as a reminder; headings can include the student's name, the date, the title and author of the text, a question, a prompt, a topic, and so on. Headings also serve as the structural glue of notebooks, connecting entries on the same text and making it easier for students to find specific entries that they might want to revisit to add information or adjust their initial responses.

Figure 3.3—A fifth-grade student in group three shows her ability to infer and use excellent vocabulary.

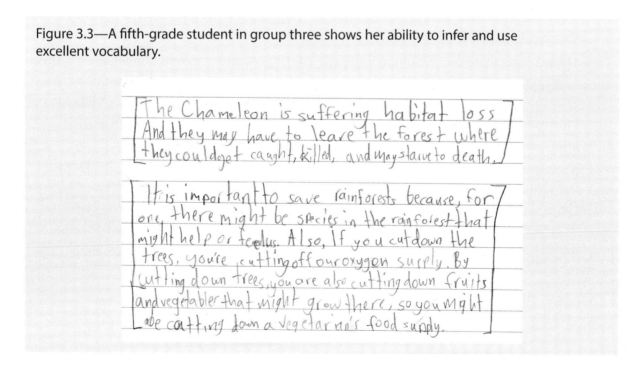

Because students' notebooks are their personal journeys into reading, and the goal is for them to write with honesty and depth, keep these suggestions in mind as you review notebook entries:

- **Don't** mark up students' notebooks by correcting punctuation and grammar. **Do** keep a list of punctuation and grammar errors in the back of your teacher's notebook, and use this information to develop whole-class and small-group focus lessons in writing. Here's a list of focus lessons Laura Robb created after reviewing fifth-grade reader's notebooks at the end of the first six weeks of school.

Focus lessons for whole class: When to use a comma in compound sentences; adding —ed and —ing to these base words: stop, brag, release

Focus lessons for five students: Start sentences with an uppercase letter; when to use uppercase letters

- **Don't** rewrite students' writing about reading in their notebooks to show what the responses should contain. **Do** discuss with students how they can improve their notebook entries, and jot suggestions on sticky notes as a reminder.

- **Don't** list ways in which students' writing about reading isn't working in their notebooks or on sticky notes. **Do** write a few positives that you noticed on sticky notes. Then, set priorities and invite students to consider improving one or two areas.

- **Don't** assign a grade to notebook entries. **Do** assign a grade to journal entries that students complete on separate paper after they have practiced that type of entry and are ready to complete one independently.

- **Don't** state that you're looking for specific interpretations, as this can negatively affect the quality and content of students' responses and reactions. If you make this kind of statement, they will start thinking about what you're looking for instead of writing their own ideas. **Do** invite students to explore diverse interpretations and support their thinking with text evidence.

Keep in mind that a goal of notebook writing is for students to practice and refine how they think and write about texts and communicate their ideas with clarity and depth. The result will be improved comprehension (Graham, Harris, and Santangelo 2015). Students' writing can be used for formative assessment as entries can reveal their levels of comprehension, understanding of literary elements (see appendix I), and application of reading strategies (Graham and Hebert 2010; Robb 2017).

What Teachers Can Learn from Students' Notebook Writing

Keep your teacher's notebook close by while reading students' notebook entries, as it will refresh your memory about the expectations you established for content. The purpose of assessing students' notebook work is to identify what they do well along with areas that require extra practice and support. Remember, you can assign grades to work completed by students on separate paper—work that they know will receive a grade. Figure 3.4 shows a checklist for assessing students' notebooks. Use the checklist to determine whether the content meets your expectations for organization, thinking, and comprehension. Assess by choosing one to three items from the list, based on what students have practiced. Remember that the primary purpose of this assessment is to inform your next instructional moves. You can also write one to three items on the board and have students self-evaluate by choosing one to reflect on and write about on separate paper. After you've read the self-evaluations, have students tape them into their notebooks so they have a record of all their writing-about-reading experiences.

> Using a single-point rubric will allow you to develop a grade for entries that students write on separate paper (not their notebook entries). See page 71 in chapter 7 for an example of a single-point rubric that you can use or adjust to your specific needs.

Conferring about Notebook Entries

When you confer with students, you have an opportunity to get inside their heads to better understand how they think about a text. Two kinds of conferences enable you to respond to students' needs and provide support that can improve their writing about reading:

1. **Making-the-rounds:** After you've presented both focus lessons for a set of differentiated lessons, while students are completing their differentiated work, circulate among them. In addition to working with students who require scaffolding, notice and offer feedback to students who are successfully completing the work on their own. Though it's natural to focus on the students who require our support, it's important to remember to notice and comment, as much as possible, on the work of *all* students.

2. **Short, scheduled conferences:** Sometimes, students require more support than the brief encounter offered by a making-the-rounds conference. Schedule brief conferences with these students while they are completing their differentiated work. Limit these to three or four minutes; if a student requires additional time, meet again during the next day. To maintain privacy, have these conferences in an area away from other students, and ask students to bring their notebooks and lesson materials.

Figure 3.4—Checklist for Assessing Students' Notebooks

Each time you assess, choose one to three items from the list, based on what students have practiced.

The student:

- provides adequate text evidence to support a point, position, or idea
- cites text details that are specific and in their own words
- can apply the reading strategy to their own poem, short text, or other instructional text
- explains how the reading strategy improves comprehension
- understands the word work modeled in a focus lesson
- can figure out an unfamiliar word's meaning by using context clues
- understands figurative language (simile, metaphor, alliteration, onomatopoeia)
- can explain how figurative language enhances visualization and a text's meaning
- can write in depth about a text
- completes pair-shares before writing when asked to do so
- plans writing paragraphs
- understands that planning makes writing easier
- can defend a thesis or position statement by citing supporting text details in their own words
- understands that an inference is not in the text but is an implied meaning
- can list key details discussed after a partner or small-group discussion
- can connect literary elements to narrative texts with specific text examples
- can review several notebook entries and explain their progress
- shows an understanding of genre structure
- can show and explain how their writing about reading has improved over time
- sets goals for writing about reading based on self-evaluation and/or teacher-student conferences

It's helpful to document the outcomes of scheduled conferences. Monitor progress by using the form in appendix G. Decide on the topic for the conference using the student's input, questions, and/or their written work.

Guidelines for Successful Conferences

Use a positive and supportive tone so students will be candid about their needs and ask questions that indicate the kind of feedback they need. These guidelines will help ensure that a conference is successful:

- **Choose a single topic.** Set priorities. With the student, select and focus on the topic that will have the most impact on their writing about reading. Start with a question or an "I notice" statement. For example, "Can you help me understand why you're not including text evidence?" Or, "I notice that you listed one inference when the guidelines called for three."

- **Offer think time.** When you ask students to respond, give them adequate time to think and organize their ideas. You might want to fill the silence with solutions, but this won't support students. Though waiting might feel like an eternity, give students the time they need to think before they respond.

- **Be a good listener.** Avoid interrupting a student while they are talking. Listen carefully, and on the conference form, note questions you have, then ask those questions once the student has finished.

- **Make affirming comments.** Use positive comments to point out progress, such as "I noticed that you found two examples in the text to support your inference." Always close a conference with positive statements.

- **Negotiate a goal.** With the student, decide on a goal, write it on a sticky note, and place the note on the entry being discussed.

- **Ask for a recap.** Invite the student to retell the highlights of the conference to ensure that their recall is solid. If the student can't recall, you can recap the key points.

The goal of conferring is not only to support students but also discover how they think and write about texts. It's also important to reserve time to confer with students who understand and can work independently—they also benefit from your feedback and need to hear positive statements that increase their self-confidence and independence.

Your teacher's notebook is a resource for students when you display an entry under a document camera and use it to model and review your process before inviting students to respond to a text in their notebooks. Your notebook is also a resource when you make it accessible for students to refer to during partner work, to refresh their thinking or review a process. Students' notebooks are safe places for them to try ideas, adjust or change their thinking about a text, or express their feelings about an event, character, or topic. You can also ask students to use their notebooks to document discussions with partners. To gain insights into the impact of student discussions, post one or more of the following prompts on the board:

- How did the discussion change your thinking?
- What new ideas did you learn from the discussion?
- Did the discussion raise questions? If so, what are they?
- How did questions raised affect your thinking?
- Did the discussion change your feelings about a topic? Explain.

When students have opportunities to have partner discussions and then write about their reading, they can not only improve their comprehension but also use reflection as a tool for clarifying and interpreting texts.

Take Time for Reflective Conversations

Reflect on these questions independently, then discuss them with colleagues:

- How does a teacher's notebook support students' notebook writing?
- What can teachers learn about students' reading from their notebook writing?
- Why is it important to make the rounds while students complete work?
- How can scheduled conferences improve students' writing about reading?

Chapter 4

Practice and Performance

Finally, Friday afternoon had arrived! Students in Jason Carter's fourth-grade class had been anticipating and preparing for their poetry slam all week. On Monday, Mr. Carter told students they would celebrate the first week of school by having a poetry slam on Friday. He read poems about school and the beginning of the school year and then asked the students to choose poems to present at the slam. Students could choose to do a solo read, or they could work and present with one or more classmates.

Over the next three days, Mr. Carter gave students time to rehearse their poems. During this time, he circulated through the room, providing advice and encouragement. Student teams explored various and creative ways of performing their chosen poems—reading chorally, alternating voices, inserting dramatic pauses, and so forth. "What amazed me the most was how eager students were to rehearse," Mr. Carter said, "Knowing that they would be performing for an authentic audience on Friday afternoon gave them a real reason to practice. Parents told me later that many wanted to practice their poems at home as well." Mr. Carter also made sure to talk with students about appropriate behavior and etiquette for a poetry slam.

On Friday afternoon, Mr. Carter rearranged the classroom with a stage at the front of the room. Chairs were brought in for the guests—the school's principal, parents, and other family members. And then, one after another, students performed their poems with expression, enthusiasm, and pure joy. Their reward was the snapping of fingers and clapping of hands that ended each performance. Students left school that afternoon feeling like stars!

Later, Mr. Carter reflected on what had occurred in his classroom. "I did this poetry slam as a way to get the school year off to a good start. But seeing how well students responded to the opportunity to practice and perform poetry, I know I am going to make this a regular part of my classroom curriculum. At least once a month, we will choose a theme, or perhaps a featured poet, and go through the week rehearsing and eventually performing the poetry. I want my students to feel like stars, and this is certainly one way to make that happen."

Research Supporting Practice and Performance

The research supporting practice and performance is found in the research on reading fluency. Reading fluency is a critical competency for success in reading. It consists of two sub-competencies: (1) the ability to read words in texts automatically or effortlessly (LaBerge and Samuels 1974) and (2) the ability to read orally with appropriate expression and phrasing that reflect the meaning of the passage (Rasinski and Young 2024; Schreiber 1980). Repeated reading and assisted reading are two key instructional methods for developing both automaticity in word recognition and expressive or prosodic reading (Rasinski 2010):

- **Repeated reading** involves having readers read a text multiple times until they achieve a level of reading that approximates the reading of a proficient reader.
- **Assisted reading** involves a reader reading a text while simultaneously hearing a fluent oral rendering of the same text by a proficient reader.

Reviews of research suggest that both methods are effective in improving fluency and overall reading performance (Rasinski et al. 2011; Stevens, Walker, and Vaughn 2017).

The challenge for teachers is to implement these fluency instructional methods in ways that are authentic and engaging for students. An alternative way to think of repeated reading and assisted reading is as rehearsal and performance. If readers know they will eventually be asked to perform a text for an audience, they have a natural reason to engage in rehearsal or practice. Moreover, the rehearsal—consisting of both repeated and assisted reading—is not aimed simply at reading the words in the text accurately and automatically; the goal is also to achieve a level of expression that reflects the meaning of the text and is satisfying for an audience. Whether the performance is a lecture, a poetry performance, or a theatrical play, the performers have an intrinsic motivation to engage in rehearsal. Thus, the notion of practice and performance as described in this chapter is not only science but also artful.

Benefits of Practice and Performance

When done on a regular basis, practice and performance have been found to lead to improvements in a variety of reading competencies (Young et al. 2019). These include word recognition accuracy and automaticity, prosodic reading, comprehension, motivation for reading, and confidence in oneself as a reader. Certainly, standing and performing in front of an audience can be a daunting task, even for adults. By performing regularly for classmates and others, students will develop a sense that they have the ability to read well and in such a way that a listening audience will find meaning and satisfaction in their performances. Confidence and success in one performance breed higher levels of confidence and success in subsequent performances.

Implementing Practice and Performance

So, how can you begin to implement practice and performance reading in your classroom? The great thing about this approach is that regardless of the grade level or age of students you may be working with, the process is generally the same. First and foremost, you need to develop an authentic reason for students to want to practice reading a text. Simply asking students to read a text four or five times with no real purpose in mind will not engage and motivate them. The notion of performance is the key. If students know that they will eventually perform their assigned text, they have a natural and powerful reason to practice or rehearse. In thinking about how students will perform, ask yourself these questions:

- Do you envision students performing daily, weekly, or monthly?
- Where will the performances take place? Will they happen in your classroom or in the school auditorium, or might students' performances be recorded in a studio for streaming online?

Once you have a sense of where students' performances will happen, you can complete the rest of the planning (see page 32 for a sample practice and performance protocol).

Finding Engaging Texts

Consideration must be given to the types of written texts used for practice and performance. Certain texts are meant to be read orally with good expression and performed for an audience. These include but are not limited to the following:

- Poetry
- Songs and song lyrics
- Reader's theater scripts
- Speeches and oratory
- Monologues
- Dialogues and interviews

At the end of this chapter, you'll find five poems by David L. Harrison to use for practice and performance in your classroom. Indeed, any of the texts in this book can be used for practice and performance. If you'd also like students to practice and perform with reader's theater scripts, see the box for suggestions.

Reader's Theater Scripts for Practice and Performance

Folktales on Stage: Children's Plays for Reader's Theater with 16 Scripts from World Folk and Fairy Tales and Legends, Including Asian, African, and Native American by Aaron Shepard (2017)

Foods for the Future by Saskia Lacey (2016)

Reader's Theater . . . and So Much More! (Grades 5–6) by Brenda McGee and Debbie Keiser Triska (2010)

With these various types of materials available, you can begin to plan the types of performance you wish to have in your classroom—for example, one week you might do poetry, the next scripts, and the next speeches. Or perhaps you might want to mix and match the various genres of materials you use, organizing them around particular themes, times of the year, or poets/authors.

In a fifth-grade classroom, for instance, the teacher selected a patriotic theme near the beginning of November in honor of Veterans Day. Various students practiced and performed patriotic poetry, especially poems in honor of veterans, and another group of students performed a script based on Abraham Lincoln's Gettysburg Address (which was first performed by President Lincoln in November 1863). The entire performance was bookended by the whole class singing patriotic songs—*God Bless America* and *This Land Is Your Land*.

The following week, the teacher chose the theme of gratitude in anticipation of Thanksgiving, and students read and performed poetry that matched that theme. Some students even wrote their own gratitude poetry, which they also performed on the Tuesday before Thanksgiving.

A Multiday Practice and Performance Protocol

When you can turn your practice and performance instruction into a regularly occurring routine, students will have a better understanding of the actual protocol used for bringing a text to performance. Here's a simple five-day routine that should take no more than 20 to 30 minutes per day of class time. Of course, students would also be expected to continue to practice on their own at school and at home.

- **Monday:** Introduce students to the texts for the week and model reading the texts for students while they follow along on their own copies of the texts or a text displayed on the board.

- **Tuesday:** As a class, read all the texts for the week chorally and discuss content and how the texts could be performed. Students choose or are assigned their texts.

- **Wednesday:** Circulate through the room, providing formative feedback and encouragement, while students rehearse in small groups.

- **Thursday (Dress Rehearsal):** Students go through a practice performance and iron out any potential problems or difficulties.

- **Friday (Grand Performance):** Students perform their assigned texts for classmates and any visitors to the class.

No doubt, it will take several rounds of practice and performance before students become familiar with the routine. As you develop the routine with students, discuss appropriate behavior during presentations. The goals are to create a regular end-of-the-week performance that replicates what might be found in the real world and for students to have justifiable pride in their performances and their work leading up to their performances.

Assessing Practice and Performance

Practice and performance routines are primarily intended to improve students' reading fluency—the ability to read words automatically and with appropriate expression or prosody that reflects the meaning of the text. Traditionally, reading fluency has been assessed by using reading speed as a proxy for automatic word recognition. While such an approach taps into the one aspect of fluency, it neglects the prosodic, expressive part of fluency. Indeed, if students aim to improve their reading speed, expression often suffers as students race through their assigned reading.

Practice and performance routines are primarily intended to improve students' reading fluency—the ability to read words automatically and with appropriate expression or prosody that reflects the meaning of the text.

We recommend the use of a rubric that allows teachers to use their own best judgment to assess students' fluency development. Figure 4.1 shows a commonly used rubric called the Multidimensional Fluency Scale, developed and adapted by Jerry Zutell and Tim Rasinski (1991) and available at timrasinski.com/resources.html. Although this rubric may not assess all parts of the practice and performance routine, it provides you with a starting place for assessing students on fluency. You may wish to add other categories, such as "engages in authentic rehearsal and practice during assigned times," "displays confidence when performing," or "is attentive and responsive as an audience member." In addition, you could work with students to create a student-friendly rubric that they can use to assess their own practice and performance. Imagine such a rubric put on display in your classroom and regularly used by students to track their own progress in reading fluency. Rubrics such as the Multidimensional Fluency Scale are particularly valuable because they allow teachers and students to develop a true eye and ear for what really matters when becoming a fluent reader.

Figure 4.1—Multidimensional Fluency Scale

	1	2	3	4
Expression and Volume	Reads in a quiet voice, as if to get words out. The reading does not sound natural, like talking to a friend.	Reads in a quiet voice. The reading sounds natural in part of the text, but the reader does not always sound like they are talking to a friend.	Reads with volume and expression. However, sometimes the reader slips into expressionless reading and does not sound like they are talking to a friend.	Reads with varied volume and expression. The reader sounds like they are talking to a friend, with their voice matching the interpretation of the passage.
Phrasing	Reads word by word in a monotone voice.	Reads in two- or three-word phrases, not adhering to punctuation, stress, and intonation.	Reads with a mixture of run-on phrases, mid-sentence pauses for breath, and some choppiness. There is reasonable stress and intonation.	Reads with good phrasing; adhering to punctuation, stress, and intonation.
Smoothness	Frequently hesitates while reading, sounds out words, and repeats words or phrases. The reader makes multiple attempts to read the same passage.	Reads with extended pauses or hesitations. The reader has many rough spots.	Reads with occasional breaks in rhythm. The reader has difficulty with specific words and/or sentence structures.	Reads smoothly with some breaks, but self-corrects with difficult words and/or sentence structures.
Pace	Reads slowly and laboriously.	Reads moderately slowly.	Reads generally at an appropriate rate throughout the reading.	Reads at an appropriate conversational pace throughout the reading.

Note: A total score of 10 or more indicates that a student is making good progress in fluency.

What Teachers Can Learn from Students' Practice and Performance

The instructional focus of practice and performance is the development of students' reading fluency. Through regular use of a rubric over time, you can determine how students are performing in each area of the rubric and the extent to which they are making progress as well.

However, practice and performance can also be used to determine other important competencies, such as the following:

- The student is able to speak orally to an audience with confidence.
- The student is able to work with others in developing a performance.
- The student is able to respond positively to formative feedback provided by the teacher and others.
- The student is able to listen attentively and supportively to others as they perform.

Conferring with Students about Practice and Performance

Conferring with students is an important part of the practice and performance routine. This conferring should focus on the performance—the end goal of the practice. The teacher may review the script with students to identify different points at which emphasis, volume, pacing, or some other aspect of expressive reading may change. What do students want their performance to look and sound like? The teacher may listen to a performance and give formative feedback and encouragement to students. Considering that students may not have had much past experience in authentic performances, they will likely need many ideas on how to make their performance unique and appealing to an audience. Conferences can take place with individual students, in small groups, or with the entire class. Brainstorming with class members is a great way to encourage and acknowledge creativity among students. (Refer back to chapter 3 for more suggestions on how to make conferences with students productive and positive.)

Involving Family Members

Practice and performance offer wonderful opportunities to involve family members in their children's literacy development. First, to reach a point where students can perform their texts with confidence, fluency, and meaning, they will need to practice more than perhaps they have done in the past. The key here is to inform family members of the importance of being supportive practice audiences for their children's rehearsal and provide guidelines for support. Here are some ideas to share with students' families:

- Set a regular time for children to practice (rehearse) with you.
- Learn ways to support children during reading—you can model reading to children, read with children, and, of course, listen to children read.
- Provide positive and formative feedback for children's reading at home.

Figure 4.2 shows an adaptation of the Multidimensional Fluency Scale rubric that students developed for working with classmates and for practicing at home. Families can also use this rubric when chatting with children about their reading.

Figure 4.2—The Multidimensional Fluency Scale: Student Edition

	1	2	3	4	Score
Expression and Volume	Too quiet, no expression	Less quiet, some expression	Volume generally good, adequate expression	Just-right volume, very expressive	
Phrasing	Word by word	Two- or three-word phrases	Generally good phrasing	Excellent phrasing	
Smoothness	Very choppy	Choppy	Generally smooth	Very smooth	
Pace	Very slow (or very fast)	Slower or faster than normal	Generally good pacing	Just-right pacing	
Total					

Of course, family members can also play the role of the audience for children in the classroom. There are few things more motivating for students than to perform for an authentic audience—particularly an audience made up of family members. Whenever possible, plans should be made to invite families to any and all performances given by students in school.

Guidelines for Successful Performances

The goal of any practice or rehearsal students engage in is to prepare for the grand performance. Each performance needs to be well planned to make it as engaging, authentic, and fulfilling for students as possible. When preparing for a performance, consider these points:

- What space will be used for the performance?
- How will the space be arranged?
- What time of day will the performance occur?
- Who will be invited to the performance besides class members? How will the invitation be communicated?
- How will audience members be asked to act and respond to the performances—particularly in ways that students will find formative?
- Will there be a host or emcee for the performance?

- What equipment will be required for the performance (a lectern, props, background scenery and decorations, a microphone and sound amplification, recording devices, etc.)?
- How will the performance be brought to an end (a song sung by all students, refreshments afterward, etc.)?

On the following pages, poet David L. Harrison presents several poems that can easily be rehearsed and performed by students to build fluency and overall reading achievement.

Take Time for Reflective Conversations

In this chapter, we present the notion of authentic performance of texts by students that will require practice—practice not aimed at reading as fast as possible but practice focused on delivering a meaningful, expressive, and satisfying oral performance for an audience.

Reflect on these questions independently, then discuss them with colleagues:

- How will you fit practice and performance into your literacy curriculum?
- What texts will work best for practice and performance in your literacy instruction?
- How will you include conferencing with students about practice and performance in your curriculum?
- What role will home involvement have in your practice and performance program?

Name: _____   Date: _____

Poem for Two Voices: "Finding the Right Word"

Directions: Read, practice, and perform the poem.

Finding the Right Word

by David L. Harrison

First Voice

Good thing for bugs, a
welcome mat is thick.

We know the right word isn't
quick; it's quickly.

Poets face such vexing
problems daily.

Second Voice

If it were thin, our feet would
squash them quick.

But then to rhyme, we'd say
the mat was thickly.

Finding words for what we
want to sayly.

Name: _____   Date: _____

Poem for Two Voices: "Two Birds under a Park Bench"

Directions: Read, practice, and perform the poem.

Two Birds under a Park Bench
by David L. Harrison

First Bird	**Second Bird**
What do you think?	
	About what?
Those seeds.	
	What about them?
Should we?	
	Should we what?
That man is throwing seeds. Should we go get some?	
	No.
He's giving them away! Free seeds! Don't you want some?	
	No.
I can't believe this!	
What is it you don't get about free seeds?	
	I get it.
Simple question.	
What can you possibly not like about free seeds?	
	I eat worms.

Poem for Two Voices: "Mr. Lincoln's Speech"

Directions: Read, practice, and perform the poem.

Mr. Lincoln's Speech
by David L. Harrison

First Voice (Child learning the speech)

I'm learning Mr. Lincoln's speech.

The way he talks sounds serious,
sad, but just right.
Four score and seven mean 87,
but his way sounds more important.

America was a young country
when he gave this speech,
only 87 years old!

Just think about it.
The young nation
was fighting a war to decide
if it was going to make it
as one united country.

Second Voice (from the Gettysburg Address)

Four score and seven years ago . . .

. . . our fathers brought forth on this
continent, a new nation. . . .

. . . Now we are engaged in a great
civil war, testing whether that nation,
or any nation so conceived and so
dedicated, can long endure . . .

(continued)

Poem for Two Voices: "Mr. Lincoln's Speech" *(continued)*

Directions: Read, practice, and perform the poem.

First Voice (Child learning the speech)

Hundreds of thousands of people died
in the fight to keep the U.S. together.
President Lincoln is telling Americans
to never forget the price they paid
to live in a free country.

I may not get all the words,
but I sure get what they mean.
America will never give up!
No matter what, Americans will
do what it takes to always be
the land of the free.

Second Voice (from the Gettysburg Address)

. . . We here highly resolve that these
dead shall not have died in vain . . .

. . . that government of the people,
by the people, for the people, shall
not perish from the earth.

Poem for Three Voices: "The Picnic"

Directions: Read, practice, and perform the poem.

The Picnic
by David L. Harrison

First Voice	**Second Voice**	**Third Voice**
The problem with a picnic is the ants.		
	As quickly as the cloth is on the table,	
		You'll feel the first one crawling up your pants.
People never really stand a chance.		
	Food without intruders is a fable.	
		The problem with a picnic is the ants.
They'll find you if they have to crawl from France.		
	No one understands how fast they're able.	
		You'll feel the first one crawling up your pants.
Around the food, they do a victory dance,		
	A buggy boogie, if you need a label.	
		The problem with a picnic is the ants.

(continued)

Poem for Three Voices: "The Picnic" (continued)

Directions: Read, practice, and perform the poem.

First Voice	Second Voice	Third Voice
Their teeny-tiny voices utter chants.		
	I heard this from my buggy Auntie Mabel.	
		You'll feel the first one crawling up your pants.
The way they rudely push and shove and prance		
	Makes you think they grew up in a stable.	
		The problem with a picnic is the ants.
You'll feel the first one		
	Crawling	
		Up your pants.

Name: _____   Date: _____

Poem for Three Voices: "A Poem Is . . ."

Directions: Read, practice, and perform the poem.

A Poem Is . . .
by David L. Harrison

First Voice	Second Voice	Third Voice
Blue jay wing Red rose		
	Baby toes Leaves in spring	
		Deer tracks Puppy eyes
Chocolate cake Lemon drop		
	Pork chop Shake and bake	
		Taste of paste French fries
Marching band River bends		
	Old friends Grandstand	
		Tardy bell Yellow flowers

(continued)

Poem for Three Voices: "A Poem Is . . ." (continued)

Directions: Read, practice, and perform the poem.

First Voice	Second Voice	Third Voice
Skinned knee Cold brook		
	New book Honeybee	
		Chocolate pudding Sudden showers
A poem is Beyond measure		
	Found treasure A poem is	
		A tire swing— Anything
[All voices together] A poem . . . is.		

Chapter 5

Student-Led Discussions

A change from teacher- to student-led discussions in Ms. Brockton's class started with a fifth-grade student. Ms. Brockton was leading a discussion of The Blossoming Universe of Violet Diamond *by Brenda Woods. Jacelynn raised her hand. Instead of answering the question that Ms. Brockton had posed, Jacelynn asked, "When can we discuss our questions?" Silence. Then, Ms. Brockton unfroze. "Let's start right now," she said. "Turn-and-talk and agree on a question with your partner. Then, write it on the whiteboard, and groups can choose a question to discuss."*

In the moment, Ms. Brockton switched gears from a teacher-controlled discussion to respecting her students' need to pose and discuss their questions. It was a light bulb moment for her! That evening, Ms. Brockton wrote this entry in her journal:

> Jacelynn's question pushed me to rethink how I conduct discussions. At first, I felt shocked and hurt. But then I thought, why shouldn't students want to write and discuss their questions? Some of the discussions I observed showed great enthusiasm. Students listened to their peers and even questioned them. We'll move forward by learning together.

This journal entry reveals that Ms. Brockton used reflection to explore her feelings and decision to invite students to ask questions. Her response also showed students that she heard their request. By allowing them to try this student-centered process immediately, Ms. Brockton silently telegraphed this message to her students: "I trust your thinking and value the questions this book raised in your minds."

In this chapter, you'll learn specific techniques for supporting student-led literary conversations that develop students' agency; improve their ability to create high-level, open-ended questions; and help them become active listeners who respond to their peers' comments instead of focusing solely on answers to prepared questions. Many of these techniques are part of the lessons in Part II.

Some of the content of this chapter has been adapted from *Read, Talk, Write: 35 Lessons That Teach Students to Analyze Fiction and Nonfiction* by Laura Robb (Corwin, 2017).

Five Kinds of Student-Led Discussions That Improve Comprehension

When students have little to no experience with composing and discussing questions related to their reading, they will need a variety of opportunities to practice (Daniels 2002; Robb 2017). There are five ways to allow students to lead discussions of texts and resources such as teacher read-alouds, poems, short texts, books, photographs, and videos (Robb 2017):

1. **Turn-and-talk** is a 1- to 3-minute discussion that can occur frequently during the day, offering students multiple opportunities to exchange thoughts and feelings about a text.

2. **Partner talk** is a 5- to 10-minute discussion with a partner about the same text or two different texts in the same genre or with similar themes.

3. **Whole-class discussions** are 10 to 20 minutes and simulate a conversation. Students don't raise their hands; instead, they listen to their peers carefully and respond to what their classmates say. Responses can include a question, a call for text evidence, or a different way of looking at an idea. The teacher can jumpstart the discussion with an open-ended question or a statement that activates thinking.

4. **Small-group discussions** are 10 to 20 minutes and work well after students have had opportunities to engage in partner talk and whole-class discussions. These discussions are ideal for book clubs and literature circles, where students have conversations about the same text by using open-ended questions they have created.

5. **In-the-head conversations** occur while students read and include mental comments on specific details in a text, questions the text raises, and connections to other materials.

For each type of discussion, it's important to remind students to supply text evidence to support their thinking and develop the habit of backing up hunches with text evidence. The goal is for students to create questions that stimulate diverse responses and use these as they lead discussions about a text.

Initiating Discussions with Interpretive Questions

Research shows that students who are taught to generate their own questions after reading develop a deeper understanding of the text than students who do not receive this training and practice (Robb 2017; Rothstein and Santana 2011; Zimmerman and Keene 2007). Deep comprehension develops because students must have a thorough knowledge of the reading material to create interpretive or open-ended questions. Moreover, by using their own questions, students engage in authentic discussions of a text and also develop greater independence and agency.

Explain to students that there are two kinds of questions: (1) open-ended, interpretive questions that have more than one possible answer, and (2) closed questions that have one correct answer. Suggest verbs that signal questions or statements that have more than one answer: *why, how, evaluate, assess, compare and contrast, conclude, analyze, hypothesize, develop, justify, argue for or against,* and *interpret.* You can display these words in your classroom as a reminder for students to include them in the questions they create.

Think aloud and show students an open-ended question using a read-aloud text or one of the focus lesson texts in this book. Here's an example for the focus lesson text on inferring ("Making the World a Better Place" in chapter 9): "Why are some young people motivated to change the world in positive ways?" Next, show students how you test a question by finding two different answers: (1) some young people have directly experienced an area that needs change, like Malala Yousafzai wanting education for girls in Pakistan, and (2) some young people have developed a vision for change with a cause they're passionate about and know they can help. Explain that if the question has two possible answers, it's open-ended. It might have other responses as well, but knowing there is more than one answer is enough for students to include the question in discussions and create additional questions.

Guidelines for Student-Led Discussions

Discussions led by students require some guidelines because students are in control of the process. Post the following guidelines on the board or chart paper, review them with students prior to their first small-group discussion, and use the guidelines as reminders:

- Come prepared for the discussion. Complete the reading assignment, and bring the text, your reader's notebook, and a pencil.

- Work with a partner or small group to compose open-ended questions about the text.

- Choose a moderator whose job is to keep the discussion moving forward. The moderator can use prompts for maintaining the flow of a discussion. (Note: See appendix M for a guide with these prompts.)

- Participate in the discussion, being respectful of others. Listen carefully, ask questions to help a speaker clarify an idea, and cite text evidence to support your points and inferences.

Increasing Students' Discussion Capacity

Here are some suggestions for gradually moving students to independence with student-led conversations:

- Start with the turn-and-talk strategy so students have brief talking encounters and can experience sharing, questioning, and listening. Use the prompts in the differentiated lessons in Part II or develop your own.

- Move to a whole-class discussion and motivate students to talk by using an open-ended question that starts the conversation. Tell students that instead of raising their hands, they can participate by adding thoughts or asking questions once a student who is speaking has finished.

- Debrief after the first whole-class discussion, and ask students to reflect on what worked and what could be improved.

Invite students to design guidelines for productive discussions. Revisit the guidelines after two or three months so students can make adjustments based on their experiences. Here are the guidelines that a fifth-grade class developed early in the school year:

Come prepared; do the reading; bring your notebook.

About two months later, the students added this:

Listen and react to what a classmate says; call for text evidence.

These guidelines reveal how much these fifth-grade students value conducting discussions on their own and how much they understand the importance of listening, responding, and raising questions. Continue using turn-and-talk to give students the experience of sharing ideas with and listening carefully to partners.

WAYS TO CONTRIBUTE TO A DISCUSSION

If students have difficulty maintaining a conversation, provide the following ideas for contributing to conversations about texts. It's helpful to post these suggestions on a whiteboard and review them with students before they begin discussing.

- **Restate the speaker's idea.** If a student would like to clarify an idea, they can restate it in their own words and ask the speaker if that was the intended meaning. ("I heard you say _____. Does that sound about right?")

- **Ask a question.** If a student would like the speaker to elaborate on or clarify their thinking, or if a student is curious about a speaker's take on a related issue, the student can ask a question. ("Can you say more about _____?" or "I'm not sure what you meant when you said _____. Can you help me understand?" or "What do you think about _____?")

- **Connect to the speaker's idea.** Students can build on a speaker's idea by first connecting to it. ("I like the point you made about _____, and I have this to add," or "I had a similar idea. Here's how my idea differs from yours.")

- **Offer a different view.** Students can acknowledge the speaker's contribution and then share their own perspectives in a respectful way. ("I hear what you're saying about _____, but I had a different thought when I read the part when _____," or "I see that scene differently. Here's how I see it.")

- **Disagree respectfully.** Sometimes, students will disagree with one another, and that's fine as long as they can frame the talk respectfully. Teach them language they can use to respectfully disagree. ("I didn't see it that way. Instead, I think _____," or "I don't agree; I think it means _____ because _____.")

- **Refer to the text.** When you want students to ground their thinking in the text, encourage them to refer to the text during the discussion, either to provide evidence for an idea or as a point of discussion. ("When it says _____, I infer _____ because _____.")

Repairing Derailed Discussions

If student behavior derails a discussion, address the issue as soon as it arises. Here are suggestions for helping students move to positive, collaborative behavior that respects everyone's ideas and promotes their desire to share them:

- **If no one talks:** First, ask students why they aren't responding; they might tell you they can't recall details or didn't read the selection. If the text is at their instructional or independent reading level, suggest that they read it again to deepen their recall. If the text is too difficult, offer a different text or read it aloud to students. If preparation and readability are not the issues, try a different prompt.

- **If one student repeatedly interrupts:** Have a private discussion with the student, explaining what you noticed and giving the student strategies to help them resist the urge to interrupt. Before a discussion starts, provide a reminder by giving the student an index card with this message on it: "Remember to be a good listener and share ideas when the person speaking has finished."

- **If one student talks over another student:** Confer with the student and ask them to step into the other person's shoes to consider how the person might perceive the situation. Suggest that when ideas pop into the student's head, they can jot them on paper to remember and share when the other student has finished.

Polite Ways to Disagree

Students might find it helpful to have prompts that show how to politely disagree with a peer's idea. Remind students that a main goal of these conversations is to shine a light on and be respectful and encouraging of diverse interpretations that can be supported with text details. Moreover, valuing other points of view makes a discussion richer and opens students to hearing ideas they might not have explored. On the flip side, when students feel their ideas are not valued, they are likely to refrain from engaging in discussions. Students can use these prompts to disagree respectfully:

- "I understand your idea, but I have a different interpretation."
- "That's an interesting point that I did not think of, and here's my idea."
- "I find that idea interesting, but I'm not sure you can support it with text evidence."
- "Even though our positions seem different, I believe they have common points. Let me explain."
- "It's okay that we have more than one interpretation. Here's what I think."
- "Your idea intrigues me, and I think my idea grows out of it. Let me explain."

DEVELOPING SELF-ADVOCACY

Self-advocacy is when students develop the ability to speak and act on behalf of themselves, such as asking for help with a word ladder, or on behalf of a cause, such as protecting endangered species or slowing the effects of climate change. During conferences, help students learn to share their needs by encouraging them to ask for help with tasks or with their interactions with peers. For example, perhaps a student shies away from participating in student-led conversations because they fear the negative comments of a peer. Help the student find the words to respond in a positive way and invite them to practice with you. Suggest statements such as: *I respect your ideas, and I'm hoping you'll hear mine*, or *You don't have to agree with me, but I'd like you to hear my interpretation*. After students implement what they practiced, hold a follow-up conference to discuss their experience and feelings about it.

Self-advocacy includes students asking for help if they don't understand a lesson or how to respond to questions or directions. Many students don't know how to self-advocate. However, they can learn more about the process through your coaching and by discussing and analyzing how characters in texts self-advocate.

Helping students find the confidence and strength to stand up for their needs during specific learning situations takes time. Build students' confidence to self-advocate by noticing their progress and celebrating each time they use positive language to speak up for themselves.

When Students Listen Actively, Literary Conversations Blossom

To become active listeners during discussions, students need multiple opportunities each week to practice talking with partners and the whole class. All participants should listen actively during discussions, but this doesn't come naturally for everyone. Take some time to define active listening, discuss why it's important, and model it for students by including the following three points in your think-aloud. Explain that when someone else is talking, listeners should do the following:

- Keep focused on what the speaker is saying.
- Set aside any distracting thoughts that arise.
- Respond to what the speaker says in a question, call for text evidence, or disagree politely, and then offer their own ideas.

Encourage listeners to jot notes in their notebooks to help them remember what the speaker said, but the focus should be on understanding the ideas the speaker is conveying first and then reacting to and responding to them.

When students discuss a text in pairs or small groups, they have a responsibility to keep the discussion moving forward. We recommend that you have students tape or staple *Prompts That Keep a Discussion Moving Forward* (appendix M) in the back of their reader's notebooks. Students can practice using these prompts during whole-class discussions and then during small-group conversations. The prompts support self-advocacy by giving students language to politely challenge the thinking of their peers as well as state their own positions with confidence.

Before students are invited to lead their own conversations, they will benefit from these experiences (Robb 2017):

- Teach students to compose open-ended interpretive questions using poems or texts from the differentiated lessons on visualizing, inferring, and comparing and contrasting.
- Have students turn-and-talk frequently during daily read-alouds and while you read aloud texts in the focus lessons.

- Invite students to practice writing interpretive questions about a poem or short text they read in the lessons and then practice discussing the questions, always offering text evidence.
- Lead whole-class discussions using texts from the teacher-led focus lessons or other read-aloud texts. Have students practice composing open-ended questions, listening actively while discussing the questions, and providing text details to support their thinking.

Offer students frequent opportunities to practice writing and discussing open-ended questions using the texts in this book, your daily read-alouds, and books used during instructional reading lessons.

Student-Led Discussions Using the Fishbowl Technique

You might decide to focus on turn-and-talk, partner talk, and whole-class discussions until you observe that students feel comfortable. For students in third and fourth grade, this may be as far as you want to go. However, for students in fifth grade, we encourage you to consider trying student-led small-group conversations using the fishbowl technique.

The fishbowl technique allows students to observe a student-led conversation and develop a mental model of the process (Fisher et al. 2007). Students who participate in the discussion sit in a circle, while the rest of the class forms a circle of observers and listeners around them. Allow 10 minutes for the discussion and 5 minutes to debrief and set goals. To implement the fishbowl technique, we suggest the following steps:

- Select a text from one of the focus lessons you've presented so that all students will be familiar with it.
- Create an open-ended or interpretive question to jumpstart the conversation.
- Set up the classroom with an inner circle of four to six chairs. These chairs are for students who will discuss the text.
- For the first fishbowl discussion, choose students who are comfortable discussing ideas in texts and citing text evidence as support. Have them bring the text, their notebooks, and pencils.
- Establish goals for students observing and listening in the outer circle, and have them bring their notebooks and pencils so that they can jot thoughts on their observations and share them with the class. You can assign specific practices students should watch for, or let the students choose. Practices could include asking open-ended questions, active listening, responding to what peers say, disagreeing politely, asking questions, keeping the discussion moving forward, and calling for text evidence.
- Review discussion guidelines. Remind students that one person talks while others listen. All participants should respond respectfully and use text evidence to support their point of view.
- Hold the discussion.
- Have students in the outer circle share their ideas and questions after students in the inner circle have completed their discussion.

- Have students write the date and title of the text on a page in their notebooks. Then, invite students to write two to four key ideas from the discussion.

- Debrief by asking students what they have learned. Require that students not refer to classmates by name but instead focus on what participants said during the discussion.

- Based on the debriefing discussion, have students write goals for the next fishbowl discussion in their notebooks.

You may want to have more than one fishbowl discussion using this procedure, especially if students would benefit from extra practice. For students in grades 3, 4, and 5, we recommend having one fishbowl group at a time. Students' debriefings and goals can help you understand when they are ready to work on their own.

Teacher Guidelines for Groups Meeting at the Same Time

Once you start using student-led discussions and have three or four groups meeting at the same time, you'll be able to observe and listen to one or two of the groups. Ask students in the other groups to write what they learned from the discussion in their notebooks so you have a clear picture of their conversation with peers. After students experience two to three student-led discussions, have them assess their participation using a discussion checklist (see appendix J). Encourage students to be honest with their self-assessment; explain that it won't receive a grade and it's meant to help them grow as readers and writers.

Following these steps each time student-led conversations occur will refresh students' memories of the process and remind them of your expectations:

- **Review what students need.** Remind them to bring the text, their notebooks, and their pencils.

- **Explain what you'll do.** Identify the one or two groups you'll watch as a silent observer.

- **Remind students of the guidelines.** Review how to develop open-ended questions, as this is the first task groups will complete. Then, remind students to be active listeners who can disagree, raise a question, or call for text evidence.

- **Have students complete a notebook entry.** You can invite them to write what they learned from the discussion or have them note two to four things they discussed.

- **Invite students to debrief and set a goal for their next discussion.** Ask students to discuss everything that worked during the conversation, set one goal for the next time they meet, and jot their thoughts and goals in their notebooks. Have students share with the class.

- **Wrap up with a summary of what you noticed.** Summarize the content of the conversations you observed and then point out all the positives you noticed, such as active listening, asking open-ended questions, responding to what peers say, providing text evidence, and disagreeing politely.

The more practice students have with leading conversations about the poems and short texts in this book, the less reminding and directing you'll need to do. If you and your colleagues want to learn more about student-led discussions, consider a book study on one of the professional texts listed in the box below.

Literature Circles: Voice and Choice in Book Clubs and Reading Groups by Harvey Daniels (2002)

Quality Talk about Text: Discussion Practices for Talking and Thinking about Text by Ian A. G. Wilkinson and Kristin Bourdage (2021)

Read, Talk, Write: 35 Lessons That Teach Students to Analyze Fiction and Nonfiction by Laura Robb (2017)

Take Time for Reflective Conversations

Reflect on these questions independently, then discuss them with colleagues:

- What do students learn when they engage in literary conversations that they lead?
- How does the fishbowl technique help students?
- What are the benefits of having students compose and discuss their own questions?
- Why can student-led conversations become derailed or not work?

Chapter 6

Assessment-Driven Interventions

It's the week before Thanksgiving break. Ms. Springer and her fifth-grade teammates are meeting about their students' progress in reading. At the start of the school year, with 60 minutes planned each day for literacy, the teachers felt they had enough time to address the needs of all students. However, on this chilly November day, the teachers' frustration is palpable as these words echo: "I'm spending so much time lifting readers who are below grade level that there's not enough time to consistently meet with other students." The culprit seems to be time—not enough of it. The reality is that schedules won't change, and the teachers' challenge has become adjusting how to use the time available to them. Their goal is to continue supporting students who are reading below grade level but also to have enough time to meet with students who are reading at and above grade level.

This chapter shows you how to plan for and find time to meet with all students to provide extra practice and support after students complete a set of differentiated lessons on a specific strategy, such as drawing conclusions. To provide extra practice and support to students, you'll need to set aside 60 or 90 minutes of your reading block for three to five days, depending on the amount of time your students need (see figure 6.1). Use the remaining time in your reading block to have students work on your ELA curriculum.

Based on our experiences, we suggest that you study and interpret formative assessments and create an intervention plan soon after completing a set of lessons and before introducing a new set of lessons and reading strategy. Formative assessments such as students' questions, their participation in focus lessons, their notebook writing, and observation of their discussions will drive your decisions for organizing students into three to four flexible groups for additional intervention. The word *flexible* is key because, although the differentiated lessons are designed for students reading

> If you notice that some students need support during one of the lessons, make time to help them right away so a small confusion doesn't grow and impede their progress.

below, at, or above grade level, your formative assessments identify students from *any group* who will benefit from additional support with a targeted reading strategy, vocabulary, or word work.

An article in *Education Week* notes that since 2017, scores from the National Association of Educational Progress (NAEP) show an increasing number of basic and below-basic readers—that is, developing readers who require support because they read below grade level. These below-grade-level readers are in grades 4 and 8 at all socioeconomic levels (Sparks 2021). According to P. David Pearson, professor emeritus in the School of Education at the University of California, Berkeley, reading comprehension should be taught alongside decoding and word study skills from the start:

> We can fall into an either-or track, so comprehension and word recognition become a kind of a zero-sum game. And we want to discourage that. . . . Just because we're teaching them word recognition doesn't mean that we can't teach comprehension. And just because we're focusing on building knowledge doesn't mean that we have to de-emphasize strategy instruction. . . . We want to think of the various instructional components and activities as complementary and integrated rather than completely separated and independent of one another (as quoted in Sparks 2021, para. 14).

The differentiated lessons in this book build on Pearson's suggestions. Applying strategies for deeper comprehension, enlarged vocabulary, fluency practice, and word study are integral parts of the lessons. Core curriculum teachers can meet all students' needs with the differentiated lessons because each group reads accessible texts and applies the same strategies and skills in the context of their text. Providing interventions based on formative assessments allows you to support and scaffold students who are reading below grade level as well as stretch the thinking and reading skills of students who are reading near, at, and above grade-level.

A list of suggested formative assessments to evaluate students' progress can be found on page 75 of chapter 7. As students work with their partners during both the focus lessons and while using the differentiated texts, assess their progress and answer any questions they raise. While students are discussing texts and writing in their notebooks, circulate with your clipboard in hand to jot your observations and make notes that can inform your instructional decisions, including how you will group students for intervention after completing a set of lessons. These assessments help you decide whether all students are ready to move on or whether certain students need targeted support on a specific strategy or skill, no matter what their group placement was for the differentiated lessons. Even above-grade-level readers might require support with applying strategies that foster critical and analytical thinking. Reserve time to reflect on the assessments you've gathered and make instructional decisions that benefit all readers.

> Reserve time to reflect on the assessments you've gathered and make instructional decisions that benefit all readers.

As you reflect on students' level of understanding and the individual needs revealed by the formative assessments, use the information to organize students into three intervention groups:

1. Students who need scaffolding and/or reteaching

2. Students who can deepen their understanding and expertise with extra practice

3. Students who can be engaged in enrichment that stretches their critical thinking and collaborative skills

The grouping of students is not only *flexible* but also *fluid*; it will change depending on students' understanding of the content in the differentiated lessons.

Implementing assessment-driven interventions after completing a set of differentiated lessons on a specific strategy such as inferring or visualizing can increase students' capacity to successfully experience future lessons. For example, understanding inferences supports students' ability to compare and contrast, draw conclusions, and brainstorm lists of connotations for specific words. When you use specific evidence about students' learning to make instructional decisions, your first step is to set aside time to support or extend learning for each intervention group. Adapting instruction based on formative assessments allows students to gain the understanding needed to apply what they've practiced to lengthier texts in ELA and across the curriculum.

Research indicates that core curriculum teachers can successfully support 80 percent of their students (Howard 2009; Owocki 2010). The differentiated lessons in this book, combined with assessment-driven interventions and students' daily independent reading, can help you move beyond this 80-percent benchmark.

However, finding time to schedule additional practice and support for multiple groups can feel daunting. The scheduling ideas that follow suggest how to organize time with the goal of reaching and teaching all students in your class. Most interventions in this book are designed to occur over two to four days. If your class is large and you have more than three intervention groups, you might need one or two additional days.

Scheduling Assessment-Driven Interventions

To teach reading, most third- and fourth-grade teachers have 90 to 120 minutes per day, and some fifth-grade teachers have 60 to 90 minutes per day (Shanahan 2019). The scheduling suggestions presented here show how interventions might fit into your daily literacy block. If you have more than three groups, you will need additional time to meet with all the groups.

> Intervention groups of five or six students are ideal for scaffolding, support, and enrichment. If you have more than six students in any group, you may need to divide it in half and present the lesson twice.

Three Intervention Groups in a 60-Minute Literacy Block

In a 60-minute literacy block, you can schedule intervention groups over three days. Figure 6.1 shows what this schedule might look like.

Figure 6.1—Three Intervention Groups in 60-Minute Schedule

	15 minutes	15 minutes	25 minutes	5 minutes
Monday–Wednesday	Independent reading	Reteaching lesson; read-aloud	Instructional reading: Teacher meets with one group while the other groups work independently.*	Wrap-up, with teacher giving positive feedback
Thursday–Friday	Independent reading	Reteaching lesson; read-aloud	Instructional reading: Teacher meets with one group that needs extra help or returns to the reading curriculum.	Wrap-up, with teacher giving positive feedback

*Students working independently should also be focused on reading; their choices could include independent reading, writing about reading, or other assignments.

Three Intervention Groups in a 90-Minute Literacy Block

Having 90 minutes allows you to meet with one or two intervention groups each day and still have two additional days left in the week to support students who would benefit from even more scaffolding. Figure 6.2 shows what this schedule might look like.

Providing students with extra practice and feedback helps them acquire the knowledge and skills needed to apply what they've practiced and learned to other texts. Save copies of your plans so you can revisit them if students need to refresh their recall later in the year.

Planning Assessment-Driven Interventions

When planning interventions for students, ask yourself these questions:

- Am I planning work for students based on my formative assessments?
- Should I prepare models for students to use as resources?
- Are directions clear?
- Can I estimate how much time students will need? How does this affect the scheduling of groups?

Figure 6.2—Three Intervention Groups in a 90-Minute Schedule

	20 minutes	15 minutes	50 minutes	5 minutes
Monday	Independent reading	Reteaching lesson; read-aloud	Instructional reading: Teacher meets with two groups for 20 to 25 minutes each while the other groups work independently.*	Wrap-up, with teacher giving positive feedback
Tuesday–Wednesday	Independent reading	Reteaching lesson; read-aloud	Instructional reading: Teacher meets with one or two groups for 20 to 25 minutes each while the other groups work independently.*	Wrap-up, with teacher giving positive feedback
Thursday–Friday	Independent reading	Reteaching lesson; read-aloud	Instructional reading: Teacher works with one group that needs more help or returns to the reading curriculum.	Wrap-up, with teacher giving positive feedback

*Students working independently should also be focused on reading; their choices could include independent reading, writing about reading, or other assignments.

- Have I planned to remind students of the materials they'll need (reader's notebook, pencil, and independent reading book)?
- Will students understand that if others are still working when they complete their work, they can read their self-selected independent reading book?

Once you've addressed these planning questions, identify materials students will use in their intervention groups. As you plan for all groups, decide whether students should use a text they've practiced with already or whether it would be more helpful for them to work with different accessible texts. When the text is easy to read, students can focus on the reading strategy or word work. Materials for students can also include visuals, videos, and online articles (all of which you should preview to ensure that they're appropriate). It's helpful to compile a set of poems and short texts for use when students need extra practice or for reteaching the entire class.

If students require additional practice with reading informational texts, find books in your classroom or school library, in the digital resources available to your school, or identify other appropriate texts. Poems, dramatizations of short stories, folktales, plays, and so forth can be found online. Work with your librarian and colleagues to find materials that meet students' needs; for quick online access, create a list of websites and online videos and texts you've identified. The goal is to use a variety of short texts for interventions with students to continually improve their reading and listening skills.

Resources for Additional Short Texts and Poems

- *Out of Wonder* by Kwame Alexander (2021)
- *A Pocketful of Poems* by Nikki Grimes (2018)
- *The Random House Book of Poetry for Children* by Jack Prelutsky (2007)
- *Hoop Kings* by Charles R. Smith (2007)
- *Cricket*: cricketmedia.com
- Poets.org/Poems for Kids: poets.org/poems-kids
- *OWL*: owlkids.com
- *Storyworks*: storyworks.scholastic.com
- *Time for Kids*: timeforkids.com
- *Zoobooks*: rangerrick.org/magazines/zoobooks

Providing Groups with Directions and Resources

Planning to support three or more different intervention groups means that directions to each group need to be crystal clear. Before you start working with one group, clarify directions and expectations for all groups so students understand their assignments. Reserve time for students to ask questions, and provide resources with models of your expectations to boost independence in learning. These resources could include the following:

- A notebook entry you created and have discussed with students displayed using a document camera.
- A video for students that reviews a process such as inferring.
- A student resource such as a list of literary elements, the procedure for figuring out words' meanings using context clues, a list of words using a Greek or Latin root, and so on.
- Examples of word building that students will practice displayed using a document camera (multiple forms of words, homophones, homonyms, building word families, creating lists of words starting with a specific prefix, and so on).
- A student resource that reviews key points and a short text selection to help students review and practice a previously taught strategy.

While teaching members of an intervention group, keep chart paper or a small whiteboard handy to turn your thoughts into visuals and to note students' ideas. As you support a group of students, focus on listening to and watching them so you can ask questions that help them clarify their ideas. Remember that students should do most of the work. Offer specific feedback so students can identify their progress and areas in which they require continued practice.

Assessing Students' Progress

Working with students in small groups lets you know how much they understand and offers opportunities for you to provide positive feedback during and after the assessment-driven intervention. Noticing students' level of comprehension of a reading strategy, word-study skills, discussion of a text, or their notebook writing sends a powerful message: you value their thinking, questions, active listening, willingness to take risks, self-corrections, and how they support one another. Your feedback can increase students' self-confidence as you shine a spotlight on their thinking, problem solving, and process (Robb 2017).

Use "I notice" statements that are specific to what students have done to help them understand that a mindset of "I can work hard" can result in progress—for example, "I notice how you've included text evidence to infer," "Your list of words starting with the prefix *dis–* is comprehensive and accurate; I noticed you checking some of them in your online dictionary," or "I noticed the discussions with your partner about visualizing included your statement that what you visualize you understand."

> Avoid generalizations such as "great work" or "I'm proud of this." The content of students' writing, visuals, and discussions and your observations should drive feedback.

Avoid generalizations such as "great work" or "I'm proud of this." The content of students' writing, visuals, and discussions and your observations should drive feedback. Students improve, grow, and gain independence with learning when your comments help them realize that they've successfully applied a strategy to a particular text, as well as when your comments identify areas that need more attention. Feedback carries these benefits for students' growth and improvement:

- It shows that you value students' writing and thinking, which in turn boosts self-confidence and their ability to risk trying new strategies and word-learning skills.

- It enables them to know when their comprehension is on target and when and how they can refine or adjust a reading strategy or word work.

- It focuses students on the thinking, problem solving, writing, discussing, and word work, rather than getting a grade.

- It informs students that they can successfully apply reading strategies independently or with the support of a peer.

When you close each group's intervention lesson with positive feedback, you empower students by increasing their self-efficacy—the belief that with continual effort and your guidance, they can internalize a strategy or skill and transfer it to other texts and learning situations. By continually observing and interacting with students while they read, discuss, and write in their notebooks, you'll collect the information needed to decide whether to place students in a different group *after* they complete a set of differentiated lessons. Grouping for the differentiated lessons is flexible. For example, if a student who began the year in a near- or at-grade-level group increases their volume in reading and makes significant progress after completing two differentiated units, you can consider moving that student into an above-grade-level group. Before you move a student to a different group, reflect on their work to ensure it indicates they'll experience success (see pages 75–76). Above-grade-level readers won't move to a higher group, but you can continually offer them choices that build their vocabularies, background knowledge, and abilities to think critically and problem-solve.

Sample Plans for Three Groups in Grade 4

To demonstrate how to use assessment-driven interventions in practice, let's examine the decisions a fourth-grade teacher made based on her assessments of students after completing the differentiated lessons on inferring. Students' questions and their notebook writing revealed that inferring personality traits was a challenge for 12 students—six students reading below grade level, four students reading at grade level, and two students reading above grade level. The teacher placed the 12 students who needed extra practice and support with identifying personality traits into Group 1 and split it into two groups of six. She planned scaffolding for Group 1. She placed the remaining students in the class into two other groups and planned additional practice for Group 2 and enrichment for Group 3.

Review and reflect on the chart the fourth-grade teacher developed for the three groups (see figure 6.3). Most students needed reteaching and more practice with connotations of words and phrases, so the teacher reserved time for reteaching everyone and having students practice with partners. Because volume in reading strongly correlates to students' improved reading skills and enlarges their vocabulary, while the teacher worked with one group, the other groups read self-selected independent reading books (Allington and McGill-Frazen 2021; Krashen 2004; Samuels and Wu 2004).

Students' notebook writing revealed their level of understanding of inferring personality traits and their ability to support each identified trait with text evidence. The teacher read the T-charts in students' notebooks to check that they were able to successfully identify personality traits and supply text evidence for each one. For the enrichment group, students should have been able to state two themes and how characters shaped each one. After the teacher identified a few students who would benefit from additional practice, she reserved time to work with those students before moving on to a new set of differentiated lessons. The rest of the class completed independent reading of self-selected books. The teacher did this to ensure that all students would have the level of understanding needed to successfully practice a different reading strategy and complete new word work. The teacher also took time to reflect on students' grouping for the next set of differentiated lessons and used students' discussions, written responses, and word work to decide whether anyone was ready to move to a different group.

Figure 6.3—Sample Schedule for Additional Support with Inferring

Group 1: Teacher Support, Scaffolding, 20 to 25 Minutes
(Two sets of six students meet over two consecutive days)

Reteaching lesson for both sets of students

The teacher starts inferring by using real-life situations to practice identifying personality traits such as bossy, determined, fearful, kind, shy, or patient.

The teacher explains that inferences are unstated meanings that aren't written in a text and models the difference between physical and personality traits. Next, the teacher models and involves students in inferring personality traits and citing text evidence, using the focus lesson text from the differentiated lesson.

Scaffolded practice for first set of students	Scaffolded practice for second set of students
The teacher then pairs students and has them infer, using a short text, while the teacher observes and scaffolds. Notebook writing: Students explain what they know about inferences. (Students do independent reading when not working with the teacher.)	The teacher discusses what students know about inferring and clarifies as needed. The teacher does a quick review of the reteaching lesson and encourages students to ask questions. Next, the teacher has students read a short narrative text and work on their own to make two inferences about the main characters, offering text evidence. The teacher supports and scaffolds as needed. Notebook writing: Students write all they understand about inferring. (Students do independent reading when not working with the teacher.)

Group 2: Additional Practice, 20 to 25 Minutes

Students watch a video on inferring and discuss it. Students then read a short folktale to practice inferring personality traits, first with partners, then on their own.

Notebook writing: T-chart: Students choose two characters and infer two personality traits for each one, including text evidence on the T-chart.

(Students do independent reading when their work is completed.)

Group 3: Enrichment, 20 to 25 Minutes

The teacher organizes students into pairs and invites them to read a short text. Students infer three or four personality traits for the protagonist and offer text evidence to support each inference. Students discuss two themes of the story and offer details that support each theme.

Notebook writing: T-chart: On the left side of the chart, students write a theme; on the right side, they explain how people and events shaped the theme. Students then repeat these steps for a second theme.

(Students do independent reading when their work is completed.)

Take Time for Reflective Conversations

Reflect on these questions independently, then discuss them with colleagues:

- How do assessment-driven interventions support students?

- How do models or examples you provide support students' learning?

- Why is it beneficial to ensure that all students understand the elements presented in your focus lessons before moving on to new topics?

- How can personalized learning support students' progress with reading?

Part II

The Differentiated Lessons

Chapter 7

Using the Differentiated Lessons

The differentiated reading lessons in chapters 8–11 provide students with the practice they need to improve their reading skills, enlarge their vocabularies, and deepen their abilities to comprehend and connect ideas. Texts and poems are provided for students reading below grade level, at grade level, and above grade level. Students who improve and move from reading below grade level to reading at grade level can use the texts in that section, and readers at grade level can use texts that are above grade level when they're ready. Above-grade-level students continue with those texts. Offer choices of reading materials and videos for students in this group who finish early. When students read, discuss, and write about poems and short informational and narrative texts, they experience the success that leads to increasing their reading stamina and self-confidence.

> When students read, discuss, and write about poems and short informational and narrative texts, they experience the success that leads to increasing their reading stamina and self-confidence.

The lessons on visualizing and drawing conclusions use poems, and the lessons on inferring and comparing and contrasting use short texts, to provide students with opportunities to practice reading, thinking, writing, and word work with both genres. Each set of lessons starts with two interactive focus lessons that ask you as the teacher to model and think aloud comprehension strategies and word work using a poem or short text. The differentiated practice lessons for students build on the interactive focus lessons they observe and experience. Figure 7.1 shows a table of the differentiated lessons.

You will need these materials for the lessons:

- **Materials for teachers:** A document camera or computer to project the focus lesson text and to model writing about reading in your teacher's notebook. You also have the option of giving students copies of the focus lesson text.

- **Materials for each student:** A reader's notebook, a file folder for storing materials for each lesson, *Reading and Enjoying Poems* (page 69), the poem or short text for their group, and the lesson directions.

Figure 7.1—The Differentiated Lessons

	Visualizing Lessons (Chapter 8)		
	Below Grade Level	*At Grade Level*	*Above Grade Level*
Grade 3	The Blue Whale (p. 85)	Hummingbird (p. 88)	Octopus (p. 91)
Grade 4	The Book or the Snake (p. 94)	The Lizard Catcher (p. 97)	A Mosquito (p. 100)
Grade 5	Desert (p. 103)	Rain Forest (p. 106)	Winter in the Mountains (p. 109)

	Inferring Lessons (Chapter 9)		
	Below Grade Level	*At Grade Level*	*Above Grade Level*
Grade 3	The Crow (p. 123)	There's More to a Worm (p. 128)	The Sea Bear (p. 132)
Grade 4	The Storyteller (p. 136)	The First Cave Artist (p. 140)	Was There a Real Alice? (p. 144)
Grade 5	Climate Strike (p. 148)	How Old Do You Have to Be? (p. 152)	Who Wants to Make Life Better? (p. 157)

	Drawing Conclusions Lessons (Chapter 10)		
	Below Grade Level	*At Grade Level*	*Above Grade Level*
Grade 3	What the Bumblebee Doesn't Know (p. 172)	The Grass and the Butterfly (p. 175)	Don't Forget (p. 178)
Grade 4	Down the Fence Row (p. 182)	Rolling (p. 187)	The Stream (p. 190)
Grade 5	Tiger (p. 194)	Milkweed and Monarchs (p. 197)	Your Eyes (p. 201)

	Comparing and Contrasting Lessons (Chapter 11)		
	Below Grade Level	*At Grade Level*	*Above Grade Level*
Grade 3	Spring, Summer, Fall, Winter (p. 216)	More Bees, Please (p. 220)	There Are Dogs, and There Are Dogs (p. 225)
Grade 4	It All Depends on Who You Are (p. 229)	I'm Thinking about It (p. 234)	Climbing Back (p. 238)
Grade 5	A Nation's Symbol (p. 242)	The Nature of Zoos (p. 247)	What Does an Eel Have for Breakfast? (p. 252)

Organize students within each group into reading partnerships. These pairs should work together for an entire unit. Partners can remain the same through all units, or you can change partnerships before starting a new set of differentiated lessons. Expect variations in the amount of time partners need to complete their assignments. As students let you know they're done, read their notebook entries to check that they've followed directions. Those who finish early can read their independent reading book to increase their volume in reading.

Modeling How to Read a Poem During the Focus Lesson

Distribute copies of *Reading and Enjoying Poems* (page 69) to students. Read the guidelines aloud and have students follow along silently. Answer any questions students raise. Then show them how you apply the suggestions to a poem.

Model how to read the poem for the first focus lesson you present by displaying the poem on the board. Think aloud and discuss the meaning of the title, your feelings, and the mental images you picture (pointing out the words and phrases that conjure these images). Underline key words, note the number of stanzas, point out any variations in line length, and explain how punctuation guides how you read aloud. During your final rereading of the poem, compare how you felt after the first reading to this reading—include feelings, thoughts and ideas, and specific words that raised emotions and helped your understanding. Then, ask students to read the poem chorally with you so that you can support and assist their initial reading of the poem.

Repeat this process during each focus lesson until you feel confident that students can follow the process without a refresher from you. As partners collaborate, circulate among the groups and listen to students reading and discussing their assigned poems. Notice and tell them what's working. Your positive observations will increase their effort, enjoyment, and understanding of each poem they read.

Name: _____   Date: _____

Reading and Enjoying Poems

When you read and reread a poem many times, you enjoy it more. You might laugh or react with feelings. Rereading deepens your understanding of what the poet is saying.

Look at the poem's shape:

- Is it one long poem with no breaks between lines? Are lines grouped into stanzas?

Look at these parts of the poem:

- Are the poem's lines all the same length? Are some long and others short?

- Look for end-of-line punctuation. Do lines end with a comma, dash, or period? The punctuation asks you to pause for a moment.

- If there is no end-of-line punctuation, you read on to the next line. Sometimes you read on for two or more lines to understand the meaning.

Read the poem aloud:

- Whisper-read the poem. Listen to the sounds the words make and the pictures they create in your mind.

- Read the poem aloud with your partner.

- Try to hear what's happening in the poem. The more you read the poem, the better you'll understand how it speaks to you.

- Listen for words that begin with the same sounds.

- Listen for words that make sounds, paint pictures, and cause feelings. Think about how these words help you enjoy the poem.

Talk about the poem with your partner:

- Start with the title. What does it mean to you? How does it link to the words and ideas in the poem?

- Read one stanza at a time and discuss the content.

- Ask questions and discuss the answers. What ideas came out of your discussion?

Reread the poem:

- Whisper-read the poem to yourself again. Compare this reading to your first reading.

- Discuss this question with your partner: How did rereading the poem affect your understanding?

Assessing Students' Notebooks with a Single-Point Rubric

Give students a single-point rubric before they start the writing tasks so they know your expectations and can check their writing against the items listed on the rubric. Students can tape the rubric into their notebooks. A single-point rubric lists standards students need to meet; however, it is more open-ended than a rubric that assigns points to specific skills. When using a single-point rubric that divides a writing task into categories, students can check their writing to ensure it meets the rubric's standards and revise it if necessary before you assess their work. This type of rubric takes students' focus off grades by not creating the numbered boundaries found in traditional rubrics. Because single-point rubrics are more open-ended and can include students' input or be created by students for a specific task, students develop their creativity and critical thinking as they craft writing that fulfills the assignment. This type of rubric also encourages you to offer feedback that enables students to revise their writing by addressing specific suggestions. You can use the rubric to evaluate students' notebook writing, as well as analytical paragraphs.

Figure 7.2 shows an example of a single-point rubric for notebook entries that you could complete with students during brief conferences; students could also complete the rubric themselves, then use it to confer with you. The notes you write under "Things to Improve" tell students what they need to reflect on and revise. What you write under "Things That Were Beyond Basic Expectations" celebrates students' excellent writing and thinking.

Using Shared Writing to Model How to Compose Analytical Paragraphs

Collaborate with students to write an analytical paragraph so that they can observe and experience the entire process. Start by planning the paragraph with students, then use the plan to collaboratively compose the paragraph and concluding sentence.

Provide a thesis or position statement to open the paragraph. Ask for two or three pieces of support from the text. For the focus lesson poem "The Nature of Nature" on page 83, Laura Robb and her fourth-grade students incorporated three pieces of support from the poem to create the following writing plan:

- **Thesis statement:** Human beings weren't the first ones to inhabit Earth.
  - Ancient lizards lived before humans.
  - Snakes were here before humans.
  - Pesky mosquitoes were here before humans.
- **Conclusion:** Animals are reminders of what came before us.

Point out to students how much easier the writing is when you have a plan. Compose the plan in your teacher's notebook, posting it on the board as you think aloud and write. Invite students to use the plan to compose sentences for the paragraph.

Figure 7.2—Single-Point Rubric for Notebook Entries

Things to Improve	Assessing Notebook Entries	Things That Were Beyond Basic Expectations
	Complete heading: includes name, date, title of text, and prompt or question	
	Supporting evidence: selects enough evidence in the text to support position; writes evidence in own words	
	Lists: generates a range of ideas	
	Connections: connects ideas to details in the text	
	Reading strategy: applies the reading strategy—infer, compare/contrast, visualize, or draw conclusions—to a poem or short text. Understands how the strategy supports reading comprehension; uses strategy to improve comprehension	
	Word work: completes word work for each lesson successfully	
	Figurative language: identifies simile, metaphor, onomatopoeia, and alliteration; understands how figurative language improves understanding of the text	

Here's what fourth graders dictated when collaborating with Laura Robb:

> ### They Came Before Us
>
> Human beings weren't the first ones to inhabit Earth. David L. Harrison tells why in his poem "The Nature of Nature." Ancient lizards lived long before humans came on Earth. Snakes were here before humans, too. Mosquitoes bugged animals before humans. Harrison says humans need to sit, look, and listen. Then they will know that many other creatures lived on Earth before humans did.

With third-grade students, you will most likely be collaborating as a group, or "sharing the pen." If they're ready to write on their own, allow them to do so. Fourth- and fifth-grade students can share the pen with you two or three times and then work independently. Here's what fourth graders dictated when collaborating with Laura Robb: Circulate among students as they work independently and offer support and positive feedback. Post one of the plans and collaborative paragraphs from your notebook on the board as a model for students. Adjust the details of the single-point rubric to align with your expectations for writing analytical paragraphs (see figure 7.3 for an example).

Complete the assessment together with the students for two or three pieces. Then students can assess themselves with the help of partners. Note that the single-point rubric offers guidance but far less direction from the teacher, leaving room for students to approach the writing from their unique points of view. This type of rubric also provides space for the teacher's feedback and/or students' self-evaluation.

Helping Developing Readers Experience Success

You may find that some developing readers can't work independently or with partners on texts and notebook work. Meet with this small group of developing readers while other students work with partners or independently. Read the poem or short text to students, then invite them to chorally read it with you. Next, help students read and understand the directions in *Reading and Enjoying Poems*, then ask them to discuss the text with partners and complete their notebook work. As students gain confidence and enlarge their reading and thinking vocabularies, you can gradually release responsibility to them.

Figure 7.3—Single-Point Rubric for Analytical Paragraphs

Things to Improve	Assessing Analytical Paragraphs	Things That Were Beyond Basic Expectations
	Title: creates a title that introduces the topic	
	Thesis or position statement: states position clearly and accurately	
	Supporting evidence: selects powerful evidence to support the thesis or position statement	
	Conclusion: not only wraps up the position but also leaves something more for the reader to think about that emerges from the topic	
	Length of paragraph: includes an introduction, the required number of supporting details, and a conclusion	
	Grammar and usage: punctuates sentences correctly; varies sentence openings	

Teaching with Word Ladders

Word ladders are a great way to improve students' word decoding and spelling and increase their vocabularies—all in ways that students will find fun and engaging. Word ladders are easy to do with students and very time efficient. All of the lessons in this book include word ladders. The teacher-led focus-lessons contain word ladders that you will complete with students to build their mental model of the process. During the differentiated lessons, students will support one another while they complete the word ladders. While partners work on their word ladders, circulate among students to answer questions and offer support. If you want to extend the lesson by asking students to sort words, model the word work using the focus lesson word ladder so that students have the experience needed to successfully work with partners later on.

Here are the steps for teaching a word ladder lesson:

1. Distribute copies of the word ladder activity sheet to students.

2. Draw students' attention to the first word at the bottom of the ladder. Then read the word to students, and have them read and spell the word chorally. Discuss the word's meaning and any important orthographic (spelling) patterns and features.

3. Guide students in working their way up the ladder. For each step, have students read the clue and spell the new word (or you can read the clues to students).

    a. The clue includes the spelling changes required to turn the current word into the new word—students may need to change one or more letters, add one or more letters, subtract one or more letters, or rearrange letters.

    b. Each clue also includes a hint about the meaning of the new word. You may also want to provide other clues or a sentence that includes the word in a meaningful context.

    c. If a word is particularly challenging, you may want to provide additional clues such as what specific letter(s) need to be changed, added, or taken away; or you could simply say the word to students to avoid frustration. Have them write the word from your pronunciation. Then check spelling and discuss the word's meaning.

    d. You may wish to discuss words as they are written by students, elaborating on the meanings of the words as well as their spelling and sound structures to foster orthographic mapping.

4. The final word in each word ladder is related to the first word in some way and is also related to the text students have just read. Students love the challenge of figuring out the words step by step.

That is a word ladder lesson in a nutshell. It should take no longer than 10 minutes. Once the lesson is complete, you may wish to extend it by having students sort the words into various categories that you provide, such as the following:

- Grammatical categories (e.g., words that are nouns and words that are not nouns)
- Word structure (e.g., words that have one syllable, two syllables, or three or more syllables; words that contain a long vowel sound and those that don't; words that contain a consonant blend and those that don't)
- Word meaning (e.g., words that express what a person can do or feel and those that don't; words that reflect what a person might do or wear and words that don't)
- Alphabetical order (not technically a word sort, but useful nonetheless)

This additional analysis through categorization will help students continue to analyze the words more deeply (i.e., orthographic mapping) and gain even greater control and understanding over these and related words. We also suggest that you and your students choose some of the most interesting (and perhaps unusual) words from each word ladder lesson and display them on a classroom word wall. Words on the word wall are read and referred to regularly, and students should be encouraged to use the words in their oral and written language. Most of all, word ladders are about having fun while playing with and learning about words. As Fred Rogers once said, "For children, play is serious learning. Play is really the work of childhood."

Formative Assessment

Formative assessment includes a variety of methods that teachers use to monitor students' learning needs during a unit or a series of lessons. These methods can include observations, listening, and reading students' writing-about-reading and their self-evaluations. The purpose of collecting information from formative assessments is to improve students' understanding quickly by adjusting instruction and/or planning scaffolds and interventions that catch and repair students' confusions before they become obstacles to moving forward. Formative assessment can occur as you circulate around the room, clipboard in hand for jotting notes while students work. You can pause to answer questions and have on-the-spot conversations with students who aren't engaged with the task. Support students who require more than a few minutes of your time by scheduling one or more conferences to work closely with them.

Formative Assessment During the Focus Lessons

Observing students during the focus lessons can help you determine which students understand your modeling and the practice you invite them to complete. Here are some questions to reflect on that can help you to make instructional moves and decisions to best catch students' confusions early:

- **Participation:** Do the students answer questions? Do their answers show understanding?

- **Questions:** Do the questions the students ask show a need for clarification or do they reveal confusion?

- **Comprehension Practice:** Can the students apply the reading strategy to the text? Do the students cite text evidence to support their positions? Are there students who don't participate all?

- **Literary Elements:** Can the students link specific literary elements to the text they are reading? Does students' work reveal a clear understanding of specific literary elements? Appendix I provides definitions of literary elements.

- **Word Work Practice:** Are students able to complete (with partners or independently) the word work the teacher modeled in the focus lesson? What do students' oral and written responses reveal about their understanding of the word work?

Offering support at this point in the lessons helps ensure that students will be able to work productively with partners, discussing and writing about their poem or short text as well as completing the word work related to their reading.

Formative Assessment During the Differentiated Lessons

While students complete the lessons and interact with partners, assess items from the following list.

- Students' discussions of the poem or text and responses to the questions. (For more about conferring, see page 25 and appendix C.)

- Notebook entries, including applying the reading strategy, analyzing the text by responding to questions, and successfully completing the word work. (For a list of items to assess in students' notebook writing, see page 26.)

- Written paragraphs (in students' notebooks), which can be summaries of the text or analytical paragraphs. (See appendix D and appendix H.)

- Fluent and expressive reading as students read aloud to each other. (See chapter 4 for ways to improve fluency.)

- Completion of word ladders and the Thinking Challenges (to evaluate students' use of phonics and word meanings).

Partner Work or Individual Work

During the differentiated lessons, students will work with partners and independently. Sometimes you'll ask students to complete notebook writing independently and other times you might invite them to seek support from partners. However, to assess students' level of understanding, there will be times when you'll want them to complete the work in the lessons or answer one or two comprehension questions on their own. You also might do this to see whether a student should move into a different group or to evaluate the progress they've made in a specific area. You are the best person to make this decision because you have been monitoring students' progress using a variety of formative assessments.

Chapter 8

Visualizing

This chapter provides 11 lessons on using visualization to develop a deeper understanding of a text. The chapter begins with two interactive focus lessons, during which the teacher demonstrates how to read poems and provides students with a mental model of how to engage in visualization and related word work. The focus lessons ask students to practice what the teacher models, so that they can apply the reading, thinking, and writing processes to their own reading. Following the focus lessons are nine differentiated lessons for students to work through independently or with partners.

Readers who can use their imaginations to visualize settings, characters, and events reveal their understanding of a text, because they can only picture in their minds what they comprehend. Using imagination to visualize also invites readers to include some or all of the five senses. Onomatopoeic words such as *bang* and *squish* add sound to visualizations, while words like *velvet* and *sandpaper* incorporate touch. Poems that include all or a few of the five senses can enrich the visualizing experience for readers and increase their comprehension.

> Readers who can use their imaginations to visualize settings, characters, and events reveal their understanding of a text, because they can only picture in their minds what they comprehend.

Review visualizing, onomatopoeia (words that make sounds), simile (a comparison of two unlike things that have something in common using *like* or *as*, as in "snagging bugs with tongues quick as lightning"), and metaphor (a comparison without *like* or *as* that equates two unlike things using the verbs *is* or *are*, as in "many think humans are kings and queens of the world") with students.

Learn What Students Know about Visualizing

Before starting your focus lessons, find out what students know about viualizing by asking them to head a page in their reader's notebooks and write everything they think they know about it. By reading these entries, you'll quickly identify students who might benefit from extra support. We suggest that you have students return to this entry at the end of the unit and write what they now understand about visualizing, comparing their end-of-unit explanation to their initial entry.

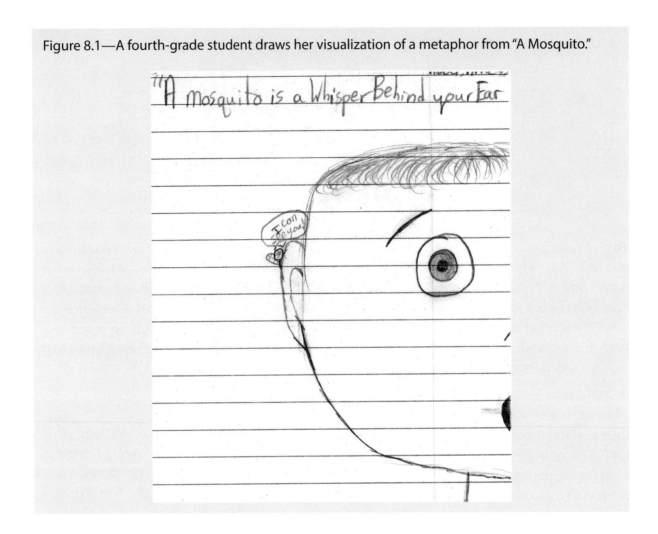

Focus Lesson: Visualizing to Show Comprehension

In this focus lesson, you will review the five senses, read the poem "The Nature of Nature" aloud, discuss its structure, think aloud to show students how you interpret the poem, and model how specific words and phrases in the poem help you visualize. Then, using the third stanza, you'll invite partners to practice.

The Teacher Models: Reading a Poem

1. Organize students into partners. Review the five senses and post them on the board: *sight, smell, touch, sound, taste*. Display the poem "The Nature of Nature" (page 83) on the board. Discuss the poem's title and explain the two meanings of the word *nature* in the title.

2. Look at the poem and point out that there are three stanzas; the first is short, and the second and third stanzas have both long and short lines. Also note that lines 10 and 11 don't have end punctuation, which means they should be read without pausing at the end of each line. Read the poem aloud twice, and, in a think-aloud, connect the title to the poem's content. Explain why the poet cautions us to remember that we weren't the first ones on Earth.

3. Underline the words and phrases in the second stanza that create pictures in your mind, such as *lazing, snagging bugs, slithered soundlessly, tickling the air, stealing blood*. Describe what you see and point out words that stir your senses in addition to sight: *tasting, scent of prey*. Reread the simile "snagging bugs with tongues quick as lightning," and explain that by comparing the lizard's tongue movements to lightning, readers understand the speed of this action.

Students Practice

1. Distribute copies of the poem (page 83) to students. Invite partners to discuss the third stanza and underline the words and phrases that paint pictures in their minds, as well as identify the sense stirred by each word or phrase. Invite pairs to share their mental pictures and the words and phrases that helped form them.

2. Introduce metaphor, a cousin of simile, by underlining the phrase "Today, many think humans are kings and queens." Show how the poet uses the word *are* to equate humans to kings and queens. In your teacher's notebook, write an explanation of metaphor as a resource for students (something like this: "'Many think human beings are kings and queens of the world.' This metaphor uses the word *are* to equate, or make equal, human beings and kings and queens who rule countries. Metaphors compare two unlike things using *is* or *are*."). Next, invite partners to discuss and then share their responses to this question: What does this metaphor say about human beings' place in nature?

The Teacher Models: Notebook Writing

Demonstrate your expectations for writing about visualizing by completing a cold write in your teacher's notebook. Head the page, write the title of the poem, and, using words only, write your visualization of the second stanza. Then, using drawings and words, write your visualization of the third stanza. Explain that students can use words only or drawings and words for their visualizations. Your cold write will become a refresher and resource for students when they write in their own notebooks.

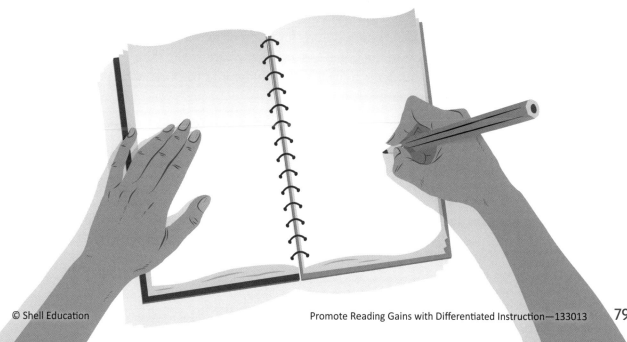

Focus Lesson: Connotations and Synonyms

Writers have tools to help readers create mental pictures or images in their minds. You've already introduced simile, metaphor, and words that stir the five senses. Another image-making technique is when poets incorporate connotations, or words and phrases that readers associate with specific words, in a poem. For example, some connotations for *king* and *queen* in the second stanza of "The Nature of Nature" are *rulers, in charge, powerful*, and *control*. Readers of poetry often think of connotations while reading and discussing, and this not only enhances the imagery but can also deepen their understanding of what the poet is saying.

Synonyms of words often create different mental images; consider *snagging bug*s versus *catching bugs* or *stealing blood* versus *taking blood*. Synonyms offer writers a range of word choices. However, the pictures created by words and their connotations are what support writers' word choices.

In this focus lesson, you'll help students understand that word choice in writing affects the detail of visualizations and the depth of comprehension.

The Teacher Models: Connotations

1. Have students head a page in their reader's notebooks with the date and the name of the poem.

2. Write these lines from "The Nature of Nature" on the board, and read them out loud: "Today, many think humans are kings and queens of the world."

3. Think aloud and share some associations with *kings and queens*, such as *rulers, powerful, control, in charge of lives, make the laws and rules*. Explain that these associations are called *connotations* and that words have connotations that can affect the reader's understanding of a poem.

Students Practice

1. Ask partners to turn-and-talk and link the connotations for *kings and queens* to the poem's first stanza and lines 18 through 20.

2. Next, invite partners to find connotations for *scent* or for *stealing* and discuss how the connotations connect to the poem. As partners share, write their ideas in your teacher's notebook for students to use as a reminder and resource when they work independently in their own notebooks.

The Teacher Models: Synonyms

1. Review the meaning of synonyms and discuss word choice with students by posting these pairs of words on the board: *lazing* and *resting*, *slithered* and *crept*.

2. Have partners discuss the difference in imagery between the words David L. Harrison used in the poem (*lazing* and *slithered*) and the synonyms you provided (*resting* and *crept*).

Students Practice

1. Ask partners to choose two words from this list of words in "The Nature of Nature": *slithered, scent, stealing, quiet, look.*

2. Next, invite partners to brainstorm and write in their notebooks two or three synonyms for each word.

3. Ask students to share their ideas with the class, and, under a document camera, write their suggestions in your teacher's notebook. Then ask pairs to discuss this question: Could the poet have used other words to help you visualize and comprehend? Have pairs share their ideas with the class.

Completing the Word Ladder

1. Distribute copies of *"The Nature of Nature" Word Ladder* (page 84) to students.

2. Start at the bottom of the ladder. Say the word "listen," and have students pair-share to discuss what they know about the word. In addition to its meaning, point out that the word has two syllables and is a verb.

3. Guide students as they work their way up the ladder. Model how you use the clues to identify "glisten." Again, have pairs discuss the word.

4. Continue supporting students. However, when you see that they can complete the ladder without your assistance, have them work with partners or independently, completing one word at a time.

5. The Thinking Challenge: The word ladder starts with *listen* and ends with *look.* Reread the third stanza and think aloud to show students that these words are in the poem. Next, on a page of your teacher's notebook, link both words to a big idea in the poem, such as in these ways: "We have to look and listen to understand and connect to the natural world," "When we look and listen, we can better understand our position in the natural world," or "When we look and listen, we can see that human beings weren't the first ones on Earth."

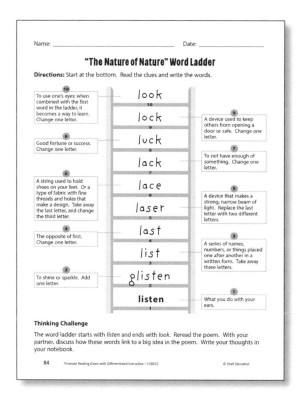

Turning the Differentiated Lessons over to Students

If students' responses to the interactive focus lessons indicate that all students or a group would benefit from review and/or reteaching, take time to boost their understanding. Pausing to do this will enable students to complete their work independently or with partners while using the resources you display from your teacher's notebook and the reminders you give to support students (see below).

The Differentiated Lessons

The content of the differentiated lessons always follows what you've modeled and what students practiced during the interactive focus lessons. Each differentiated lesson has three parts: 1) the poem; 2) directions for students to engage in visualization and word work; and 3) a word ladder that connects to the poem.

Visualizing Lessons			
	Below Grade Level	**At Grade Level**	**Above Grade Level**
Grade 3	The Blue Whale (p. 85)	Hummingbird (p. 88)	Octopus (p. 91)
Grade 4	The Book or the Snake (p. 94)	The Lizard Catcher (p. 97)	A Mosquito (p. 100)
Grade 5	Desert (p. 103)	Rain Forest (p. 106)	Winter in the Mountains (p. 109)

Reminders to Support Students

To prepare students for working through the differentiated lessons independently or with partners:

- Remind students of the writing on visualizing and the word work in your teacher's notebook, and display the notebook so students can refer to it as needed. Tell them they can use your notebook as a resource while they work.

- Review simile and metaphor. Remind students that both are comparisons of two unlike things. Similes use *as* or *like* to compare. Metaphors use *is* or *are* because a metaphor equates two things.

- Write these terms on the board: *connotations* and *synonyms*. Review how to pronounce both words and what they mean.

- Write these terms on the board: *visualize* and *visualizing*. Review how to pronounce these words, and explain that when readers visualize while reading, they make pictures in their mind.

- Remind students to use quiet voices when talking with their partners.

Name: _____   Date: _____

Focus on Visualizing

Directions: Read the poem and follow your teacher's directions.

The Nature of Nature
by David L. Harrison

1   The thing we need to remember is,
2   we were not the first ones here.

3   Long before we came along,
4   lizards went about their quiet lives,
5   lazing in the sun, snagging bugs
6   with tongues quick as lightning.
7   Snakes slithered soundlessly
8   through brush, tickling the air,
9   tasting the scent of their prey.
10 Mosquitoes developed tools
11 for their trade, learned the tricks
12 of stealing blood.

13 Today, many think humans are
14 kings and queens of the world,
15 but ancient lizards know better.
16 Slithering snakes and humming mosquitoes
17 know better. We only have to sit for a while,
18 look and listen for a while,
19 and they will show us, remind us,
20 we were not the first ones here.

"The Nature of Nature" Word Ladder

Directions: Start at the bottom. Read the clues and write the words.

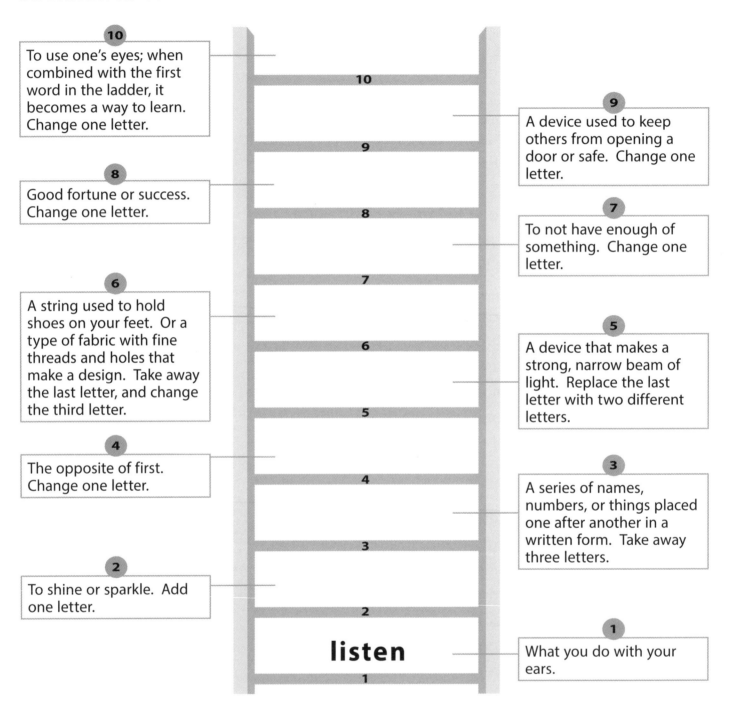

10 To use one's eyes; when combined with the first word in the ladder, it becomes a way to learn. Change one letter.

9 A device used to keep others from opening a door or safe. Change one letter.

8 Good fortune or success. Change one letter.

7 To not have enough of something. Change one letter.

6 A string used to hold shoes on your feet. Or a type of fabric with fine threads and holes that make a design. Take away the last letter, and change the third letter.

5 A device that makes a strong, narrow beam of light. Replace the last letter with two different letters.

4 The opposite of first. Change one letter.

3 A series of names, numbers, or things placed one after another in a written form. Take away three letters.

2 To shine or sparkle. Add one letter.

listen

1 What you do with your ears.

Thinking Challenge

The word ladder starts with *listen* and ends with *look*. Reread the poem. With your partner, discuss how these words link to a big idea in the poem. Write your thoughts in your notebook.

Visualizing: "The Blue Whale"

Directions: Read the poem and complete the activities.

The Blue Whale
by David L. Harrison

1	Down where
2	there is no light
3	and the water is cold,
4	the great blue whale
5	minds its own business.
6	It sings,
7	and its voice rumbles
8	in the gloom, one of the
9	loudest noises
10	of any living thing.
11	Nothing else—
12	not an elephant
13	or a dinosaur—
14	has ever been bigger,
15	on land or air or sea.
16	For food,
17	it eats tiny things like shrimp.
18	Its babies
19	are bigger than a car.
20	It comes up
21	for air and goes
22	back down.
23	All the blue whale wants is
24	to mind
25	its own business.

Thinking about "The Blue Whale"

Directions: Complete these activities. For each activity, label a page in your notebook with the date, the title of the poem, and which activity you are completing.

Activity 1: Making Mental Pictures by Visualizing

1. Review "Reading and Enjoying Poems." Use the tips to read "The Blue Whale."

2. Reread "The Blue Whale." Underline words that help you create pictures in your mind. Discuss these words with your partner.

3. In your notebook, write four things you learned about the blue whale.

4. Reread the first, second, and third stanzas. Visualize or imagine the blue whale in its home, singing. Draw a picture or use words to describe what you see.

5. Reread the fourth stanza. Notice the metaphor—a comparison between two unlike things using the words *is* or *are*. Discuss with your partner: What picture in your mind does this comparison create?

6. Discuss with your partner: Why do you think the blue whale has few enemies who try to attack it? Write your ideas in your notebook.

Activity 2: Word Work: Synonyms and Connotations

1. Write the word *synonym*. Explain what a synonym is.

2. Choose two of these words from the poem: *cold, gloom, sea, tiny*. Write the words on their own lines. Talk with your partner. Find synonyms for your words. List two to four synonyms next to each word.

3. Think about the word *connotation*. Refresh your memory by rereading your teacher's notebook. Write what *connotation* means.

4. Choose two of these words from the poem: *water, dinosaur, shrimp, noises*. Write one word in your notebook. Skip three lines, then write the other word.

5. Brainstorm connotations for the two words. Write your connotations under each word.

6. Choose one of the words. Use the connotations to make a picture in your mind. Draw the picture or use words to describe what you see.

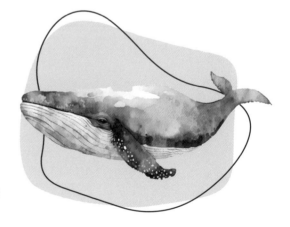

Name: _____   Date: _____

"The Blue Whale" Word Ladder

Directions: Start at the bottom. Read the clues and write the words.

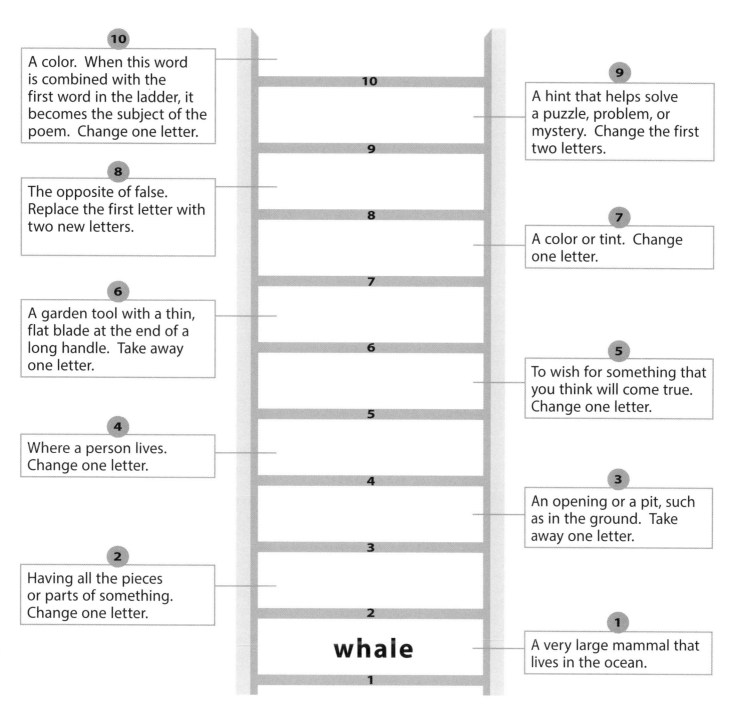

10 A color. When this word is combined with the first word in the ladder, it becomes the subject of the poem. Change one letter.

9 A hint that helps solve a puzzle, problem, or mystery. Change the first two letters.

8 The opposite of false. Replace the first letter with two new letters.

7 A color or tint. Change one letter.

6 A garden tool with a thin, flat blade at the end of a long handle. Take away one letter.

5 To wish for something that you think will come true. Change one letter.

4 Where a person lives. Change one letter.

3 An opening or a pit, such as in the ground. Take away one letter.

2 Having all the pieces or parts of something. Change one letter.

1 A very large mammal that lives in the ocean.

whale

Thinking Challenge

The word ladder starts with *whale* and ends with *blue*. Reread the poem. With your partner, discuss what you learned about the blue whale. Explain how the blue whale minds its own business. Write the ideas in your notebook.

Visualizing: "Hummingbird"

Directions: Read the poem and complete the activities.

Hummingbird
by David L. Harrison

1	Darts past
2	windowsill.
3	Whir of hurry.
4	Seldom still.
5	Color flash.
6	Blurred zoom.
7	Feathered streak.
8	Bright bloom.
9	Quick pause.
10	Stolen sip.
11	Wing hum.
12	Gone, zip.
13	Here, there.
14	Hardly heard.
15	Dipping, diving.
16	Hummingbird.

Name: _____ Date: _____

Thinking about "Hummingbird"

Directions: Complete these activities. For each activity, label a page in your notebook with the date, the title of the poem, and which activity you are completing.

Activity 1: Making Mental Pictures by Visualizing

1. Review "Reading and Enjoying Poems." Use the tips to read "Hummingbird."

2. Reread "Hummingbird." Underline words and phrases that create images in your mind. Discuss these words and phrases with your partner.

3. Reread the first, second, and third stanzas. Use the words from these stanzas to imagine the hummingbird. Draw a picture or use words to describe what you imagine.

4. Discuss with your partner: Why does the poet call the hummingbird's sip a "stolen sip?" Write your ideas.

5. Reread the poem. List three things you learned about hummingbirds.

Activity 2: Word Work: Synonyms and Connotations

1. Write the word *synonym*. Explain what a synonym is.

2. Choose two of these words from the poem: *darts, hurry, blurred, diving*. Write the words on their own lines. Talk with your partner. Find synonyms for your words. List two to four synonyms next to each word.

3. Think about the word *connotation*. Refresh your memory by rereading your teacher's notebook. Write what *connotation* means.

4. Choose two of these words from the poem: *hurry, seldom, pause, hum, diving*. Write one word in your notebook. Skip three lines, then write the other word.

5. Brainstorm connotations for the two words. Write your connotations under each word.

6. Choose one of the words. Use the connotations to make a picture in your mind. Draw the picture or use words to describe what you see.

Name: _____ Date: _____

"Hummingbird" Word Ladder

Directions: Start at the bottom. Read the clues and write the words.

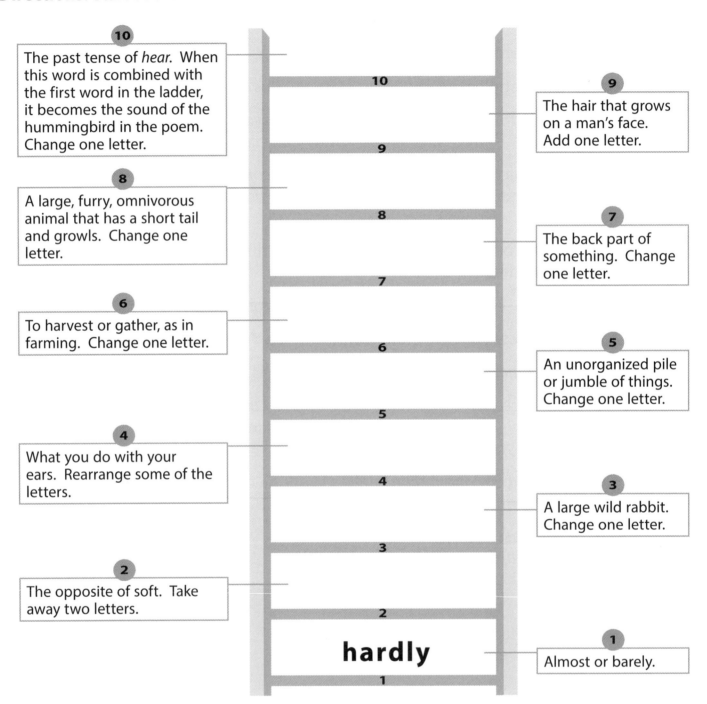

10 The past tense of *hear*. When this word is combined with the first word in the ladder, it becomes the sound of the hummingbird in the poem. Change one letter.

9 The hair that grows on a man's face. Add one letter.

8 A large, furry, omnivorous animal that has a short tail and growls. Change one letter.

7 The back part of something. Change one letter.

6 To harvest or gather, as in farming. Change one letter.

5 An unorganized pile or jumble of things. Change one letter.

4 What you do with your ears. Rearrange some of the letters.

3 A large wild rabbit. Change one letter.

2 The opposite of soft. Take away two letters.

hardly

1 Almost or barely.

Thinking Challenge

The word ladder starts with *hardly* and ends with *heard*. With your partner, discuss why the hummingbird is hardly heard. Write your explanation in your notebook.

Name: _____ Date: _____

Visualizing: "Octopus"

Directions: Read the poem and complete the activities.

Octopus
by David L. Harrison

1   Octopus, octopus,
2   escape-artist octopus,
3   ink-squirting octopus,
4   magician of the sea.

5   Octopus, octopus,
6   color-changing octopus,
7   shape-changing octopus,
8   jetting through the sea.

9   Octopus, octopus,
10 coral-creeping octopus,
11 squeeze-in-cracks octopus,
12 hide and seek at sea.

13 Octopus, octopus,
14 eight-limbed octopus,
15 blue-blooded octopus,
16 slyest in the sea.

17 Octopus, octopus,
18 three-hearted octopus,
19 nine-brained octopus,
20 genius of the sea.

Name: _____ Date: _____

Thinking about "Octopus"

Directions: Complete these activities. For each activity, label a page in your notebook with the date, the title of the poem, and which activity you are completing.

Activity 1: Making Mental Pictures by Visualizing

1. Review "Reading and Enjoying Poems." Use the tips to read "Octopus."

2. Reread "Octopus." Underline words and phrases that create images in your mind. Discuss these words with your partner.

3. Reread the first four stanzas of the poem. Create a mental picture for each stanza.

4. Choose two stanzas. Using your mental images, illustrate each stanza or write your own words describing what you see.

5. Write five things the poem taught you about the octopus. Discuss them with your partner.

6. Discuss with your partner: Why does the poet call the octopus "magician of the sea" and "genius of the sea"? Write the two phrases. Explain why you think the poet used each one.

Activity 2: Word Work: Synonyms and Connotations

1. Write the word *synonym*. Explain what a synonym is.

2. Choose two of these words from the poem: *escape*, *hide*, *seek*, *jetting*. Write the words on their own lines. Talk with your partner. Find synonyms for your words. List two to four synonyms next to each word.

3. Think about the word *connotation*. Refresh your memory by rereading your teacher's notebook. Write what *connotation* means.

4. Choose two of these words from the poem: *magician*, *slyest*, *genius*, *shape-changing*. Write one word in your notebook. Skip three lines, then write the other word.

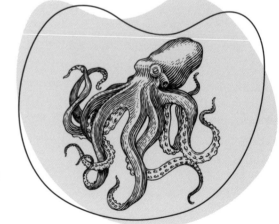

5. Brainstorm connotations for the two words. Write your connotations under each word.

6. Choose one of the words. Use the connotations to make a picture in your mind. Draw the picture or use words to describe what you see.

Name: _____ Date: _____

"Octopus" Word Ladder

Directions: Start at the bottom. Read the clues and write the words.

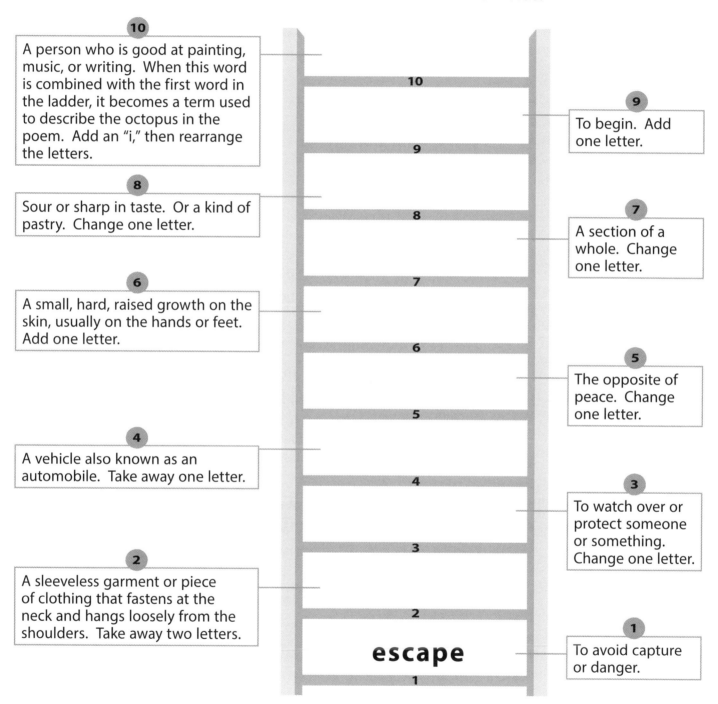

10 A person who is good at painting, music, or writing. When this word is combined with the first word in the ladder, it becomes a term used to describe the octopus in the poem. Add an "i," then rearrange the letters.

9 To begin. Add one letter.

8 Sour or sharp in taste. Or a kind of pastry. Change one letter.

7 A section of a whole. Change one letter.

6 A small, hard, raised growth on the skin, usually on the hands or feet. Add one letter.

5 The opposite of peace. Change one letter.

4 A vehicle also known as an automobile. Take away one letter.

3 To watch over or protect someone or something. Change one letter.

2 A sleeveless garment or piece of clothing that fastens at the neck and hangs loosely from the shoulders. Take away two letters.

1 To avoid capture or danger.

escape

Thinking Challenge

The word ladder starts with *escape* and ends with *artist*. With your partner, discuss why "escape artist" is the perfect phrase to describe the octopus. Write your explanation in your notebook.

Name: _____   Date: _____

Visualizing: "The Book or the Snake"

Directions: Read the poem and complete the activities.

The Book or the Snake
by David L. Harrison

1   Sitting on the deck, keeping
2   cool under the fan, wishing
3   I had more chip and dip, but
4   don't want to go get it.

5   Tired of this book, yawning
6   so hard my eyes squish shut, and
7   when I open them, a little black
8   snake is crawling across the deck.

9   Snakes don't scare me much, but
10 I don't like one coming toward me, so
11 I hop like a toad on my chair, but
12 the snake keeps coming.

13 I jump onto the table, but
14 the snake keeps coming, and
15 my chip and dip bowl falls off, and
16 my book smacks down on the floor.

17 The snake curls 'round a table leg, so
18 I yell, as the table tips and crashes down, and
19 the snake crawls off like it's late for dinner, and
20 I decide my book may be better, after all.

Thinking about "The Book or the Snake"

Directions: Complete these activities. For each activity, label a page in your notebook with the date, the title of the poem, and which activity you are completing.

Activity 1: Making Mental Pictures by Visualizing

1. Review "Reading and Enjoying Poems." Use the tips to read "The Book or the Snake." Reread the poem. Underline words that help you create pictures in your mind. Discuss these words with your partner.

2. Reread the first and second stanzas. Write the feelings of the narrator or "I" in the first stanza. Explain why the feelings change in the second stanza.

3. Reread the third stanza. In your notebook, write the simile from the stanza and answer these questions: What picture or image does the simile create? How does the simile show the feelings of the narrator or "I"?

4. Reread the fifth stanza. Write the simile from the stanza and answer these questions: What words in the simile help you picture how the snake crawls? How does the narrator or "I" feel? Use details to support your idea.

5. Discuss with your partner: Did the poem make you laugh? Explain why.

6. Choose the first and second *or* the fourth and fifth stanzas. Reread the stanzas and create pictures in your mind. Draw or use words to show what you picture.

Activity 2: Word Work: Synonyms and Connotations

1. Write the word *synonym*. Explain what a synonym is.

2. Choose two of these words from the poem: *jump, tired, scare, smacks*. Write the words on their own lines. Talk with your partner. Find synonyms for your words. List two to four synonyms next to each word.

3. Think about the word *connotation*. Refresh your memory by rereading your teacher's notebook. Write what *connotation* means.

4. Choose two of these words from the poem: *cool, hop, crashes, late*. Write one word in your notebook. Skip three lines, then write the other word.

5. Brainstorm connotations for the two words. Write your connotations under each word.

6. Choose one of the words. How do your connotations help you picture the poem? How do they help you understand the "I" of the poem? Write your thoughts.

"The Book or the Snake" Word Ladder

Directions: Start at the bottom. Read the clues and write the words.

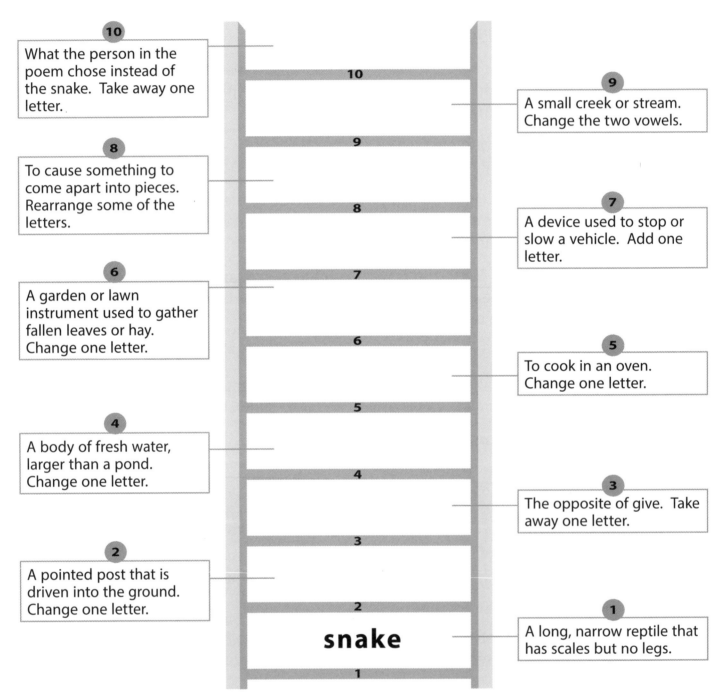

10 What the person in the poem chose instead of the snake. Take away one letter.

9 A small creek or stream. Change the two vowels.

8 To cause something to come apart into pieces. Rearrange some of the letters.

7 A device used to stop or slow a vehicle. Add one letter.

6 A garden or lawn instrument used to gather fallen leaves or hay. Change one letter.

5 To cook in an oven. Change one letter.

4 A body of fresh water, larger than a pond. Change one letter.

3 The opposite of give. Take away one letter.

2 A pointed post that is driven into the ground. Change one letter.

1 A long, narrow reptile that has scales but no legs.

snake

Thinking Challenge

The word ladder starts with *snake* and ends with *book*. In your notebook, write "snake to book." Explain how both words link to the story the poem tells. Explain why the narrator decides, "My book may be better, after all."

Name: _____   Date: _____

Visualizing: "The Lizard Catcher"

Directions: Read the poem and complete the activities.

The Lizard Catcher
by David L. Harrison

1   The boy was here yesterday
2   but couldn't catch any of the lizards
3   that sunned like small dinosaurs
4   baking on the warm walks
5   and clinging to tree trunks,
6   the skin below their throats
7   ballooning in and out like bellows.

8   No matter how carefully he crept,
9   on feet as silent as a Lakota hunter
10 might have stalked a bison or a bear,
11 each lizard escaped his lunging fingers,
12 vanished into dense ground cover.

13 Today the boy comes prepared—
14 fish-tank net bought with his allowance,
15 two empty pickle jars to hold his prizes,
16 backpack to carry them home.
17 Today he has all he needs, except
18 one—his mother's permission
19 to keep a live lizard—and two—
20 he still can't catch a lizard.

Thinking about "The Lizard Catcher"

Directions: Complete these activities. For each activity, label a page in your notebook with the date, the title of the poem, and which activity you are completing.

Activity 1: Making Mental Pictures by Visualizing

1. Review "Reading and Enjoying Poems." Use the tips to read "The Lizard Catcher." Reread the poem. Underline words and phrases that create images in your mind. Discuss these words and phrases with your partner.

2. Write the simile in line 3 of the first stanza. Discuss with your partner: How does the comparison help you visualize lizards?

3. Use a dictionary to look up the noun *bellows*. Write what it means. Discuss with your partner: How does knowing what a *bellows* is help you picture the lizards' throats?

4. Find the simile in the second stanza, and write it in your notebook. Discuss with your partner how the simile helps you imagine the boy catching lizards.

5. Reread lines 17 to 20 of the poem. Discuss with your partner: What do these lines tell you about the mother's feelings?

6. Choose and reread two of the stanzas in the poem. Visualize what you read. Draw the pictures or use words to describe what you imagine.

Activity 2: Word Work: Synonyms and Connotations

1. Write the word *synonym*. Explain what a synonym is.

2. Choose two of these words from the poem: *catch, crept, vanished, silent, stalked*. Write the words on their own lines. Talk with your partner. Find synonyms for your words. List two to four synonyms next to each word.

3. Think about the word *connotation*. Refresh your memory by rereading your teacher's notebook. Write what *connotation* means.

4. Choose two of these words from the poem: *baking, clinging, escaped, prepared, permission*. Write one word. Skip three lines, then write the other word.

5. Brainstorm connotations for the two words. Write your connotations under each word.

6. Choose one of the words. How do your connotations help you make a picture in your mind? How do your connotations help you better understand the boy in the poem? Write your thoughts.

Name: _____   Date: _____

"The Lizard Catcher" Word Ladder

Directions: Start at the bottom. Read the clues and write the words.

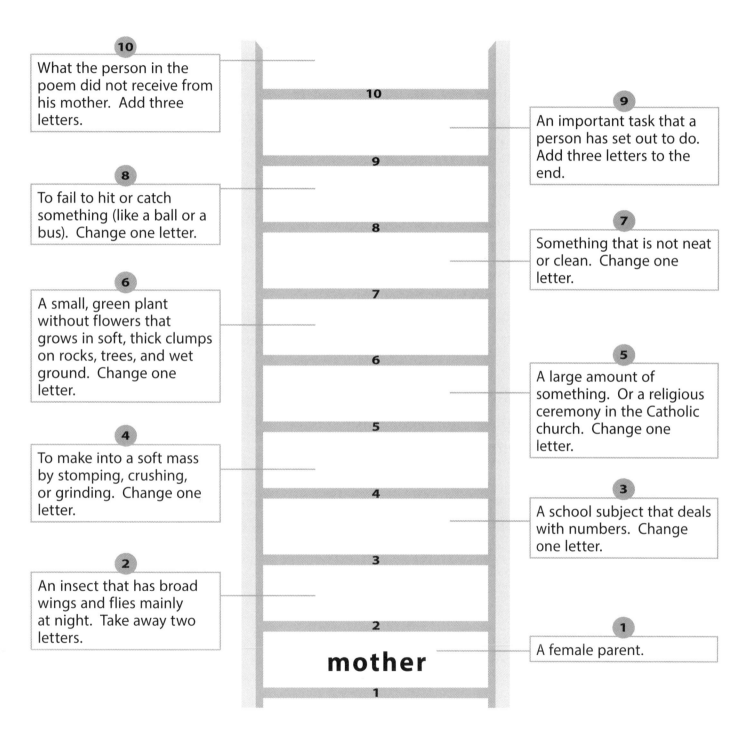

10 What the person in the poem did not receive from his mother. Add three letters.

9 An important task that a person has set out to do. Add three letters to the end.

8 To fail to hit or catch something (like a ball or a bus). Change one letter.

7 Something that is not neat or clean. Change one letter.

6 A small, green plant without flowers that grows in soft, thick clumps on rocks, trees, and wet ground. Change one letter.

5 A large amount of something. Or a religious ceremony in the Catholic church. Change one letter.

4 To make into a soft mass by stomping, crushing, or grinding. Change one letter.

3 A school subject that deals with numbers. Change one letter.

2 An insect that has broad wings and flies mainly at night. Take away two letters.

1 A female parent.

mother

Thinking Challenge

The word ladder starts with *mother* and ends with *permission*. In your notebook, write "mother to permission" and link both words to the title of the poem and the third stanza.

Name: _____ Date: _____

Visualizing: "A Mosquito"

Directions: Read the poem and complete the activities.

A Mosquito
by David L. Harrison

1   A mosquito is a whisper behind your ear,
2   a slender silhouette on your leg in the dark under the table,
3   a vampire's light touch assessing your cheek.

4   A mosquito is a fiery itch on your elbow,
5   an unreachable welt in the center of your back,
6   a knuckle you can't stop scratching.

7   A mosquito is stagnant green water,
8   the reason you flee indoors on a windless night,
9   why you can't sleep if one's around.

10   A mosquito is evil-smelling spray,
11   adores your blood, detests the person's beside you.
12   A mosquito is why you hate mosquitoes.

Name: _____   Date: _____

Thinking about "A Mosquito"

Directions: Complete these activities. For each activity, label a page in your notebook with the date, the title of the poem, and which activity you are completing.

Activity 1: Making Mental Pictures by Visualizing

1. Review "Reading and Enjoying Poems." Use the tips to read "A Mosquito." Reread the poem. Underline words that create pictures in your mind. Discuss these words with your partner.

2. Refresh your knowledge of metaphors. Read the definition and example in your teacher's notebook. Discuss with your partner what you know about metaphors.

3. Identify the three metaphors in the first stanza. Discuss each one with your partner. Write how the metaphors help you make mental pictures. Explain how these metaphors show the poet's feelings about mosquitoes.

4. Discuss with your partner: What pictures do the metaphors create in the second, third, and fourth stanzas? What do you learn in these stanzas about the poet's attitude toward mosquitoes?

5. Write what you learn about the poet's feelings toward mosquitoes. Include details from the poem to support your ideas.

6. Illustrate two of the four stanzas. Use the metaphors and details to draw your pictures, or use words to describe what you see.

Activity 2: Word Work: Synonyms and Connotations

1. Write the word *synonym*. Explain what a synonym is.

2. Choose two of these words from the poem: *whisper, unreachable, stagnant, adores*. Write the words on their own lines. Talk with your partner. Find synonyms for your words. List two to four synonyms next to each word.

3. Think about the word *connotation*. Refresh your memory by rereading your teacher's notebook. Write what *connotation* means.

4. Choose two of these words from the poem: *whisper, flee, stagnant, windless, detests*. Write one word in your notebook. Skip three lines, then write the other word.

5. Brainstorm connotations for the two words. Write your connotations under each word.

6. Choose one of the words. How do your connotations help you make pictures in your mind? In your notebook, draw the pictures or use words to describe what you see.

Name: _____ Date: _____

"A Mosquito" Word Ladder

Directions: Start at the bottom. Read the clues and write the words.

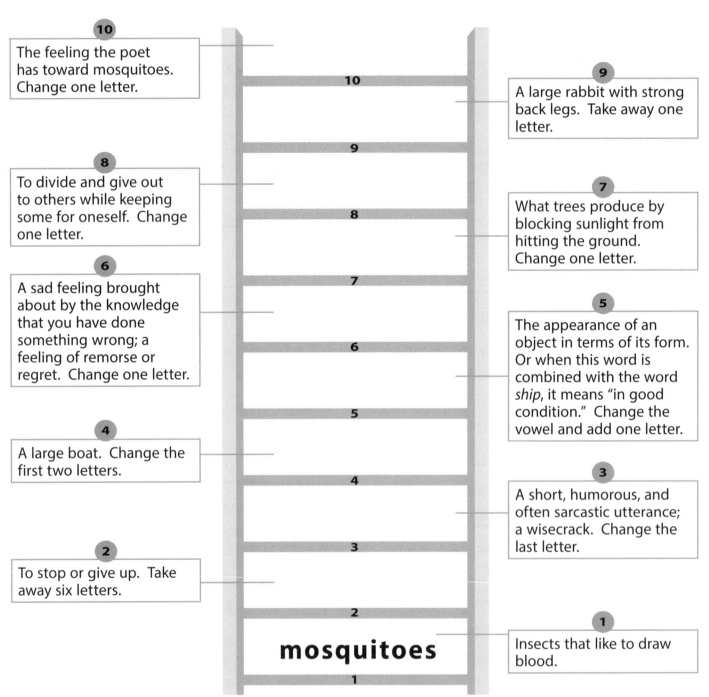

10 The feeling the poet has toward mosquitoes. Change one letter.

9 A large rabbit with strong back legs. Take away one letter.

8 To divide and give out to others while keeping some for oneself. Change one letter.

7 What trees produce by blocking sunlight from hitting the ground. Change one letter.

6 A sad feeling brought about by the knowledge that you have done something wrong; a feeling of remorse or regret. Change one letter.

5 The appearance of an object in terms of its form. Or when this word is combined with the word *ship*, it means "in good condition." Change the vowel and add one letter.

4 A large boat. Change the first two letters.

3 A short, humorous, and often sarcastic utterance; a wisecrack. Change the last letter.

2 To stop or give up. Take away six letters.

mosquitoes

1 Insects that like to draw blood.

Thinking Challenge

The word ladder starts with *mosquitoes* and ends with *hate*. In your notebook, connect both words to how the poet feels about mosquitoes. Include details from the poem that show the poet's feelings.

Name: _____ Date: _____

Visualizing: "Desert"

Directions: Read the poem and complete the activities.

Desert

by David L. Harrison

1   The desert is not for worriers.
2   Look around.

3   See that scorpion?
4   Over there?
5   Tail in the air?
6   Ready for war?
7   She'll eat her own young
8   if she's hungry.

9   Hear that rattle?
10 Stay where you are.
11 That's a warning,
12 not a dance tune.

13 Cactus plants
14 armed with needles,
15 double-dog dare you
16 to touch them.

17 Looking for water?
18 Not much of that.
19 Looking for heat?
20 Plenty of that.
21 Looking for sand, sun-heated hot?
22 Don't forget your boots.

23 The desert is not for worriers.
24 Look around.

Name: _____ Date: _____

Thinking about "Desert"

Directions: Complete these activities. For each activity, label a page in your notebook with the date, the title of the poem, and which activity you are completing.

Activity 1: Making Mental Pictures by Visualizing

1. Review "Reading and Enjoying Poems." Use the tips to read "Desert." Reread the poem. Underline the words that help you create pictures in your mind. Discuss these words with your partner.

2. Reread the second stanza. In your mind, picture what you see. Discuss with your partner: What do the last two lines tell you about scorpions? What does the word *war* tell you about scorpions?

3. List reasons why you would or would not want to meet a scorpion.

4. Reread the third stanza. With your partner, discuss what reptile this stanza is about. What clues helped you figure this out?

5. Write how the sound of the rattle can save your life.

6. Reread the fourth and fifth stanzas. Create a picture in your mind. Draw the picture or use words to describe what you see.

7. Discuss with your partner: Why does the poet open and close the poem with the same two lines? Write your ideas.

Activity 2: Word Work: Synonyms and Connotations

1. Write the word *synonym*. Explain what a synonym is.

2. Choose two of these words from the poem: *plants, water, look, hungry*. Write the words on their own lines. Talk with your partner. Find synonyms for your words. List two to four synonyms next to each word.

3. Think about the word *connotation*. Refresh your memory by rereading your teacher's notebook. Write what *connotation* means.

4. Choose two of these words from the poem: *war, eat, needles, heat*. Write one word in your notebook. Skip three lines, then write the other word.

5. Brainstorm connotations for the two words. Write your connotations under each word.

6. Choose one of the words. How do your connotations help you make pictures in your mind? Write your thoughts in your notebook.

Name: _____   Date: _____

"Desert" Word Ladder

Directions: Start at the bottom. Read the clues and write the words.

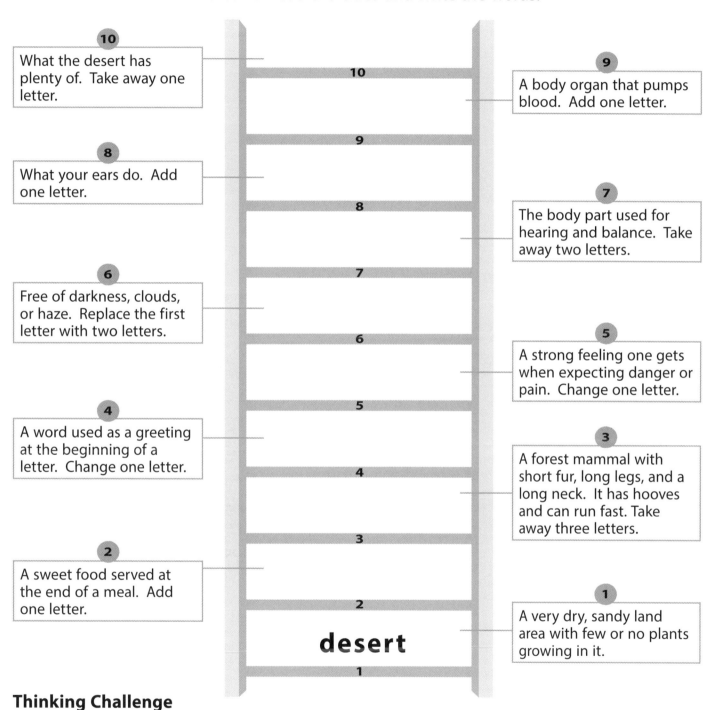

10 — What the desert has plenty of. Take away one letter.

9 — A body organ that pumps blood. Add one letter.

8 — What your ears do. Add one letter.

7 — The body part used for hearing and balance. Take away two letters.

6 — Free of darkness, clouds, or haze. Replace the first letter with two letters.

5 — A strong feeling one gets when expecting danger or pain. Change one letter.

4 — A word used as a greeting at the beginning of a letter. Change one letter.

3 — A forest mammal with short fur, long legs, and a long neck. It has hooves and can run fast. Take away three letters.

2 — A sweet food served at the end of a meal. Add one letter.

1 — A very dry, sandy land area with few or no plants growing in it.

desert

Thinking Challenge

The word ladder starts with *desert* and ends with *heat*. Reread the poem. With your partner, discuss why heat causes the poet to say, "The desert is not for worriers." Find other lines in the poem that support the poem's opening line. Write three reasons why "the desert is not for worriers."

Name: _____ Date: _____

Visualizing: "Rain Forest"

Directions: Read the poem and complete the activities.

Rain Forest
by David L. Harrison

1   The rain forest never sleeps.
2   While some nap, others creep.
3   Some climb, swim, fly,
4   hide, hunt, flee, die.
5   Some growl, crouch, leap.
6   The rain forest never sleeps.

7   The rain forest, ever green,
8   is home to plants no one has seen.
9   Home to creatures no one knows,
10 secret spots where no one goes.
11 Eyes peering through jungle screen,
12 the rain forest, ever green.

13 The rain forest, where monsoons roar
14 their wild-thing songs on jungle floor.
15 Sodden soil where droplets seep.
16 Rivers twist swift and deep.
17 Night and day it pounds and pours.
18 The rain forest, where monsoon roars.

Name: _____ Date: _____

Thinking about "Rain Forest"

Directions: Complete these activities. For each activity, label a page in your notebook with the date, the title of the poem, and which activity you are completing.

Activity 1: Making Mental Pictures by Visualizing

1. Review "Reading and Enjoying Poems." Use the tips to read "Rain Forest." Reread the poem. Underline words that create images in your mind. Discuss these words with your partner.

2. Reread lines 2 to 5 in the first stanza. These lines include verbs that describe how rain forest animals move. Match a rain forest animal to each verb. For example, climb—monkey.

3. Use a dictionary to look up the noun *monsoon*. Write its meaning. With your partner, find words in the third stanza that help you visualize and hear monsoons. Write these words under your definition of *monsoon*.

4. Reread the second and third stanzas. Choose one of them. Draw a picture of what you see in your mind or use words to describe what you see.

5. Find three words in the poem that make sounds or remind you of sounds. Write them in your notebook. This kind of figure of speech is known as *onomatopoeia*.

6. Discuss with your partner how words that make sounds help you picture the rain forest. Write your ideas.

Activity 2: Word Work: Synonyms and Connotations

1. Write the word *synonym*. Explain what a synonym is.

2. Choose two of these words from the poem: *hunt, hide, swift, peering*. Write the words on their own lines. Talk with your partner. Find synonyms for your words. List two to four synonyms next to each word.

3. Think about the word *connotation*. Refresh your memory by rereading your teacher's notebook. Write what *connotation* means.

4. Choose two of these words from the poem: *creep, secret, roar, sleeps*. Write one word in your notebook. Skip three lines, then write the other word.

5. Brainstorm connotations for the words. Write your connotations under each word.

6. Choose one word. How do your connotations help you make pictures in your mind? How do your connotations help you better understand the rain forest? Write your thoughts in your notebook.

"Rain Forest" Word Ladder

Directions: Start at the bottom. Read the clues and write the words.

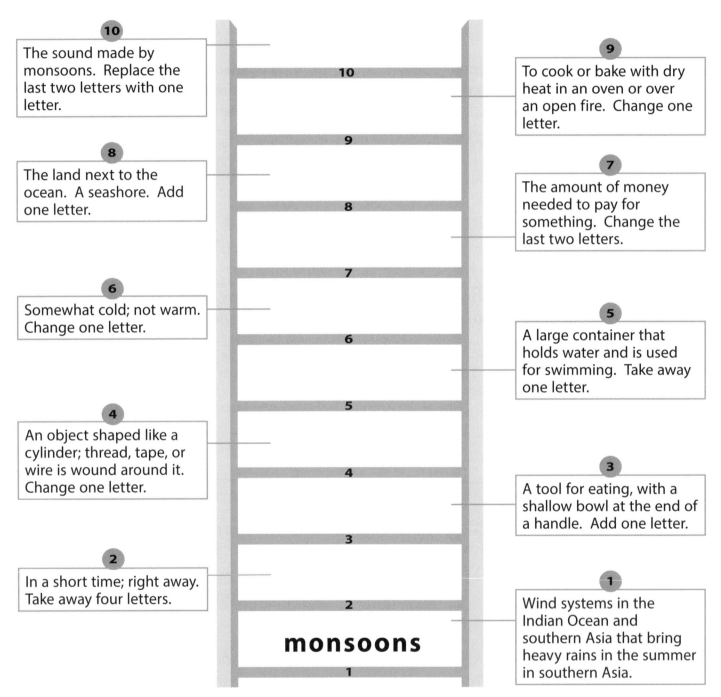

10 The sound made by monsoons. Replace the last two letters with one letter.

9 To cook or bake with dry heat in an oven or over an open fire. Change one letter.

8 The land next to the ocean. A seashore. Add one letter.

7 The amount of money needed to pay for something. Change the last two letters.

6 Somewhat cold; not warm. Change one letter.

5 A large container that holds water and is used for swimming. Take away one letter.

4 An object shaped like a cylinder; thread, tape, or wire is wound around it. Change one letter.

3 A tool for eating, with a shallow bowl at the end of a handle. Add one letter.

2 In a short time; right away. Take away four letters.

1 Wind systems in the Indian Ocean and southern Asia that bring heavy rains in the summer in southern Asia.

monsoons

Thinking Challenge

The word ladder starts with *monsoons* and ends with *roar*. With your partner, find words and phrases in the poem that apply to monsoons. In your notebook, explain the effect of monsoons on the rain forest.

Visualizing: "Winter in the Mountains"

Directions: Read the poem and complete the activities.

Winter in the Mountains
by David L. Harrison

1   Up here,
2   trees dance to whistling wind,
3   awaiting deliveries from the North
4   of fat snow hats
5   and heavy sweaters.

6   Up here,
7   valleys slumber deep in their covers.
8   Bears dream, if bears dream,
9   of cubs and blueberries
10   on sunny slopes come spring.

11   Up here,
12   you migrate, hibernate or camouflage,
13   dress for the occasion
14   or miss your meal.
15   Hungry eyes peer hard
16   for trembles in the snow
17   betraying hidden meals
18   scurrying down tunnels below.

19   Up here,
20   you have to be able to be
21   up here.

Thinking about "Winter in the Mountains"

Directions: Complete these activities. For each activity, label a page in your notebook with the date, the title of the poem, and which activity you are completing.

Activity 1: Making Mental Pictures by Visualizing

1. Review "Reading and Enjoying Poems." Use the tips to read "Winter in the Mountains." Reread the poem. Underline words that create images in your mind. Discuss these words with your partner.

2. Reread line 2. Identify the verb that shows what trees do. Now reread line 7. Identify the verb that shows what valleys do. Discuss the images each verb creates.

3. Use a dictionary to look up the verb *camouflage*. Write what it means. Reread the third stanza. Discuss with your partner why it's important for animals to "dress for the occasion."

4. Reread the second and third stanzas. Choose one of them. Draw a picture of what you see in your mind or use words to describe what you see.

5. Find a word in the poem that makes sounds or reminds you of sounds. Write it in your notebook. This kind of figure of speech is known as *onomatopoeia*. Discuss: How does the word help you hear and picture the wind? Write your ideas.

6. Reread the last three lines of the poem. With your partner, discuss what you think they mean. Write your thoughts in your notebook.

Activity 2: Word Work: Synonyms and Connotations

1. Write the word *synonym*. Explain what a synonym is.

2. Choose two of these words from the poem: *wind, dream, migrate, peer*. Write the words on their own lines. Talk with your partner. Find synonyms for your words. List two to four synonyms next to each word.

3. Think about the word *connotation*. Refresh your memory by rereading your teacher's notebook. Write what *connotation* means.

4. Choose two of these words from the poem: *camouflage, spring, hibernate, scurrying*. Write one word in your notebook. Skip three lines, then write the other word.

5. Brainstorm connotations for the two words. Write your connotations under each word.

6. Choose one of the words. How do these connotations help you make pictures in your mind and better understand winter in the mountains? Write your thoughts.

"Winter in the Mountains" Word Ladder

Directions: Start at the bottom. Read the clues and write the words.

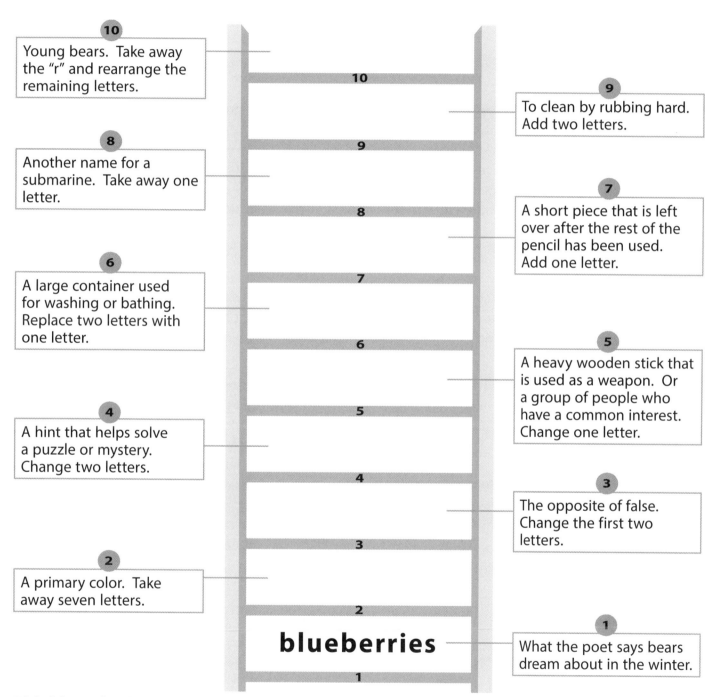

10 Young bears. Take away the "r" and rearrange the remaining letters.

9 To clean by rubbing hard. Add two letters.

8 Another name for a submarine. Take away one letter.

7 A short piece that is left over after the rest of the pencil has been used. Add one letter.

6 A large container used for washing or bathing. Replace two letters with one letter.

5 A heavy wooden stick that is used as a weapon. Or a group of people who have a common interest. Change one letter.

4 A hint that helps solve a puzzle or mystery. Change two letters.

3 The opposite of false. Change the first two letters.

2 A primary color. Take away seven letters.

blueberries

1 What the poet says bears dream about in the winter.

Thinking Challenge

The word ladder starts with *blueberries* and ends with *cubs*. Reread the second and third stanzas of the poem. Connect both words to *hibernate* and *bears*. In your notebook, explain the connections you've made.

Chapter 9

Inferring

This chapter provides 11 lessons on inferring to develop a deeper understanding of a text. The chapter begins with two interactive focus lessons, during which the teacher demonstrates how to read texts and provides students with a mental model of how to engage in inferring and related word work. The focus lessons ask students to practice what the teacher models, so that they can apply the reading, thinking, and writing processes to their own reading. Following the focus lessons are nine differentiated lessons for students to work through independently or with partners.

Inferring invites readers to use their own existing knowledge along with details in a text to find unstated meanings. When readers search for valid inferences, they deepen their comprehension and understanding (Marzano 2010; Robb 2010). When asked to find unstated or implied meanings in a text, students in grades 3 to 5 frequently find this to be a challenge. However, many students do fully understand what it means to infer.

One way of explaining inferring to students is to tell them to think like a detective and find clues—details—in the text that can help them infer or find a meaning that the author didn't explicitly state. Next, have students combine these clues with what they already know about the topic to make logical inferences. Put your detective hat on, think aloud, and show students how you find text clues and combine them with what you already know. By making your inferring process visible to students, you enlarge their mental model of what they need to do to succeed with making inferences. Inferring is a skill that students develop by reading, as the texts they read require them to infer to deepen their understanding of theme, character's or people's personality traits and decisions, the impact of setting, interactions with others, and why and how characters or people change from the beginning to the end of a text.

Learn What Students Know about Inferring

Before starting your focus lessons, find out what students know about inferring by asking them to head a page in their reader's notebooks and write everything they think they know about it. By reading these entries, you'll quickly identify students who might benefit from extra support. We suggest that you have students return to this entry at the end of a unit and write what they now understand about inferring, comparing their end-of-unit explanation to their initial entry.

The more practice students have with inferring, the easier the process becomes. Eventually, with enough practice, students infer automatically while reading, instead of consciously returning to a text to infer. The timetable for students internalizing this strategy varies and depends on their prior knowledge and the amount of practice they have inferring. In addition, the amount of independent reading learners complete at school and at home also supports the internalization of the inferring process, because as their reading volume increases, they have more opportunities to infer while reading a variety of genres.

Figure 9.1—A fifth grader weaves text evidence into his responses.

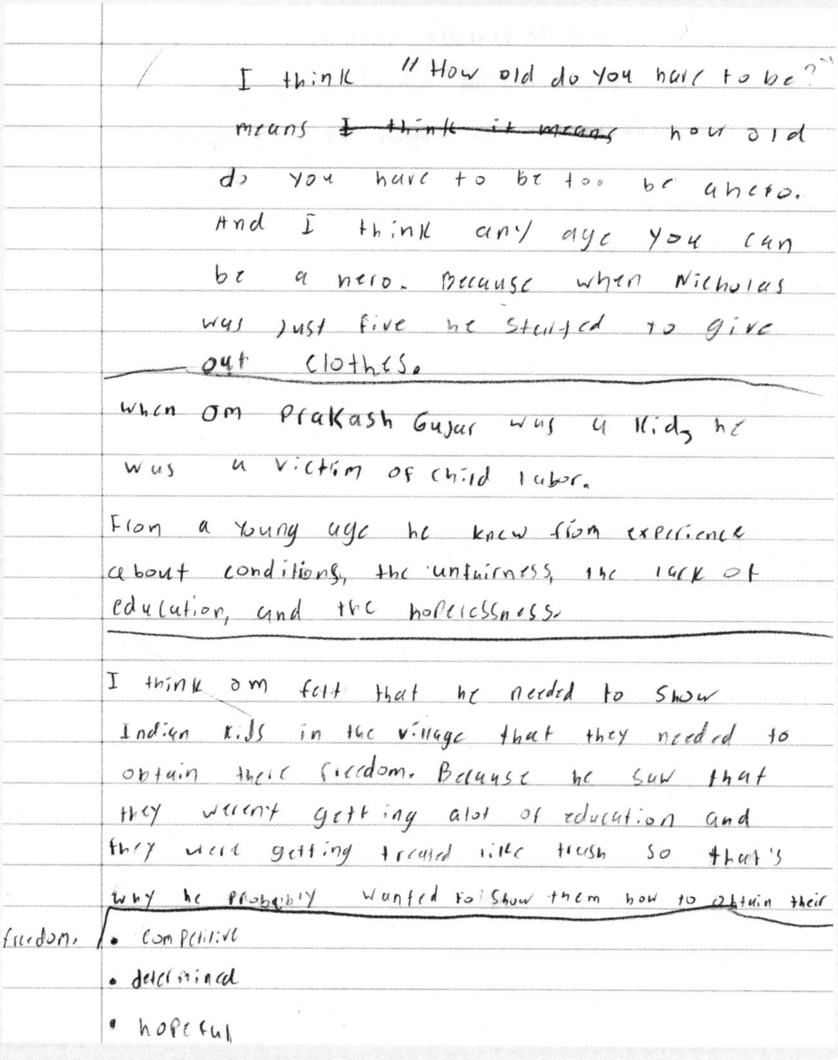

I think "How old do you have to be?" means ~~I think it means~~ how old do you have to be too be a hero. And I think any age you can be a hero. Because when Nicholas was just five he started to give out clothes.

When Om Prakash Gujar was a kid, he was a victim of child labor.

From a young age he knew from experience about conditions, the unfairness, the lack of education, and the hopelessness.

I think Om felt that he needed to show Indian kids in the village that they needed to obtain their freedom. Because he saw that they weren't getting alot of education and they were getting treated like trash so that's why he probably wanted to show them how to obtain their freedom.

- competitive
- determined
- hopeful

Review how to identify personality traits while reading, to ensure that students understand that they can identify personality traits by thinking about the following:

- Characters' and people's experiences
- Characters' and people's feelings
- Characters' and people's words and actions
- Characters' and people's interactions with others

- Characters' and people's inner thoughts
- Characters' and people's decisions
- Characters' and people's conversations with others
- Characters' and people's reactions to conflicts and problems

With some text selections, instead of inferring personality traits, students will be asked to infer unstated meanings of big ideas, concepts, and events using specific details in the text.

Continually return to the idea that inferring personality traits from a text invites students to be detectives who can see specific details as clues that enable them to figure out or infer what a person is like. As people and characters live through experiences, their personality traits can change. For example, a person might go from shy to outgoing, uncaring to kind and helpful, or bossy to considerate. When you read aloud fiction, point out the changes in characters and the causes of these changes, such as specific events, interactions with people, settings, decisions, and so on. Good fiction emulates life and reveals how and why characters grow and change.

Focus Lesson: Inferring to Find Personality Traits

In this focus lesson, you will show students how you use text details to infer personality traits and then help students understand what kinds of traits people have that lead them to make positive changes in their communities and the world. Then, you'll invite students to practice identifying personality traits with partners. You'll also model how to find synonyms and antonyms using words in "Making the World a Better Place" (pages 120–121) and introduce students to three types of compound words.

The Teacher Models: Reading a Text

1. In "Making the World a Better Place," David L. Harrison refers to people in the text as heroes. Invite students to pair-share and discuss the personality traits they believe are common to heroes.

2. Collect students' ideas on chart paper. These lists are from third graders and fifth graders:

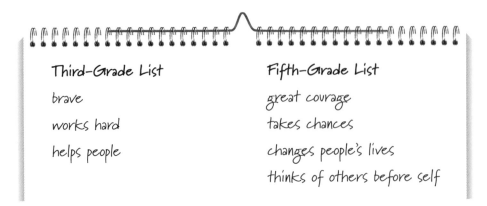

Third-Grade List
brave
works hard
helps people

Fifth-Grade List
great courage
takes chances
changes people's lives
thinks of others before self

3. Next, organize students into partners. Ask them to discuss what the title "Making the World a Better Place" means to them and what people can do to make the world a better place. Here's what a group of fifth graders suggested:

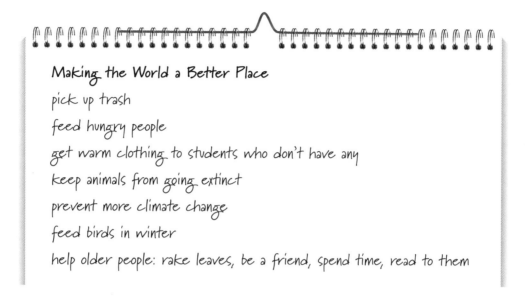

Making the World a Better Place

pick up trash

feed hungry people

get warm clothing to students who don't have any

keep animals from going extinct

prevent more climate change

feed birds in winter

help older people: rake leaves, be a friend, spend time, read to them

4. Display the text "Making the World a Better Place" on the board. Read it out loud. Have partners turn-and-talk and discuss what the people mentioned in the text have in common. Ask volunteers to share their ideas.

5. Underline the words and phrases in the first and second paragraphs that show what a person did to make the world a better place. Here are four:

Mahatma Gandhi led a nonviolent independence movement.

Emmeline Pankhurst led the movement that helped some women win the right to vote.

Martin Luther King Jr. became a leader of the U.S. civil rights movement.

Marie Curie pioneered research on radioactivity and won the Nobel Prize.

6. Ask partners to discuss and infer a personality trait common to Gandhi, Pankhurst, King, and Curie. Then invite pairs to use their lists of qualities of a hero to decide whether all or some of the four people are heroes. As an example, a group of fifth graders suggested courage as a personality trait. They said all the individuals were heroes because they worked to help people, showed great courage in their decisions, and thought of others before themselves.

7. Near the end of the unit, invite students to revisit the list of personality traits of heroes and adjust their lists based on their reading and discussions.

Students Practice

1. Invite students to volunteer to use the text posted on the board to show what the people in paragraphs 4 through 7 did to make the world a better place. Then, in a T-chart you create in your notebook, write this example for students to see how you have organized a set of details:

What the Person Did	Personality Traits
Martin Luther King Jr. kept fighting for desegregation and antiracism.	determined, persistent, resolved, organized, truthful

2. Now, invite pairs to head a page in their notebooks and create a T-chart with the same two headings as in the example. Display your T-chart on the board as a model for students. Next, ask students to choose one person discussed in paragraphs 4 through 7 and write that person's goals and accomplishments on the left-hand side of the T-chart. Then ask partners to discuss the personality traits that enabled the person to achieve their dreams and goals and list these traits on the right-hand side of the chart. Invite students to share the traits they have identified. Next, on chart paper, list the personality traits that most of the people in the text had in common, such as *caring, helpful, dedicated, persistent, empathetic, compassionate, giving,* and so on, to show the traits common to leaders who work to help the world.

The Teacher Models: Notebook Writing

In the last paragraph of "Making the World a Better Place," Harrison writes: "These heroes were not seeking fame." Demonstrate writing in your teacher's notebook about the achievements of one person whom you would classify as a hero. Display your notebook on the board and write the name of the person—for example, Martin Luther King Jr. Then share these quick notes and explain that thinking before writing and having notes makes the writing easier:

> **Notes:** hero—Martin Luther King Jr., leader of the U.S. civil rights movement; worked to end segregation that separated Black people from white people; wanted racism to end and Black people to have equal rights. Showed courage and devoted himself to a great cause—equity for all U.S. citizens—and cared about all people in the United States.

Next, use the notes to cold write your response in front of students, taking the position that King is a hero. Point out that having notes asks you to *think* before writing and makes the writing easier. Your cold writes are resources for students that can refresh their recall of the process you've modeled.

Focus Lesson: Compound Words, Synonyms, Antonyms

Word choice can make a difference in how well writers communicate ideas. When writers select a word or phrase that expresses their thinking, they consider its meaning, its connotations, and how well it fits into the ideas they want to convey. Word study for these lessons includes compound words and synonyms and antonyms. Compound words are two or more words combined to form a new word. Understanding the meaning of each word in a compound word can enable readers to better understand the new, combined word. There are three types of compound words:

- **Closed compound words** contain two independent words combined to create a new word: *houseboat, basketball, snowball.*

- **Open compound words** are two words that remain separate but together create a new meaning: *ice cream, peanut butter, living room.*

- **Hyphenated compound words** are two words joined together with a hyphen: *runner-up, merry-go-round, eighty-four.*

Studying synonyms and antonyms can enlarge students' thinking, reading, and writing vocabularies. Though similar in meaning, groups of synonyms and groups of related antonyms often have different connotations. For example, *happy* versus *elated, sad* versus *depressed, aggressive* versus *assertive*, or *kind* versus *helpful*. When students list synonyms and antonyms in their notebooks and complete word ladders, they expand their vocabularies and become aware of the nuances in meaning among similar words. In this focus lesson, you'll help students understand that word choice in writing affects how an author communicates ideas to readers.

The Teacher Models: Compound Words

1. Explain the difference between closed, open, and hyphenated compound words to students and provide examples of each type. Next, place "Making the World a Better Place" under a document camera and underline these compound words: *throughout, understanding, radioactivity*, and *homeless*. Think aloud to show students how joining the words changes their meaning.

2. Choose two compound words from "Making the World a Better Place," and think aloud as you write sentences using each word to show that you understand its meaning. Explain to students that you're *not* looking for a definition; instead, you're looking to understand the word's meaning from the details in the sentence. For example, write a sample sentence for *understanding* on the board: "Students use blocks to show their *understanding* of addition and subtraction." Next, explain that adding or taking away blocks to show the concepts of more and less can improve students' understanding of addition and subtraction with numerals.

Students Practice

1. Invite students to find additional compound words in the text, then come to the document camera and underline them. Ask students to find one hyphenated compound word.

2. Have students turn-and-talk to discuss the meanings of the underlined compound words.

The Teacher Models: Synonyms and Antonyms

1. Review synonyms and antonyms and explain to students that if they can identify a few antonyms of a word, they understand the meanings of the synonyms and their antonyms.

2. Underline *segregation* at the end of the second paragraph in "Making the World a Better Place." Think aloud as you find synonyms and antonyms to show students a set of these words, but also to show that the meanings of these words are similar and not exactly the same. Here's an example: *segregation, separation, exclusion, cliques, isolation — inclusion, collaboration, teaming, accepting*. Point out that the dash separates synonyms from antonyms.

Students Practice

1. Have students create a T-chart, writing *Synonyms* on the left and *Antonyms* on the right. Ask partners to choose one of these words from "Making the World a Better Place" and list synonyms and antonyms for their chosen word: *banned, danger, hope, abolished*. Then, ask pairs to share the words on their T-charts and discuss the differences in meanings. Next, invite the rest of the class to add synonyms and antonyms to each pair's list.

Completing the Word Ladder

1. Distribute copies of *"Making the World a Better Place" Word Ladder* (page 122).

2. Start at the bottom of the ladder. Say the word "speak," and have students pair-share to discuss what they know about the word. In addition to its meaning, point out that the word has one syllable and is a verb.

3. Guide students by helping them work their way up the ladder. Model how you use the clues to identify "peak." Again, have pairs discuss the word.

4. Continue supporting students. However, when you see that they can complete the ladder without your assistance, have them work with partners or independently, completing one word at a time.

5. The Thinking Challenge: The word ladder starts with *speak* and ends with *out*. Have students turn-and-talk to discuss how speaking out connects to "Making the World a Better Place," sharing specific examples from the text. Next, have pairs discuss the personality traits needed to speak out for a

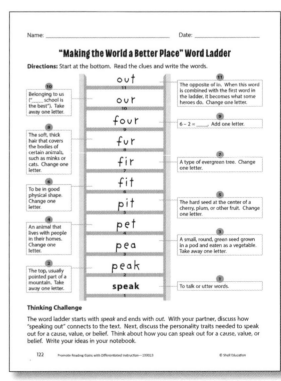

cause, value, or belief. Challenge students to think about how they can speak out for a cause, value, or belief. Have students share their thoughts and jot the traits in their notebooks. Ask students to share the personality traits they identified, and list these in your teacher's notebook. Put checks next to traits that are identified repeatedly, so students can see the personality traits common to heroes and changemakers.

Turning the Differentiated Lessons over to Students

If students' responses to the interactive focus lessons indicate that all students or a group would benefit from review and/or re-teaching, take time to boost their understanding. Pausing to do this will enable students to complete their work independently or with partners while using the resources you display from your teacher's notebook and the reminders you give to support students (see below).

The Differentiated Lessons

The content of the differentiated lessons always follows what you've modeled and what students practiced during the interactive focus lessons. Each differentiated lesson has three parts: 1) the text; 2) directions for students to engage in inferring and word work; and 3) a word ladder that connects to the text.

Inferring Lessons			
	Below Grade Level	*At Grade Level*	*Above Grade Level*
Grade 3	The Crow (p. 123)	There's More to a Worm (p. 128)	The Sea Bear (p. 132)
Grade 4	The Storyteller (p. 136)	The First Cave Artist (p. 140)	Was There a Real Alice? (p. 144)
Grade 5	Climate Strike (p. 148)	How Old Do You Have to Be? (p. 152)	Who Wants to Make Life Better? (p. 157)

Reminders to Support Students

To prepare students for working through the differentiated lessons independently or with partners:

- Remind students of the writing on inferring and the word work in your teacher's notebook, and display the notebook so students can refer to it as needed. Tell them they can use your notebook as a resource while they work.

- Write these terms on the board: *compound words*, *synonyms*, and *antonyms*. Define these terms and offer examples. Review the three types of compound words and provide examples.

- Write this term on the board: *making inferences*. Review what it means, with examples from your focus lesson.

- Remind students to use quiet voices when talking with their partners.

Focus on Inferring

Directions: Read the text and follow your teacher's directions.

Making the World a Better Place

by David L. Harrison

1   Throughout history, in times of need, heroes have appeared who have changed the world in positive ways: in the United States, President Abraham Lincoln led the efforts to abolish slavery at the cost of a great civil war.

2   India's Mahatma Gandhi led a nonviolent independence movement against British rule. In England, Emmeline Pankhurst led the movement that helped some women win the right to vote. German-born Albert Einstein greatly advanced our understanding of space, time, gravity, and the universe. Polish-born Marie Curie pioneered research on radioactivity and won the Nobel Prize twice. Martin Luther King Jr. became a leader in the U.S. civil rights movement, pursuing his dream of a United States devoid of segregation and racism.

3   But not all heroes lived in the past. Around the world, people still choose to speak out for what they believe in, to take action, and to make our world a better place. Times change and new challenges are created, but there are always those who step forward to do their part to help right wrongs and solve problems. Some of them are young.

4   When the Taliban came to her village in Pakistan, 11-year-old Malala Yousafzai's life changed forever. Girls were banned from school. When Malala objected, the Taliban shot her. She recovered from her wound and didn't let it keep her from speaking out against her oppressors. In time, she became the youngest recipient of the Nobel Peace Prize at 17 and the leader of an international movement to obtain free and equal education for girls.

(continued)

Focus on Inferring (continued)

Directions: Read the text and follow your teacher's directions.

5 While in her teens, Sweden's Greta Thunberg decided to speak out about how the environment was in danger and not enough was being done to save it. She became an international leader in a campaign to convince world leaders to move more quickly and decisively to fight climate change.

6 Jorge Muñoz, born in Colombia, was nine when his dad died. Jorge's mother moved him and his sister to the United States. Jorge saw hungry, homeless men in his neighborhood and worried about them. He decided to feed them hot meals from his own kitchen. Over time, he fed hungry people more than seventy thousand hot meals. He was awarded the Presidential Citizens Medal, the second-highest civilian honor in the land.

7 When he was four years old, Nicholas Cobb didn't like seeing people living under a bridge in his hometown of Plano, Texas. When he was older, Nicholas started raising money to buy warm coats for kids in need. As an honoree in the 2010 National Make a Difference Day, Nicholas was awarded $10,000. He used the money to buy more coats.

8 These heroes were not seeking fame. They saw wrongs they thought needed to be righted and made a decision to help. Everyone has the capacity to be someone's hero. When you turn on a lamp in a dark place, it lights the way for others. For those people, you will have made their world a better place.

"Making the World a Better Place" Word Ladder

Directions: Start at the bottom. Read the clues and write the words.

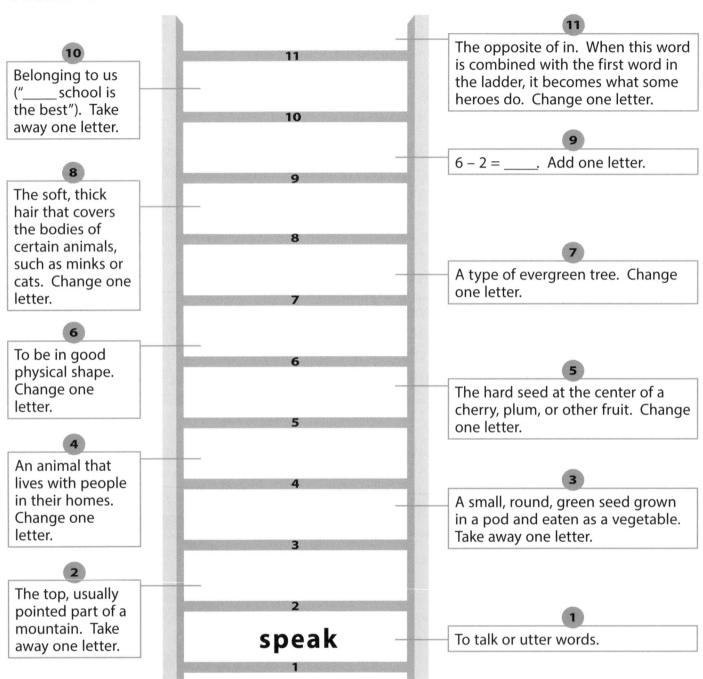

10 Belonging to us ("_____ school is the best"). Take away one letter.

8 The soft, thick hair that covers the bodies of certain animals, such as minks or cats. Change one letter.

6 To be in good physical shape. Change one letter.

4 An animal that lives with people in their homes. Change one letter.

2 The top, usually pointed part of a mountain. Take away one letter.

speak

11 The opposite of in. When this word is combined with the first word in the ladder, it becomes what some heroes do. Change one letter.

9 $6 - 2 =$ _____. Add one letter.

7 A type of evergreen tree. Change one letter.

5 The hard seed at the center of a cherry, plum, or other fruit. Change one letter.

3 A small, round, green seed grown in a pod and eaten as a vegetable. Take away one letter.

1 To talk or utter words.

Thinking Challenge

The word ladder starts with *speak* and ends with *out*. With your partner, discuss how "speaking out" connects to the text. Next, discuss the personality traits needed to speak out for a cause, value, or belief. Think about how you can speak out for a cause, value, or belief. Write your ideas in your notebook.

Inferring: "The Crow"

Directions: Read the text and complete the activities.

The Crow
by David L. Harrison

1   Crows are crowing—caw-caw.

2   Are some birds smarter than other birds? Even smarter than other kinds of animals? How can you tell? What about crows? Crows may have bird brains, but they are not birdbrains.

3   Crows are laughing—ha-ha-ha.

4   Crows are all over the place. They have big, noisy families and loud meetings. They fly around town like they own the place. They hop across your yard and perch on your roof.

5   Part clown, part outlaw.

6   Crows help themselves to your birdfeeder and trash can. They make off with shiny things to keep in their nests. They work like a gang of outlaws. While some look for food, others are the lookouts, in case a cat or a car or a sneaky kid comes along.

7   Crows are calling—caw-ha-ha.

8   Crows are not picky eaters, so they don't have to look hard to find something they like. They have lived in town so long that they have learned to like some of our food, from hot dogs to ice cream.

9   They'll eat a mouse. They'll eat a frog. They'll eat a toad or pollywog.

10   Crows are rather rough and rude. They'll steal your cat's or puppy's food.

11   They'll swipe an egg or corn or wheat. There's not a lot a crow won't eat.

(continued)

Inferring: "The Crow" (continued)

Directions: Read the text and complete the activities.

12   Crows can also do things that few other animals can. With their strong beaks, they can bend a twig or even a small piece of wire to make a hook. They use the hook as a tool to poke into holes and cracks where bugs or other small creatures are hiding. A hungry crow may take a nut in its shell to the street. Some have learned to wait for the light to turn red so that cars will stop before they walk out.

13   A crow that wants a nutty treat leaves a walnut on the street.

14   When cars and buses in a bunch have honked and zoomed and cracked its lunch,

15   the crow knows it's time to eat and pecks its tasty walnut sweet.

16   Crows like to play and tease, too. They love winter sports like sliding down roofs and car windshields after a snow. If a roof has a skylight, they will slide down it, too. They like to swing on the limbs of willow trees. At other times, they fly around doing tricks in the air, just hanging out together.

17   Not many animals have a sense of humor, but a crow does. One of the things it loves most is to play tricks. It may dive-bomb the cat or nip the dog's tail. The other animals may not like it, but the crow does. It may even swoop above a human's head. Crows can tell one person from another, and they spread the word if they spot someone who is on their "not nice to crows" list.

18   Crows are crowing—caw-caw.

19   Crows are laughing—ha-ha-ha.

20   Part clown, part outlaw.

22   Crows are calling—caw-ha-ha.

23   Are some birds smarter than other birds? Even smarter than other kinds of animals? How can you tell?

Name: _____ Date: _____

Thinking about "The Crow"

Directions: Complete this activity. Label a page in your notebook with the date, the title of the text, and "Activity 1."

Activity 1: Making Inferences

1. Work with your partner. Take turns reading the paragraphs of "The Crow" out loud. Discuss what you learn about crows.

2. Reread "The Crow." Discuss how you can infer that crows are smart.

3. The author calls crows "part clown" and "part outlaw." Discuss the meanings of *clown* and *outlaw*. Share with your partner one reason the author says a crow is a clown. Share one reason the author says a crow is an outlaw.

4. The author talks about crows' eating habits. Reread the lines that tell about their eating habits. Infer why these eating habits show that the crow is clever. Discuss with your partner.

5. Create a T-chart. On the left side, write "Inference." On the right side, write "Text Evidence."

6. Write "clever" under "Inference." Under "Text Evidence," write text details that show that crows are clever.

7. Define the word *birdbrain*. Write the definition in your notebook.

8. Add to the T-chart. Under "Inference," write "crows are birdbrains" or "crows aren't birdbrains." Write text evidence to support your choice.

9. Discuss with your partner: What details have you learned about crows that you didn't know? List the details in your notebook.

10. Reread the three questions the author asks at the end of the text. Discuss your answers with your partner.

(continued)

Thinking about "The Crow" *(continued)*

Directions: Complete this activity. Label a page in your notebook with the date, the title of the text, and "Activity 2."

Activity 2: Word Work: Compound Words and Synonyms and Antonyms

1. Write the phrase *compound words* in your notebook. Explain everything you know about compound words.

2. Reread "The Crow." List the compound words you find.

3. Choose two of the compound words. Use each one in its own sentence that shows you understand the word's meaning.

4. Think about the words *synonym* and *antonym*. Refresh your memory by rereading your teacher's notebook. Write what *synonym* means. Then write what *antonym* means.

5. Create a T-chart. On the left side, write "Synonyms." On the right side, write "Antonyms."

6. Choose two of these words from the text: *birdbrain*, *walk*, *smarter*, *tease*. On the T-chart, list synonyms and antonyms for each word you chose.

Name: _____ Date: _____

"The Crow" Word Ladder

Directions: Start at the bottom. Read the clues and write the words.

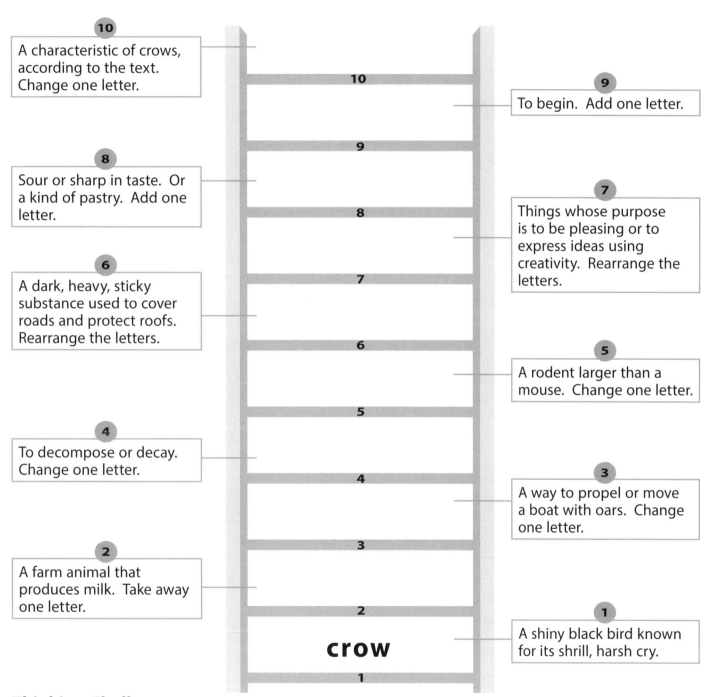

10 A characteristic of crows, according to the text. Change one letter.

9 To begin. Add one letter.

8 Sour or sharp in taste. Or a kind of pastry. Add one letter.

7 Things whose purpose is to be pleasing or to express ideas using creativity. Rearrange the letters.

6 A dark, heavy, sticky substance used to cover roads and protect roofs. Rearrange the letters.

5 A rodent larger than a mouse. Change one letter.

4 To decompose or decay. Change one letter.

3 A way to propel or move a boat with oars. Change one letter.

2 A farm animal that produces milk. Take away one letter.

1 A shiny black bird known for its shrill, harsh cry.

crow

Thinking Challenge

The word ladder starts with *crow* and ends with *smart*. With your partner, discuss ways another animal is smart. In your notebook, write some of the ways that animal and crows are alike and different.

Inferring: "There's More to a Worm"

Directions: Read the text and complete the activities.

There's More to a Worm

by David L. Harrison

1   Have you ever touched an earthworm or watched a robin hop across the grass with a worm in its beak? Have you seen a worm crawling down a sidewalk after a rain? Have you wormed one onto a fishhook? If you cut a worm in two, the front end might grow a new tail end, but the tail end cannot regrow a new front end. Guess which end has the brain in it.

2   We can see worms, and we can touch them and pick them up. They have no teeth, so they cannot bite. But there is much more to a worm than you may think. And there are many kinds of them around the world.

3   Most of a worm's life takes place in the dark, in the soil where it makes its home. What is there to eat down there, and how does the worm do it? A worm's body is mostly hollow, a tube that leads from one end of it to the other. So how is an armless, legless creature supposed to dig tunnels into the soil? And how is it supposed to get rid of the soil that it digs?

4   Nature has solved that problem. The worm eats the soil. The soil goes in through its mouth and passes slowly down the tube in the worm's body. As the soil moves along, the worm removes bits of plants and animals to live on. While that is going on, the soil is also breaking down and becoming better soil. The new and improved soil is a fertilizer that helps plants grow.

5   In a little square of land one foot long and one foot wide, as many as 25 worms may be living down there under the grass. There can be one million of them, often many times that, in one acre of land. (An acre is a little smaller than a football field.)

(continued)

Inferring: "There's More to a Worm" *(continued)*

Directions: Read the text and complete the activities.

6   The worm you see crawling down the sidewalk, along with millions and millions of others you don't see, plays a huge role in nature. Imagine all those worms and all those tunnels down where we can't see them. The tunnels crisscross in every direction. Each worm can eat through tons of soil in a year and leave droppings everywhere. All those tunnels make it easier for air to flow and for rainwater to drain into the ground. This keeps the soil looser so that the rich topsoil doesn't wash away.

7   Worms can tunnel through soil, but they cannot dig through concrete. They can crawl down a sidewalk or a driveway, but they must move elsewhere to find food and a good place to dig. Some parking lots at large shopping centers are bigger than 12 football fields. That keeps out a lot of worms.

Name: _____   Date: _____

Thinking about "There's More to a Worm"

Directions: Complete these activities. For each activity, label a page in your notebook with the date, the title of the text, and which activity you are completing.

Activity 1: Making Inferences

1. Work with your partner. Take turns reading the paragraphs of "There's More to a Worm" out loud. Discuss what you learn about worms.

2. Reread "There's More to a Worm." Discuss this question: How are worms important to humans' survival? In your notebook, write the inferences you made.

3. Use a dictionary to look up the word *fertilizer*. With your partner, discuss the definition and how worms are connected to fertilizer. Write the connection.

4. Discuss with your partner: Why is worm poop good for plants?

5. Create a T-chart. On the left side, write "Inference." On the right side, write "Text Evidence."

6. Infer how farmers feel about worms. Write your inference on the left side of the T-chart. Under "Text Evidence," write details from the text to support your inference.

7. With your partner, discuss why the title is "There's More to a Worm." List two or three reasons.

8. Why is it important for millions of worms to live in an acre of land? List the reasons.

Activity 2: Word Work: Compound Words and Synonyms and Antonyms

1. Write the phrase *compound words* in your notebook. Explain everything you know about compound words.

2. Reread "There's More to a Worm." List the compound words you find.

3. Choose two of the compound words. Use each one in its own sentence that shows you understand the word's meaning.

4. Think about the words *synonym* and *antonym*. Refresh your memory by rereading your teacher's notebook. Write what *synonym* means. Then write what *antonym* means.

5. Create a T-chart. On the left side, write "Synonyms." On the right side, write "Antonyms."

6. Choose two of these words from the text: *dark, better, large, removes*. On the T-chart, list synonyms and antonyms for each word you chose.

Name: _____   Date: _____

"There's More to a Worm" Word Ladder

Directions: Start at the bottom. Read the clues and write the words.

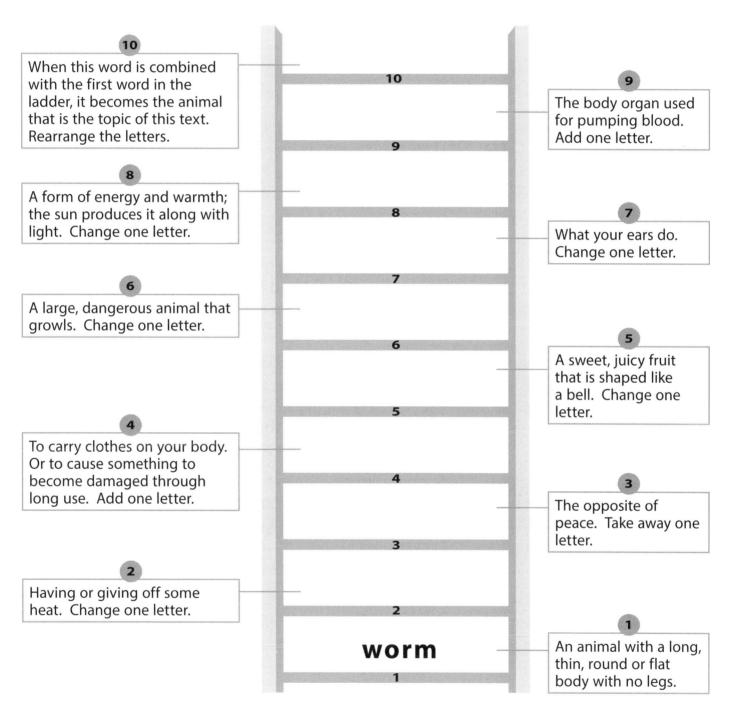

10 When this word is combined with the first word in the ladder, it becomes the animal that is the topic of this text. Rearrange the letters.

9 The body organ used for pumping blood. Add one letter.

8 A form of energy and warmth; the sun produces it along with light. Change one letter.

7 What your ears do. Change one letter.

6 A large, dangerous animal that growls. Change one letter.

5 A sweet, juicy fruit that is shaped like a bell. Change one letter.

4 To carry clothes on your body. Or to cause something to become damaged through long use. Add one letter.

3 The opposite of peace. Take away one letter.

2 Having or giving off some heat. Change one letter.

1 An animal with a long, thin, round or flat body with no legs.

worm

Thinking Challenge

The word ladder starts with *worm* and ends with *earth*. With your partner, discuss why earthworms are important to the survival of animals and human beings. In your notebook, list all your reasons.

Name: _____ Date: _____

Inferring: "The Sea Bear"

Directions: Read the text and complete the activities.

The Sea Bear
by David L. Harrison

1   What is black and white and bear all over? The polar bear.

2   The largest bear on Earth lives near the top of the world in the Arctic Circle. The coldest temperature on record there has been 93.3 degrees below zero. How can a bear live in such bone-chilling weather?

3   A thick buildup of fat just under its hide traps heat. But fat alone is not enough to keep the bear from freezing. Its skin is black, a perfect color to help soak in the sun's rays to warm the body. Like a good topcoat, over the fat and the black skin, the bear wears a heavy layer of fur, thicker than any other kind of bear's fur.

4   But that's still not enough. A second coat of fur covers the first. This is a special kind of fur with hollow hairs that make the polar bear look white. In an ice-covered area of the world, being white makes it harder for the animals that the bear hunts to see it coming.

5   The polar bear's scientific name comes from Latin words that mean "sea bear." That's a good name for a creature that spends much of its life on and around sea ice, trying to catch its favorite food, the ring seal. A polar bear knows to wait near a hole in the ice. When a seal comes up to breathe, the bear attacks.

6   The giant creature can also run 25 miles per hour across the ice and swim 6 miles per hour through icy waters. But seals are good swimmers, too, and they are not easy to catch. The hunter misses its prey far more often than it gets lucky. For every two seals a bear catches, eight others escape its giant claws and knife-sharp teeth.

(continued)

Promote Reading Gains with Differentiated Instruction—133013   © Shell Education

Inferring: "The Sea Bear" (continued)

Directions: Read the text and complete the activities.

7   For a million years or more, life for the polar bear was much the same. New ice began to form each winter as the weather grew colder. Ice fields were huge and thick and not far from land. Mama bears could dig dens on shore to give birth to their cubs, then move with them out onto the ice to hunt seals. There were always plenty of seals, and their pups were a special treat for the bears.

8   But in only a few years, much has changed in the Arctic Circle. The weather is warmer. Ice forms later in the winter and farther from land, and it breaks up earlier for the summer. A mama bear might be strong enough to swim for days to reach the ice, but her cubs may drown along the way.

9   In the huge areas where ice no longer forms, humans explore the sea floor. Many of them drill for oil. The water is not as pure now. Where some ice packs have moved, there aren't as many seals. Many bears are starving, and weaker ones may drown when they have to swim too far.

10   Time is running out for the polar bear. Unless changes are made that can save it, the great white bear may soon be gone.

Name: _____ Date: _____

Thinking about "The Sea Bear"

Directions: Complete these activities. For each activity, label a page in your notebook with the date, the title of the text, and which activity you are completing.

Activity 1: Making Inferences

1. Work with your partner. Take turns reading the paragraphs of "The Sea Bear" out loud. Discuss what you learn about polar bears.

2. Reread "The Sea Bear." Discuss text evidence you can use to infer that polar bears are endangered. In your notebook, list three reasons why they are endangered.

3. Reread paragraphs 3 and 4. List three ways the polar bear survives the cold.

4. Use a dictionary to look up the words *extinct* and *extinction*. Write the definitions in your notebook.

5. Discuss with your partner: Does the author feel that the polar bear might become extinct? Include evidence from the text.

6. In your notebook, write the reasons that support the belief that the polar bear will become extinct.

7. Discuss with your partner: What needs to happen to prevent the polar bear's extinction? Use inferences to answer the question. In your notebook, write what can be done to prevent the polar bear's extinction.

Activity 2: Word Work: Compound Words and Synonyms and Antonyms

1. Write the phrase *compound words* in your notebook. Explain everything you know about compound words.

2. Reread "The Sea Bear." List the compound words you find.

3. Choose two of the compound words. Use each one in its own sentence that shows you understand the word's meaning.

4. Think about the words *synonym* and *antonym*. Refresh your memory by rereading your teacher's notebook. Write what *synonym* means. Then write what *antonym* means.

5. Create a T-chart. On the left side, write "Synonyms." On the right side, write "Antonyms."

6. Choose two of these words from the text: *freezing, favorite, near, plenty*. On the T-chart, list synonyms and antonyms for each word you chose.

"The Sea Bear" Word Ladder

Directions: Start at the bottom. Read the clues and write the words.

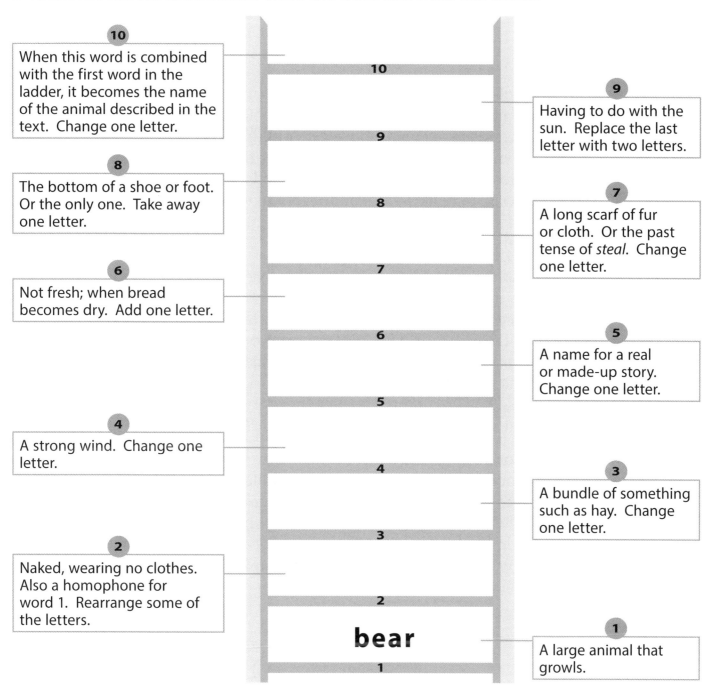

10 When this word is combined with the first word in the ladder, it becomes the name of the animal described in the text. Change one letter.

9 Having to do with the sun. Replace the last letter with two letters.

8 The bottom of a shoe or foot. Or the only one. Take away one letter.

7 A long scarf of fur or cloth. Or the past tense of *steal*. Change one letter.

6 Not fresh; when bread becomes dry. Add one letter.

5 A name for a real or made-up story. Change one letter.

4 A strong wind. Change one letter.

3 A bundle of something such as hay. Change one letter.

2 Naked, wearing no clothes. Also a homophone for word 1. Rearrange some of the letters.

bear

1 A large animal that growls.

Thinking Challenge

The word ladder starts with *bear* and ends with *polar*. With your partner, discuss how the polar bear can survive in temperatures that are 93 degrees below zero. Write in your notebook reasons why the polar bear survives in extreme cold. Next, write how warmer temperatures in the Arctic Circle are impacting the polar bear's survival.

Inferring: "The Storyteller"

Directions: Read the text and complete the activities.

The Storyteller
by David L. Harrison

1   Some of the best stories ever told were made up by people who could not read or write. No one else could read or write, either. There were no books because writing had not been invented yet. Storytellers had to remember the words for the next time they told the same story. They might draw pictures, maybe on a cave wall, to help them tell the story of when one of their hunters killed a big bear, or maybe when a big bear killed one of their hunters!

2   Storytellers who did not draw well or live near a cave needed other ways to help remember and tell their stories. They could dance. They could shuffle their feet in a certain way. They might paint their faces to look wise, old, mean, or brave. They could sing or chant some of the words. They could make up poems. They might do all those things. People who heard the stories might nod their heads. The next time they saw the storyteller, they might ask to hear that story again.

3   Some oral stories were just for fun. Others used silly animals to teach good manners and lessons about life to the young. Many stories were to help people remember the old ways, who they were, where they came from, and their history. Having a storyteller in the tribe or the village was a good thing. Sometimes the honor was passed down in the same family.

(continued)

Inferring: "The Storyteller" *(continued)*

Directions: Read the text and complete the activities.

4   After thousands of years, writing was invented. Now stories could be written down. Lucky people who learned how to read could read the stories themselves. Some stories were told on a stage, with more than one actor taking part. Times were changing. Printing was invented. Storytellers could write their stories in books. Movies were invented. At first, movies had no recorded voices. Actors used body movements and facial expressions to show what the storyteller wrote. Later, sound was added. Then television came along. Computers were invented. There were more and more ways for storytellers to tell their stories, and each way was different from the last.

5   Today, we love to hear stories more than ever. But now, instead of sitting around a campfire swatting bugs while the village storyteller chants and dances and tells us about our history, we open a book, we switch on our TV or computer or phone, or we go to a movie to enjoy stories that we choose. There are more storytellers in the world now than ever before.

6   In our own way, each of us is a storyteller. We want to tell others about ourselves and some of the things we have done. Listen to a group of friends talking among themselves. We tell stories about what we ate last night, a stinky thing our baby brother did, a trip we would love to take, our favorite song. . . . One of these days, maybe you will write your own story. Who knows?

Thinking about "The Storyteller"

Directions: Complete these activities. For each activity, label a page in your notebook with the date, the title of the text, and which activity you are completing.

Activity 1: Making Inferences

1. Work with your partner. Take turns reading the paragraphs of "The Storyteller" out loud. Discuss what you learn about storytelling.

2. Reread "The Storyteller." With your partner, discuss why storytelling is important. Then list three ways that oral storytelling helped people in the past.

3. With your partner, discuss the personality traits of storytellers.

4. Create a T-chart. On the left side, write "Inferring Storytellers' Personality Traits." On the right side write "Text Evidence." In the T-chart, list two personality traits storytellers need. Then, give text evidence for each one.

5. With your partner, discuss: Besides oral storytelling, what other ways can stories be told today?

6. In your notebook, list four things that changed the way stories can be told.

7. How do you feel about reading, watching, and listening to stories? Choose one way you enjoy stories, and write about why you enjoy it.

Activity 2: Word Work: Compound Words and Synonyms and Antonyms

1. Write the phrase *compound words* in your notebook. Explain everything you know about compound words.

2. Reread "The Storyteller." List the compound words you find.

3. Choose two of the compound words. Use each one in its own sentence that shows you understand the word's meaning.

4. Think about the words *synonym* and *antonym*. Refresh your memory by rereading your teacher's notebook. Write what *synonym* means. Then write what *antonym* means.

5. Create a T-chart. On the left side, write "Synonyms." On the right side, write "Antonyms."

6. Choose two of these words from the text: *remember, different, tell, listen, chant.* On the T-chart, list synonyms and antonyms for each word you chose.

Name: _____ Date: _____

"The Storyteller" Word Ladder

Directions: Start at the bottom. Read the clues and write the words.

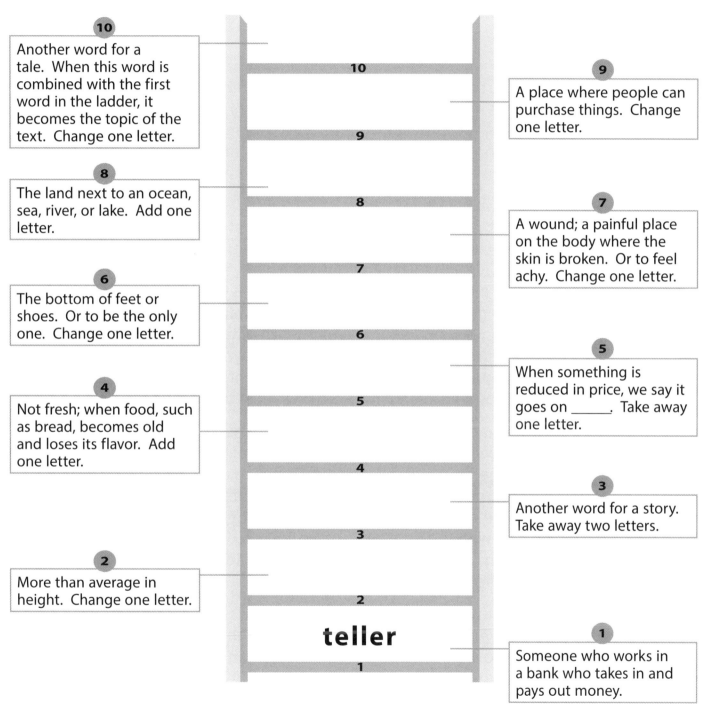

10 Another word for a tale. When this word is combined with the first word in the ladder, it becomes the topic of the text. Change one letter.

9 A place where people can purchase things. Change one letter.

8 The land next to an ocean, sea, river, or lake. Add one letter.

7 A wound; a painful place on the body where the skin is broken. Or to feel achy. Change one letter.

6 The bottom of feet or shoes. Or to be the only one. Change one letter.

5 When something is reduced in price, we say it goes on _____. Take away one letter.

4 Not fresh; when food, such as bread, becomes old and loses its flavor. Add one letter.

3 Another word for a story. Take away two letters.

2 More than average in height. Change one letter.

teller

1 Someone who works in a bank who takes in and pays out money.

Thinking Challenge

The word ladder starts with *teller* and ends with *story*. With your partner, discuss: Why are stories important? What can you learn from them? In your notebook, list reasons stories are important.

Inferring: "The First Cave Artist"

Directions: Read the text and complete the activities.

The First Cave Artist

by David L. Harrison

1   About forty thousand years ago, someone became the first artist to paint a picture on a cave wall. Life was short back then, so this person was probably young. The person might have lived in what we know today as Portugal, England, Italy, Romania, Germany, Russia, or Indonesia, but most of the four hundred caves where paintings have been found are in France and Spain.

2   Imagine that you are the original cave artist. You have been getting ready for this day for a long time. A person doesn't just stroll into a cave and paint a picture on a wall! You need a plan. What kind of pictures will you paint? What will your story be? Will you draw dangerous beasts? Bears? Lions? Mammoths? If you draw their pictures on the wall, what will that mean? Will your pictures capture their spirits? Scare them away? Keep them from hurting your people? Writing will not be invented for another thirty-five thousand years. Your pictures must tell the whole story.

3   When you decide what you want to say, you'll know what colors you need. But finding or making the colors is hard work and takes time. You may have to walk many miles to find the right kind of rocks, plants, or shells. You'll have to break and grind stone until you have enough powder to do the job. You'll have to mix the powders with the right sorts of liquids, such as juices, plant oils, sap, animal fat, bone marrow, and blood, to make pastes that will stick to the cave wall.

4   And what will you use to paint with? Your fingers? A bit of fur? A twig? A feather? A slender bone from the leg of a wolf? You might blow paste through a tube to spread the color over a larger area. You might decide to cut an outline of the animal into the wall with something sharp, like a clam shell or a chipped rock.

(continued)

Promote Reading Gains with Differentiated Instruction—133013

Inferring: "The First Cave Artist" *(continued)*

Directions: Read the text and complete the activities.

5   You'll need torches soaked in animal fat. They smoke and sputter and smell bad, but they are the best light for walking down long halls in the dark.

6   Don't forget more light! Once you find a good place to work, you'll need a different kind of light. Animal fat burns longer and cleaner in a stone lamp, so you'll need a supply of those. They're heavy, but you need to have them.

7   There is so much to think about. So much to prepare and carry. One thing is for sure: you will need help to get your supplies into the cave.

8   There you stand at the mouth of the cave, ready at last. You and your helper light the first two torches. Loaded down with the tools of your trade, you make your way deeper and deeper into the dark tunnel. In our minds, we see you there, bent to your work, a small circle of yellow light holding back the darkness. Your pictures tell us the world's oldest story. We don't know the words. How we wish we could have known you.

Name: _____ Date: _____

Thinking about "The First Cave Artist"

Directions: Complete these activities. For each activity, label a page in your notebook with the date, the title of the text, and which activity you are completing.

Activity 1: Making Inferences

1. Work with your partner. Take turns reading the paragraphs of "The First Cave Artist" out loud. Discuss what we can learn from cave drawings.

2. Cave artists needed skills that helped people understand their drawings. Infer two skills these artists needed. In your notebook, write the two skills you inferred. Next to each skill, explain why it was important.

3. Think about why drawing stories in caves took a lot of thought and planning. List what cave artists did *before* they started painting.

4. Create a T-chart. On the left side, write "Personality Traits." On the right side, write "Text Evidence." With your partner, infer the personality traits a cave artist needed.

5. On the T-chart, list three personality traits of an excellent cave artist. List text details that support these inferences.

6. The last line of the text says, "How we wish we could have known you." Why does the author end the text that way? Discuss with your partner and write your ideas.

Activity 2: Word Work: Compound Words and Synonyms and Antonyms

1. Write the phrase *compound words* in your notebook. Explain everything you know about compound words.

2. Reread "The First Cave Artist." List the compound words you find.

3. Choose two of the compound words. Use each one in its own sentence that shows you understand the word's meaning.

4. Think about the words *synonym* and *antonym*. Refresh your memory by rereading your teacher's notebook. Write what *synonym* means. Then write what *antonym* means.

5. Create a T-chart. On the left side, write "Synonyms." On the right side, write "Antonyms."

6. Choose two of these words: *short, dangerous, soaked, light, walk*. On the T-chart, list synonyms and antonyms for each word you chose.

Name: _____ Date: _____

"The First Cave Artist" Word Ladder

Directions: Start at the bottom. Read the clues and write the words.

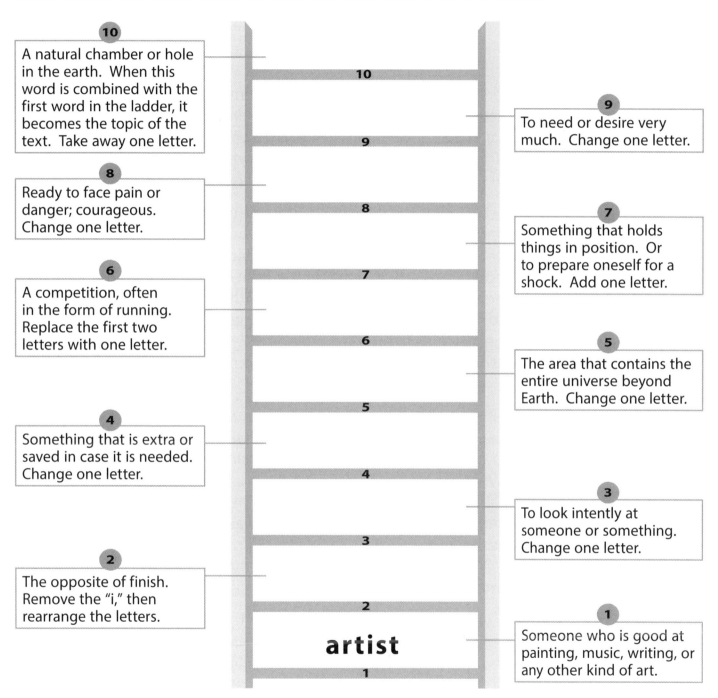

10 A natural chamber or hole in the earth. When this word is combined with the first word in the ladder, it becomes the topic of the text. Take away one letter.

9 To need or desire very much. Change one letter.

8 Ready to face pain or danger; courageous. Change one letter.

7 Something that holds things in position. Or to prepare oneself for a shock. Add one letter.

6 A competition, often in the form of running. Replace the first two letters with one letter.

5 The area that contains the entire universe beyond Earth. Change one letter.

4 Something that is extra or saved in case it is needed. Change one letter.

3 To look intently at someone or something. Change one letter.

2 The opposite of finish. Remove the "i," then rearrange the letters.

1 Someone who is good at painting, music, writing, or any other kind of art.

artist

Thinking Challenge

The word ladder starts with *artist* and ends with *cave*. With your partner, discuss: When did artists start drawing in caves? What skills did artists need to tell stories on cave walls? Write what you discuss in your notebook.

Inferring: "Was There a Real Alice?"

Directions: Read the text and complete the activities.

Was There a Real Alice?

by David L. Harrison

1   Storytellers find ideas even when they aren't looking for them. Anything—a turtle crossing a road, a bird looking in a window, a tummy ache, a child's sneeze—might spark a thought that sends the mind sailing off on a new adventure. Storytellers welcome new characters, new places, and plots they've never met before.

2   One July day in England in 1862, a 30-year-old math teacher named Charles Dodgson went for a boat ride on a river. Charles didn't know that just a few hours later, he would make up one of the most famous stories of all time. In the boat with Charles were his friend Reverend Robinson Duckworth and three daughters of another friend. Lorina was 13 years old. Alice was 10. Edith was 8. After a time, the girls must have grown restless. As the party rowed down the river, Alice begged Charles to make up a story for them.

3   Talk about pressure! There Charles sat—in a boat in July—facing a 10-year-old girl demanding that he make up a story on the spot. You can imagine the storyteller, looking around for inspiration. What did he see that stirred his imagination as the party poked along the banks of the river? All he had to start with was a name: Alice. He looked harder. There was also the sparkling water. He needed more. Maybe he spotted a rabbit, nibbling grass by the water's edge. Perhaps the rabbit hurried off when their boat came too close.

4   The girls were probably growing impatient. At last Charles began to speak. Once there was a little a girl named Alice. Alice was bored. A white rabbit came along, hurrying beside a river and muttering to himself about running late. Alice followed the curious rabbit. When he disappeared down a hole, Alice went, too. And there she had the most amazing adventures.

(continued)

Inferring: "Was There a Real Alice?" (continued)

Directions: Read the text and complete the activities.

5   The girls loved the story. When the outing was over, Alice (the real one) asked Lewis Carroll to write the story for her to read. Yes, Charles Dodgson was none other than Lewis Carroll. A private man, he went by Dodgson as a teacher and Carroll as a writer. For two years, Lewis Carroll polished his story. He added more characters and adventures, and he drew pictures for it. In 1864, he gave Alice, who was 12 by then, her own personal copy. He called it *Alice's Adventures Under Ground.*

6   Today, 160 years after he made up an amusement for three girls in a boat, Lewis Carroll's tale has become one of the most-loved stories ever written. Around the world, children can read the famous story in their own language. They follow Alice's adventures in movies, in plays, and on television. Today the story is known as *Alice's Adventures in Wonderland* or *Alice in Wonderland.* What inspired Charles Dodgson? A rabbit in the weeds? Who knows?

Name: _____ Date: _____

Thinking about "Was There a Real Alice?"

Directions: Complete these activities. For each activity, label a page in your notebook with the date, the title of the text, and which activity you are completing.

Activity 1: Making Inferences

1. Work with your partner. Take turns reading the paragraphs of "Was There a Real Alice?" Then infer two storytelling skills Charles Dodgson had. How did these help him create a story for the girls?

2. In your notebook, write the two skills you inferred. Explain why each skill is important to telling a story.

3. With your partner, discuss: What personality traits did Charles need to tell a story so quickly?

4. Create a T-chart. On the left side, write "Personality Traits." On the right side, write "Text Evidence." List two personality traits that Charles had. Then, offer evidence from the text that supports your thinking.

5. Why do you think Alice didn't want her sisters to be bored? Write your ideas.

6. Why did Alice want Charles to write the story for her to keep? Discuss with your partner and write your ideas in your notebook.

Activity 2: Word Work: Compound Words and Synonyms and Antonyms

1. Write the phrase *compound words* in your notebook. Explain everything you know about compound words.

2. Reread "Was There a Real Alice?" List the compound words you find.

3. Choose two of the compound words. Use each one in its own sentence that shows you understand the word's meaning.

4. Think about the words *synonym* and *antonym*. Refresh your memory by rereading your teacher's notebook. Write what *synonym* means. Then write what *antonym* means.

5. Create a T-chart. On the left side, write "Synonyms." On the right side, write "Antonyms."

6. Choose three of these words from the text: *looked, famous, restless, bored, late, curious.* On the T-chart, list synonyms and antonyms for each word you chose.

Name: _____   Date: _____

"Was There a Real Alice?" Word Ladder

Directions: Start at the bottom. Read the clues and write the words.

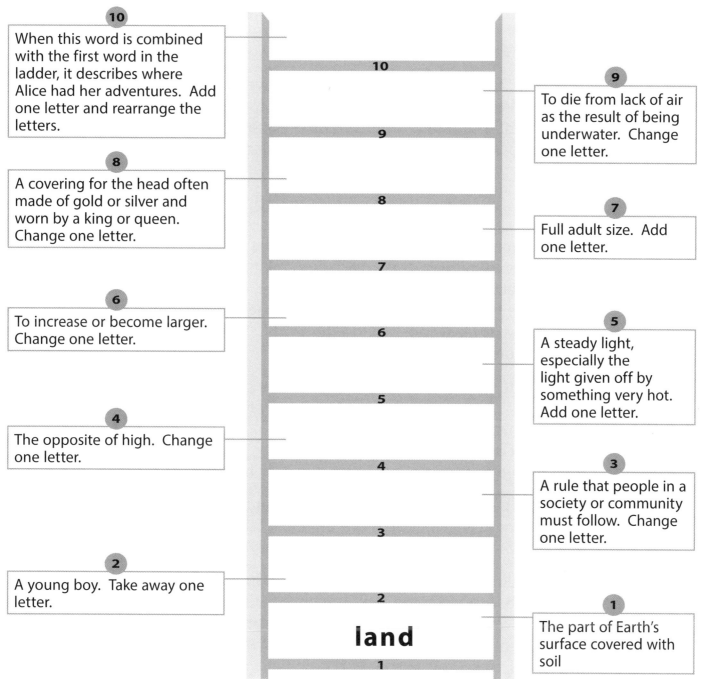

10 When this word is combined with the first word in the ladder, it describes where Alice had her adventures. Add one letter and rearrange the letters.

9 To die from lack of air as the result of being underwater. Change one letter.

8 A covering for the head often made of gold or silver and worn by a king or queen. Change one letter.

7 Full adult size. Add one letter.

6 To increase or become larger. Change one letter.

5 A steady light, especially the light given off by something very hot. Add one letter.

4 The opposite of high. Change one letter.

3 A rule that people in a society or community must follow. Change one letter.

2 A young boy. Take away one letter.

1 The part of Earth's surface covered with soil

land

Thinking Challenge

The word ladder starts with *land* and ends with *wonder*. Discuss with your partner what the text "Was There a Real Alice?" has to do with *land*. Next, discuss with your partner how *wondering* links to the text. In your notebook, write the word *land* and its connection to the text. Do the same for *wondering*.

Name: _____ Date: _____

Inferring: "Climate Strike"

Directions: Read the text and complete the activities.

Climate Strike
by David L. Harrison

1   Greta Thunberg was born in 2003 in Sweden, a country in Europe. Greta is known around the world for her work on one of the biggest problems in the world—climate change! Greta thinks about, talks about, and works to do something about this problem.

2   Earth's surface and atmosphere are getting warmer. Why? Humans burn huge amounts of coal, oil, gasoline, and natural gas. The more that is burned, the worse the problem grows. The warmer temperatures cause glaciers to melt faster. Water from melted glaciers makes sea levels rise higher. Communities beside oceans are in danger of flooding. The changing climate is causing extreme weather swings around the world. Storms are stronger and do more harm.

3   Climate change isn't only bad for every person on the planet, it's bad for plants and animals, too. Heat waves cause crops and other plants to die. Animals can't get the food they need, so they get sick or die. That goes for pets, livestock, birds . . . everything. Humans are causing the problem, and only humans can fix it.

4   Greta believes this problem will not get fixed until leaders of the countries causing it do more than just talk about it. They need to actually do something about it.

5   How did Greta start getting involved? In August 2018, when she was 15, Greta painted a sign that said SCHOOL STRIKE FOR CLIMATE. She skipped school and took a spot just outside a government building. Other students saw what she was doing. Adults did, too. Pretty soon, so did politicians. People liked what Greta was doing and how she was doing it. In 13 months, she had so many fans that four million people joined a climate strike around the world. It was the largest event like it in history!

(continued)

Promote Reading Gains with Differentiated Instruction—133013

Inferring: "Climate Strike" (continued)

Directions: Read the text and complete the activities.

6   Since that first day in 2018, Greta has given a speech at the United Nations and met with the Pope. In 2019, *Time* magazine named her Person of the Year. Her picture has been painted in murals, and her name has become known around the world. A dictionary named Greta's idea, "climate strike," the word of the year.

7   Greta is very good at focusing on one thing at a time. She self-identifies as having Asperger's syndrome and says that it helps her think outside the box about things.

8   Has Greta made a difference? So far, she has gotten promises from local and national leaders to take action. The United Kingdom passed a law requiring the country to greatly reduce how much it adds to global warming. She knows there is far more to do, but as she says, "we won't stop until we're done."

Thinking about "Climate Strike"

Directions: Complete these activities. For each activity, label a page in your notebook with the date, the title of the text, and which activity you are completing.

Activity 1: Making Inferences

1. Work with your partner. Take turns reading the paragraphs of "Climate Strike" out loud. Discuss what you learn about Greta Thunberg.

2. Reread "Climate Strike." Discuss what a strike is with your partner. In your notebook, write the title "Climate Strike" and explain how the title connects to what Greta did.

3. With your partner, discuss Greta's personality traits. Think about her decision to work on climate change. Think about the details in the text. Then, infer Greta's personality traits.

4. Create a T-chart. On the left side, write "Greta's Personality Traits." On the right side, write "Text Evidence." List three of Greta's personality traits. Write text evidence for each one.

5. Is Greta Thunberg a hero? Use the chart your class created that lists the traits of a hero. Discuss your thoughts with your partner.

6. Take a stand and write in your notebook "Greta Thunberg is a hero" or "Greta Thunberg isn't a hero." List reasons to support your position.

Activity 2: Word Work: Compound Words and Synonyms and Antonyms

1. Write the phrase *compound words* in your notebook. Explain everything you know about compound words.

2. Reread "Climate Strike." List the compound words you find.

3. Choose two of the compound words. Use each one in its own sentence that shows you understand the word's meaning.

4. Think about the words *synonym* and *antonym*. Refresh your memory by rereading your teacher's notebook. Write what *synonym* means. Then write what *antonym* means.

5. Create a T-chart. On the left side, write "Synonyms." On the right side, write "Antonyms."

6. Choose two of these words from the text: *flooding*, *harm*, *sick*, *leaders*. On the T-chart, list synonyms and antonyms for each word you chose.

Name: _____   Date: _____

"Climate Strike" Word Ladder

Directions: Start at the bottom. Read the clues and write the words.

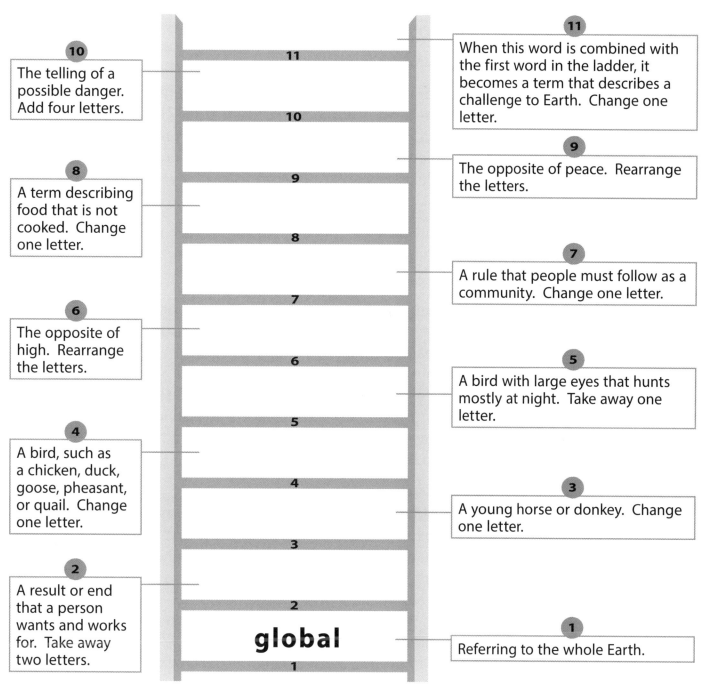

10 The telling of a possible danger. Add four letters.

8 A term describing food that is not cooked. Change one letter.

6 The opposite of high. Rearrange the letters.

4 A bird, such as a chicken, duck, goose, pheasant, or quail. Change one letter.

2 A result or end that a person wants and works for. Take away two letters.

11 When this word is combined with the first word in the ladder, it becomes a term that describes a challenge to Earth. Change one letter.

9 The opposite of peace. Rearrange the letters.

7 A rule that people must follow as a community. Change one letter.

5 A bird with large eyes that hunts mostly at night. Take away one letter.

3 A young horse or donkey. Change one letter.

1 Referring to the whole Earth.

global

Thinking Challenge

The word ladder starts with *global* and ends with *warming*. Explain what you learned about global warming from reading "Climate Strike." Think of reasons why Greta Thunberg adopted global warming as her cause and write them in your notebook.

Inferring: "How Old Do You Have to Be?"

Directions: Read the text and complete the activities.

How Old Do You Have to Be?

by David L. Harrison

1   Most ideas for making our world better come from adults. They have been around longer than kids. They have more experience. They've studied the issues and know what problems our world faces. And they have the power to reach decisions and make the solutions work.

2   But kids also pay attention to what's going on around them. Many are living with the very problems that need to be solved, so who knows those situations better than they do?

3   Here's an example: shoes. Shoes that look good. Shoes that fit. Or just having shoes at all! Most young people have at least one pair of shoes that fit their feet and blend in with shoes worn by friends and schoolmates. It can be tough to fit in with those around you. The last thing you need is to have the wrong shoes. You might get teased, even bullied. It's enough to make someone want to keep quiet, stay out of the way, not join in.

4   A five-year-old boy named Nicholas Lowinger noticed that some kids in homeless shelters in Rhode Island didn't have shoes. He learned that kids in the same family took turns sharing the same pair of shoes and going to school every other day. He did all a boy his age could do. He started giving his old shoes and clothes to children who were experiencing homelessness. When he was 12, Nicholas started an organization called Gotta Have Sole Foundation. Since that day, his foundation has provided new shoes for more than forty-five thousand children in homeless shelters.

(continued)

Inferring: "How Old Do You Have to Be?" *(continued)*

Directions: Read the text and complete the activities.

5   In India, many children experience bonded slavery, with little hope of a decent future. When he was a young child, Om Prakash Gurjar was forced to work growing and harvesting crops from dawn to dusk. With help from activists, he was finally released from his bondage. Right away, he began showing other village children how to obtain freedom. Since then, he has worked tirelessly to make life better for children who suffer the way he once did.

6   Om Prakash has fought to keep public schools free. He has worked to make sure that every Indian child is given a birth certificate to protect their rights. He has been given many awards, but to him, the most important one is knowing that countless Indian children will have better lives.

7   The list goes on. In Georgia, Mackenzie Bearup, and her brothers Alex and Benjamin began collecting books for kids living in shelters. Since 2007, they have donated thousands of books to shelters. Parker Liautaud was 15 the first time he hiked to the North Pole to raise awareness about climate change. Throughout history, in times of need, heroes of all ages have appeared and changed the world in positive ways. They still do.

Thinking about "How Old Do You Have to Be?"

Directions: Complete this activity. Label a page in your notebook with the date, the title of the text, and "Activity 1."

Activity 1: Making Inferences

1. Work with your partner. Take turns reading the paragraphs of "How Old Do You Have to Be?" Discuss what you learn about Nicholas Lowinger and Om Prakash Gurjar.

2. With your partner, discuss the meaning of the title. In your notebook, write the title and explain what it means. Find one example from the text that explains the title.

3. Infer the feelings that Nicholas had when he was five. List these feelings. Write the personality trait or traits Nicholas had that led to his feelings.

4. Discuss with your partner: Why did Om Prakash want to show Indian children how to gain freedom? Give specific reasons and write them in your notebook.

5. The author writes that Om Prakash has received many awards. The most important one to him is "knowing that countless Indian children will have better lives." What does this show about Om Prakash's personality traits? In your notebook, list two traits. Record text evidence to support each trait.

6. Discuss with your partner: Why might Mackenzie Bearup and her brothers think children need books to read? Write your answer.

7. Which one of the people in the text do you think is a hero? Review the chart your class created about the traits of a hero. Choose one person and discuss your thoughts with your partner.

8. Take a stand. In your notebook, write about the person you chose. List the reasons you believe that person is a hero.

(continued)

Thinking about "How Old Do You Have to Be?" *(continued)*

Directions: Complete this activity. Label a page in your notebook with the date, the title of the text, and "Activity 2."

Activity 2: Word Work: Compound Words and Synonyms and Antonyms

1. Write the phrase *compound words* in your notebook. Explain everything you know about compound words.

2. Reread "How Old Do You Have to Be?" List the compound words you find.

3. Choose two of the compound words. Use each one in its own sentence that shows you understand the word's meaning.

4. The compound word *bondage* combines *bond* and *age*. Reread paragraph 5. Use context clues to figure out the meaning of *bondage*. In your notebook, write the word *bondage* and its meaning.

5. Think about the words *synonym* and *antonym*. Refresh your memory by rereading your teacher's notebook. Write what *synonym* means. Then write what *antonym* means.

6. Create a T-chart. On the left side, write "Synonyms." On the right side, write "Antonyms."

7. Choose two of these words from the text: *solutions, bondage, protect, positive, shelters.* On the T-chart, list synonyms and antonyms for each word you chose.

Name: _____   Date: _____

"How Old Do You Have to Be?" Word Ladder

Directions: Start at the bottom. Read the clues and write the words.

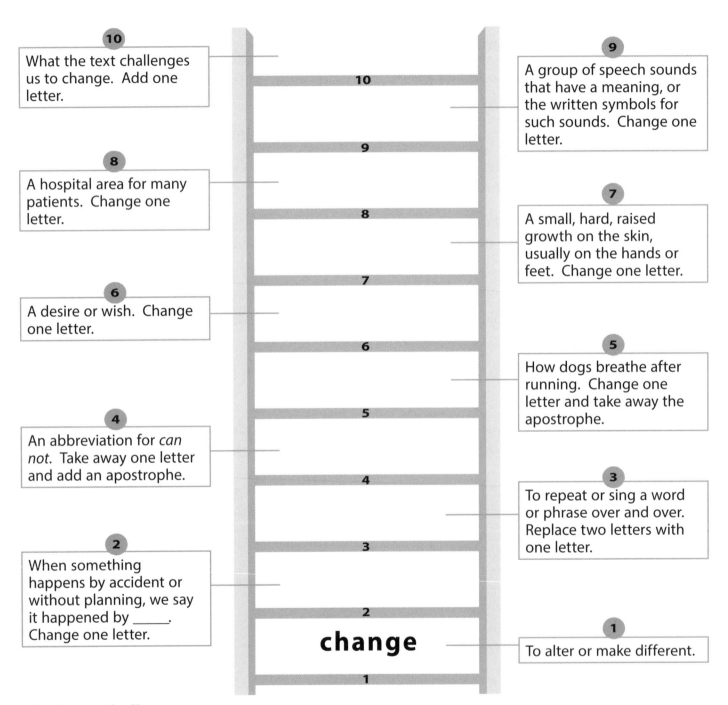

10 What the text challenges us to change. Add one letter.

8 A hospital area for many patients. Change one letter.

6 A desire or wish. Change one letter.

4 An abbreviation for *can not*. Take away one letter and add an apostrophe.

2 When something happens by accident or without planning, we say it happened by _____. Change one letter.

9 A group of speech sounds that have a meaning, or the written symbols for such sounds. Change one letter.

7 A small, hard, raised growth on the skin, usually on the hands or feet. Change one letter.

5 How dogs breathe after running. Change one letter and take away the apostrophe.

3 To repeat or sing a word or phrase over and over. Replace two letters with one letter.

change

1 To alter or make different.

Thinking Challenge

The word ladder starts with *change* and ends with *world*. In your notebook, explain how these two words connect to "How Old Do You Have to Be?" Include two examples from the text.

Inferring "Who Wants to Make Life Better?"

Directions: Read the text and complete the activities.

Who Wants to Make Life Better?

by David L. Harrison

1.   Mae Jemison was born in Decatur, Alabama, in 1956. Her father was a maintenance supervisor, and her mother was an elementary school teacher. Her parents loved and supported her. She had a good childhood.

2.   Mae was a smart kid, and from an early age she had many interests. She stuck to a goal once she set her mind to it. Watching astronauts on TV, she fretted that there were no women among them. She was still a child, but she decided that one day she would become an astronaut. Another of Mae's interests was dancing. She thought that she might want to become a professional dancer. But she loved nature and science, too. She liked so many things!

3.   After she graduated from high school, Mae attended Stanford University. At Stanford, she danced, was active in musicals, and pursued her interest in space. She never slowed down. She earned two degrees, one in chemical engineering and another in African American studies. Then she went on to medical school to become a doctor.

4.   But Mae held on to one of her original goals—to become an astronaut. When she was 29, she applied to NASA and was eventually accepted. In 1992, she circled the globe 127 times aboard the space shuttle *Endeavor*.

(continued)

Inferring "Who Wants to Make Life Better?" *(continued)*

Directions: Read the text and complete the activities.

5   Mae has achieved more amazing things since her astronaut days. In addition to her desire to succeed, she has had something else within her: a desire to serve others. During her medical school days, she traveled to Cuba to lead a medical study. She worked at a refugee camp in Thailand. She joined the Peace Corps and served as a medical officer for two years in Africa.

6   Mae started a company to encourage science, technology, and social change. She created an organization to promote science literacy for students around the world. She started an international space camp for students who are 12 to 16 years old. She also wrote children's books about her life.

7   From early in her life, Mae Jemison was loved, supported, and encouraged to follow her dreams. Lives of so many children—and adults—have been made richer because she did.

Name: _____   Date: _____

Thinking about "Who Wants to Make Life Better?"

Directions: Complete these activities. For each activity, label a page in your notebook with the date, the title of the text, and which activity you are completing.

Activity 1: Making Inferences

1. Work with your partner. Take turns reading the paragraphs of "Who Wants to Make Life Better?" out loud. Discuss what you learn about Mae Jemison.

2. Reread "Who Wants to Make Life Better?" With your partner, discuss Mae's personality traits. Give details from the text to support each trait you infer.

3. Create a T-chart. On the left side, write "Personality Traits," On the right side, write "Text Evidence." List three of Mae's personality traits. Write text evidence for each one.

4. With your partner, discuss: Is Mae Jemison a hero? Use the chart your class created that lists the traits of a hero.

5. Take a stand and write a statement that tells if you do believe or don't believe Mae is a hero. List three reasons that support your belief.

6. Look up the word *polymath*. Decide whether Mae is a polymath. State your position in your notebook. Write details from the text to support it.

Activity 2: Word Work: Compound Words and Synonyms and Antonyms

1. In your notebook, list the three types of compound words. Give two examples for each one.

2. Reread "Who Wants to Make Life Better?" List the compound words you find.

3. Choose two of the compound words. Use each one in its own sentence that shows you understand the word's meaning.

4. Think about the words *synonym* and *antonym*. Refresh your memory by rereading your teacher's notebook. Write what *synonym* means. Then write what *antonym* means.

5. Create a T-chart. On the left side, write "Synonyms." On the right side, write "Antonyms."

6. Choose two of these words from the text: *fretted*, *accepted*, *encouraged*. On the T-chart, list synonyms and antonyms for each word you chose.

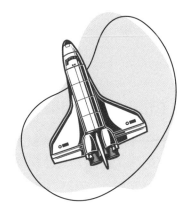

Name: _____ Date: _____

"Who Wants to Make Life Better?" Word Ladder

Directions: Start at the bottom. Read the clues and write the words.

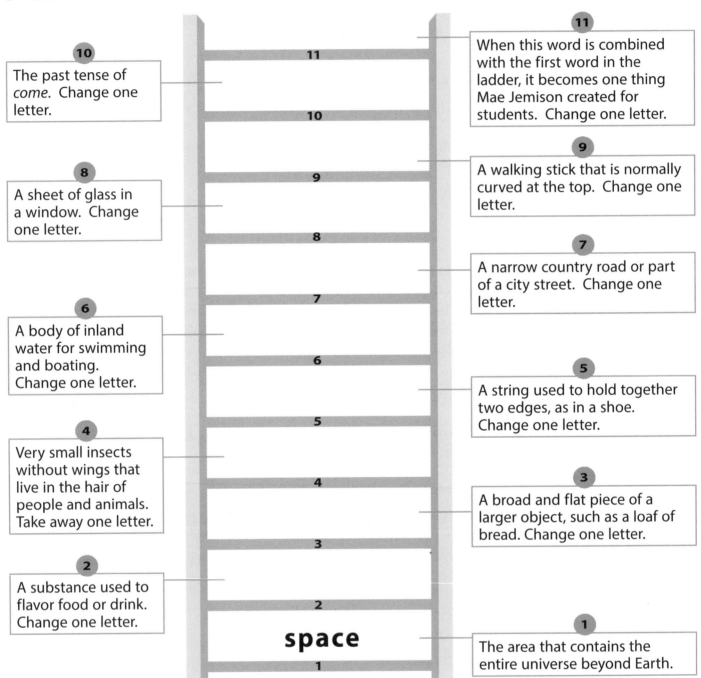

10 The past tense of *come*. Change one letter.

8 A sheet of glass in a window. Change one letter.

6 A body of inland water for swimming and boating. Change one letter.

4 Very small insects without wings that live in the hair of people and animals. Take away one letter.

2 A substance used to flavor food or drink. Change one letter.

11 When this word is combined with the first word in the ladder, it becomes one thing Mae Jemison created for students. Change one letter.

9 A walking stick that is normally curved at the top. Change one letter.

7 A narrow country road or part of a city street. Change one letter.

5 A string used to hold together two edges, as in a shoe. Change one letter.

3 A broad and flat piece of a larger object, such as a loaf of bread. Change one letter.

1 The area that contains the entire universe beyond Earth.

space

Thinking Challenge

The word ladder starts with *space* and ends with *camp*. In your notebook, explain what space camp had to do with Mae Jemison's life. Next, reread the text and take notes about ways Mae made life better for others. Then, use your notes to write a paragraph that explains how she made life better for others.

Chapter 10

Drawing Conclusions

This chapter provides 11 lessons on drawing conclusions to develop a deeper understanding of a text. The chapter begins with two interactive focus lessons, during which the teacher demonstrates how to read poems and provides students with a mental model of how to engage in drawing conclusions and related word work. The focus lessons ask students to practice what the teacher models, so that they can apply the reading, thinking, and writing processes to their own reading. Following the focus lessons are nine differentiated lessons for students to work through independently or with partners.

Drawing conclusions and making inferences both ask readers to find unstated meanings in a text. Both strategies invite readers to combine what they know about a topic with text details and then develop conclusions the author doesn't explicitly state. The dictionary defines *conclude* and *conclusion* as "using reasoning or logical thinking to arrive at an opinion or judgment that grows out of details in a text or in research," and that's what we want students to practice.

The poems in this chapter for grades three and five are ideal for helping students use logical thinking to draw conclusions about a problem that can affect the ecology of our planet, our food supply, and how animals and humans are dependent on some endangered species for food. The poems for fourth grade reveal why tigers are becoming extinct and how tossing cans and tires into streams that feed into rivers and seas causes pollution. Students can build mental models of the process of drawing conclusions when you think aloud and make your reasoning visible (see page 165 of the focus lesson). Moreover, when you build students' understanding of words such as *habitat, endangered, extinct, predator, ecology, pollination,* and *diet,* you support their abilities to draw conclusions about the endangered species in the poems.

> Drawing conclusions is related to inferring but moves beyond making inferences as students explore issues related to their conclusions.

Sometimes, drawing conclusions requires that students gather more information about the animal, its habitat, and its impact on people and the environment. For example, in these poems, students will need and want to know how the extinction of a species of butterfly, bee, or chameleon will affect other animals (including predators), people, the environment, and the natural habitat. Some lessons suggest using additional resources that can enhance students' understandings and support their conclusions. A list of possible resources is provided on page 169.

Drawing conclusions is related to inferring but moves beyond making inferences as students explore issues related to their conclusions. For example, the blunt-nosed leopard lizard is on the endangered species list. It is a predator that feeds on grasshoppers, spiders, and rodents—and one conclusion is that this lizard prevents an overabundance of these insects and animals in the environment. When any animal is endangered, another reasonable conclusion is that its habitat might also be in danger, which affects the animal's health and ability to reproduce. In addition, a conclusion for all endangered species is the importance of having scientists find ways to help increase population numbers to avoid extinction.

Learn What Students Know about Drawing Conclusions

Before starting your focus lessons, find out what students know about drawing conclusions by asking them to head a page in their reader's notebooks and write everything they think they know about it. If students feel they have no background knowledge or experience, they can write, "I don't know." It's not unusual for students to have little to no experience with this strategy. If students know little to nothing about this strategy, monitor their responses during the lessons and repeat parts as needed to build and increase their background knowledge. Taking the time to pause and discover what students have absorbed enables you to build on what they understand, so they can move forward. For this unit, enlarging students' vocabulary about concepts related to endangered species can support their ability to draw conclusions.

Focus Lesson: Drawing Conclusions

In this focus lesson, you will show students how to draw conclusions using details in a poem. Then, you'll invite students to practice drawing conclusions with partners. You'll also discuss multiple forms of words and model how to build word families.

Build Background Knowledge

To prepare students to draw conclusions when reading the poem "And What Can We Conclude?", build their background knowledge about endangered species, the environment, and animals and insects that might become extinct. Students will need to understand vocabulary that enables them to think about the animal or insect, and draw conclusions based on specific facts.

Help students understand the complex process of pollination by watching a video and observing the process in action. One such video is "Like Fruit? Thank a Bee!" (SciShow Kids), which can be found on YouTube.

Next, display on the board the sentences that follow (without the examples), and then choose two words to think aloud and model how you offer examples to show your understanding. Invite pairs to turn-and talk and discuss each underlined word. As they share, write their ideas on the chart next to "Examples."

Vocabulary for Drawing Conclusions

1. The <u>habitat</u> is the place where an animal or insect lives and grows.

   Examples: ocean, river, jungle, city, plains, mountains

2. When scientists say that a species is <u>endangered</u>, there are few of its kind left on the earth.

   Examples: honeybees, monarch butterflies, bumblebees, snow leopards

3. An animal or plant is <u>extinct</u> when there are none left on the earth.

   Examples: African black rhino, carrier Pigeon

4. <u>Predators</u> hunt and eat other animals in order to live.

   Examples: lions, eagles, snakes, wolves, tigers, sharks

5. The <u>diet</u> of animals can be leaves, vegetables, insects, unhatched eggs, or other animals.

   Examples: grasshoppers, mushrooms, berries, leaves, rodents, baby snakes

6. <u>Ecology</u> is the science of looking at how living things interact with each other and with their habitats and how these interactions affect life on earth.

   Examples: all living organisms and climate change; endangered species and their effect on food supply; endangered species as predators and their effect on controlling animal populations

After building students' background knowledge, move on to modeling how to draw conclusions using the poem "And What Can We Conclude?"

The Teacher Models: Drawing Conclusions

1. Display the poem "And What Can We Conclude?" (page 170). Explain what the poem's title asks of readers. Then, using a world map or globe, invite students to volunteer to find the places mentioned in the poem.

2. Explain that the poem has six short stanzas. Read the poem aloud twice.

3. Underline words and phrases that reveal the homes of endangered species mentioned: Australia, America, and Africa. Next, underline the endangered animals and insects: butterfly, bumblebee, and lizard.

4. Think aloud about the second stanza and explain that endangered species can be small, they are wild, and they depend on their habitats as they quietly go about living their lives. Ask students to pair-share and discuss why the author uses the adjectives small, quiet, and wild. Here's what third graders have suggested:

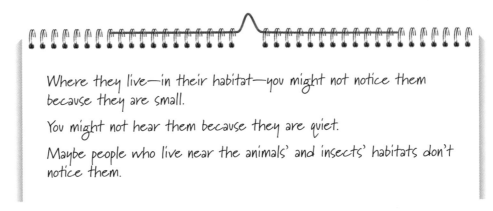

Where they live—in their habitat—you might not notice them because they are small.
You might not hear them because they are quiet.
Maybe people who live near the animals' and insects' habitats don't notice them.

5. When students show you that they can think with information, praise their thinking and point out that they have begun to draw conclusions.

Students Practice

1. Invite partners to answer the question posed in the fifth stanza, "What do they share in common?" Explain that their responses will be conclusions. Here are conclusions from third graders:

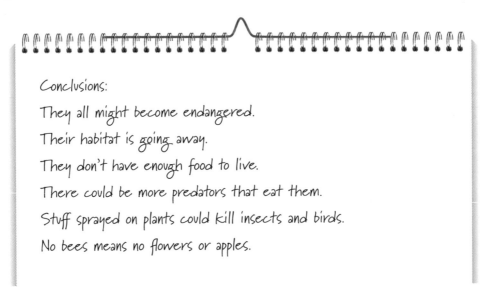

Conclusions:
They all might become endangered.
Their habitat is going away.
They don't have enough food to live.
There could be more predators that eat them.
Stuff sprayed on plants could kill insects and birds.
No bees means no flowers or apples.

2. Invite students to pair-share to discuss the meaning of the last stanza of the poem. After discussing, have students write in their notebooks the title of the poem and jot the key points of their discussions and any new ideas that popped into their minds. Ask volunteers to share.

The Teacher Models: Notebook Writing

Demonstrate your expectations for drawing conclusions by completing a cold write. Display your teacher's notebook, and write notes drawing conclusions about why scientists and people should pay attention to species that have become endangered. For example:

- the species could die out and become extinct
- the habitat could be in danger
- animals that depend on the habitat for food could starve
- diets of predators and the endangered animal could suffer because there is not enough food in their habitat

Ask students if they'd like to add any other notes. Here's what one group of third graders suggested:

- the habitat could go and never come back
- animals and insects that live there will also be gone
- other animals can lose their food

Next, write a short paragraph or create a list in your notebook of your conclusions to the question: *Why should scientists and people pay attention to endangered species?* Show students how you start your conclusions by turning the question into a statement: *There are many conclusions that show why scientists and people should pay attention to endangered species.* Your cold write is a resource for students that will refresh their recall of the process you've modeled.

Focus Lesson: Multiple Forms of Words and Word Families

The overarching purpose of providing students with not one word, such as *share*, but with multiple forms of that word—*share, shared, sharing, shares, sharer*—is to enlarge their vocabularies and show them how other forms of words work. Ultimately, the goal is for students to be able to use the words in writing and thinking. Building word families enlarges students' vocabularies by asking them to do analogous thinking. For example, if you can say *things*, then you can find other words in the "ings" word family by replacing the *th* with *br*—brings, *str*—strings, *cl*—clings, *fl*—flings, *st*—stings, *k*—kings, *r*—rings, and so on. Building word families enables readers to pronounce and create several new words in that family.

The Teacher Models: Multiple Forms of Words

1. Ask students to work with their partners and identify forms of *danger* (*dangerous, endangered, dangers*). Then invite students to use these words in sentences that you record on the board.

2. Have students pair-share to find multiple forms of *do*, and then volunteer to share. Record their responses on the board (*do, does, did, done, don't, doesn't*).

3. Next, ask students to head a page in their notebooks and use these forms in a separate sentence: *does, did, done.* Have students share and write their sentences on the board.

4. Now ask partners to develop a sentence for the contractions *doesn't* (*does not*) and *don't* (*do not*). Have pairs volunteer to share; record their sentences on the board and discuss.

Students Practice:

1. Ask partners to use the word *day* from the poem to build on the *ay* family (say, may, lay, stray, play, gray, tray, way, hay, pay, pray, ray, stay, clay, bray, nay, slay).

2. Next, have pairs work together and use *kill* and *small* to find words in the *ill* and *all* families.

3. Here's what third graders found for the *ill* family: *bill, fill, gill, hill, mill, still, pill, will, grill.* Here are words you might add and discuss with students: *shrill, dill, frill, quill, krill, trill.*

Completing the Word Ladder

1. Distribute copies of *"And What Can We Conclude?" Word Ladder* (page 171) to students.

2. Start at the bottom of the ladder. Say the word "butter," and have students pair-share to discuss what they know about the word. In addition to its meaning, point out that the word has two syllables and is a noun.

3. Guide students by helping them work their way up the ladder. Model how you use the clues to identify "batter." Again, have pairs discuss the word.

4. Continue supporting students. However, when you see that they can complete the ladder without your assistance, have them work with partners or independently, completing one word at a time.

5. The Thinking Challenge: The word ladder starts with *butter* and ends with *fly.* On a page of your teacher's notebook, model explaining how the work of butterflies is similar to what bees do. Then, discuss how the survival of humans depends on butterflies.

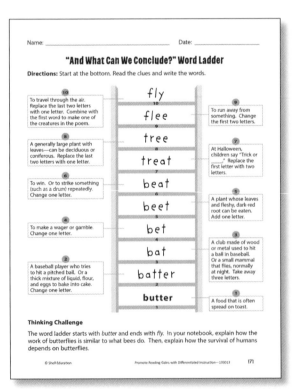

Name: _____   Date: _____

"And What Can We Conclude?" Word Ladder

Directions: Start at the bottom. Read the clues and write the words.

10 To travel through the air. Replace the last two letters with one letter. Combine with the first word to make one of the creatures in the poem.	**fly** (10)
8 A generally large plant with leaves—can be deciduous or coniferous. Replace the last two letters with one letter.	**flee** (9) — **9** To run away from something. Change the first two letters.
	tree (8)
6 To win. Or to strike something (such as a drum) repeatedly. Change one letter.	**treat** (7) — **7** At Halloween, children say "Trick or _____." Replace the first letter with two letters.
	beat (6)
4 To make a wager or gamble. Change one letter.	**beet** (5) — **5** A plant whose leaves and fleshy, dark-red root can be eaten. Add one letter.
	bet (4)
2 A baseball player who tries to hit a pitched ball. Or a thick mixture of liquid, flour, and eggs to bake into cake. Change one letter.	**bat** (3) — **3** A club made of wood or metal used to hit a ball in baseball. Or a small mammal that flies, normally at night. Take away three letters.
	batter (2)
	butter (1) — **1** A food that is often spread on toast.

Thinking Challenge

The word ladder starts with *butter* and ends with *fly.* In your notebook, explain how the work of butterflies is similar to what bees do. Then, explain how the survival of humans depends on butterflies.

© Shell Education   Promote Reading Gains with Differentiated Instruction—133013   171

Figure 10.1—A third grader answers questions about "What the Bumblebee Doesn't Know."

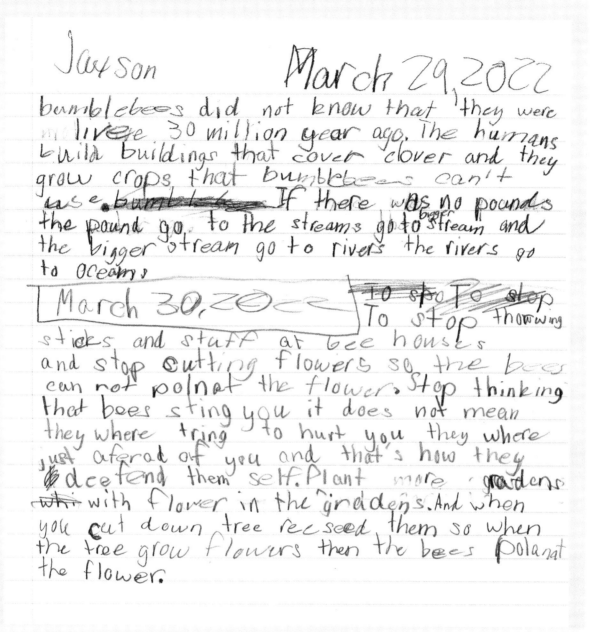

Jaxson   March 29, 2022

bumblebees did not know that they were
live 30 million year ago. The humans
build buildings that cover clover and they
grow crops that bumblebees can't
use. bumbl~~ebees~~ If there was no pounds
the pound go to the streams go to bigger stream and
the bigger stream go to rivers the rivers go
to oceans

March 30, 20cc   To stop To stop
                 To stop throwing
sticks and stuff at bee houses
and stop cutting flowers so the bees
can not polnat the flower. Stop thinking
that bees sting you it does not mean
they where tring to hurt you they where
just aferad of you and that's how they
dcefend them self. Plant more graddens
~~whi~~ with flower in the graddens. And when
you cut down tree recseed them so when
the tree grow flowers then the bees polanat
the flower.

Turning the Differentiated Lessons over to Students

If students' responses to the interactive focus lessons indicate that all students or a group would benefit from review and/or re-teaching, take time to boost their understanding. Pausing to do this will enable students to complete their work independently or with partners while using the resources you display from your teacher's notebook and the reminders you give to support students (see below).

The Differentiated Lessons

The content of the differentiated lessons always follows what you've modeled and what students practiced during the interactive focus lessons. Each differentiated lesson has three parts: 1) the poem; 2) directions for students to engage in drawing conclusions and word work; and 3) a word ladder that connects to the poem.

	Drawing Conclusions Lessons		
	Below Grade Level	**At Grade Level**	**Above Grade Level**
Grade 3	What the Bumblebee Doesn't Know (p. 172)	The Grass and the Butterfly (p. 175)	Don't Forget (p. 178)
Grade 4	Down the Fence Row (p. 182)	Rolling (p. 187)	The Stream (p. 190)
Grade 5	Tiger (p. 194)	Milkweed and Monarchs (p. 197)	Your Eyes (p. 201)

Reminders to Support Students

To prepare students for working through the differentiated lessons independently or with partners:

- Remind students of the writing drawing conclusions and the word work in your teacher's notebook, and display the notebook so students can refer to it as needed. Tell them they can use your notebook as a resource while they work.
- Write on the board: *multiple forms of words* and *word families*. Review what these terms mean.
- Write this term on the board: *drawing conclusions*. Review what it means, giving examples from your focus lesson.
- Remind students to use quiet voices when talking with their partners.

Background Information Resources

Several of the lessons that follow ask students to use resources provided by their teacher to build their background knowledge. Here is a list of videos that can be found on YouTube and used for these lessons.

Grade 3 Video Resources

"What the Bumblebee Doesn't Know" (page 172)

- "Like Fruit? Thank a Bee!" (3:46) SciShow Kids
- "Kids Learn Why Bees Are Awesome" (2:02) National Geographic
- "Why Are Bees Important? (For Kids!)" (5:03) 7NEWS Australia

"The Grass and the Butterfly" (page 175)

- "Like Fruit? Thank a Bee!" (3:46) SciShow Kids
- "Save Butterflies" (2:04) Kissesforhope69
- "Save the Bees and Butterflies" (4:29) TBR Media

"Don't Forget" (page 178)

- "How Chameleons Could Help Save Madagascar's Rainforest" (1:35) Newsy Science

Grade 4 Video Resources

"Down the Fence Row" (page 182)

- "Growing Milkweed for Monarch Butterflies" (2:16) Gardenerd

Grade 5 Video Resources

"Tiger" (page 194)

- "Here's Why Tigers Are Going Extinct" (1:30) The Dodo
- "What's Driving Tigers Toward Extinction?" (5:46) National Geographic
- "International Tiger Day 2021" (2:24) TTT Live Online

"Milkweed and Monarchs" (page 197)

- "Like Fruit? Thank a Bee!" (3:46) SciShow Kids
- "The Endangered Monarch Butterfly" (2:44) Peter Imber
- "Butterfly Garden: Grow Milkweed for Monarch Butterflies!" (1:18) Eden Maker by Shirley Bovshow

"Your Eyes" (page 201)

- "Chimpanzees | Special Report - Endangered Animals | Best Science for Kids" (2:12) AUDREY4CARE
- "First Look at Jane" (2:50) National Geographic

Name: _____   Date: _____

Focus on Drawing Conclusions

Directions: Read the poem and follow your teacher's directions.

And What Can We Conclude?

by David L. Harrison

1   In Australia,
2   in the Americas,
3   in Africa.

4   Small things,
5   quiet things,
6   wild things.

7   A butterfly,
8   a bumblebee,
9   a lizard,

10   In danger,
11   may one day
12   be gone.

13   What do
14   they share
15   in common?

16   Only humans
17   have the power
18   to save them.

Promote Reading Gains with Differentiated Instruction—133013

Name: _____   Date: _____

"And What Can We Conclude?" Word Ladder

Directions: Start at the bottom. Read the clues and write the words.

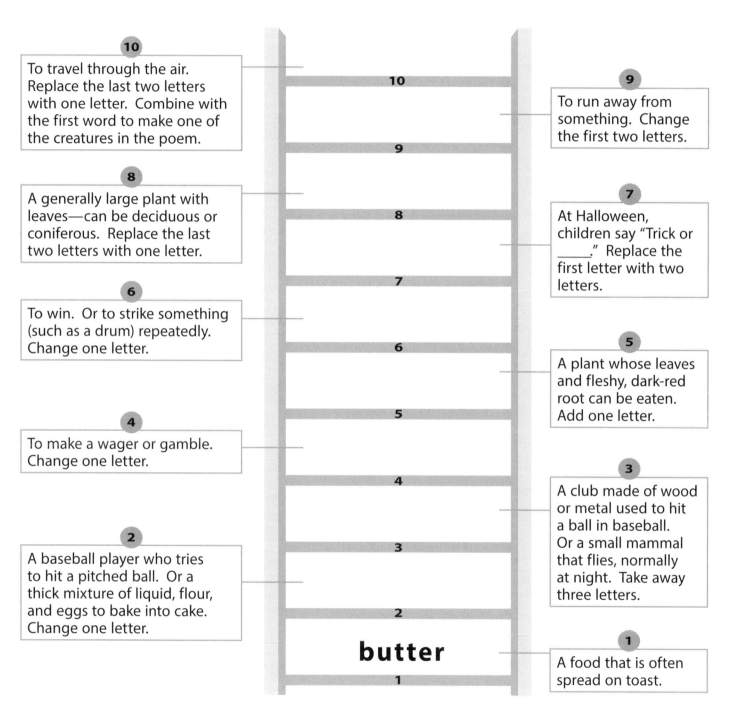

10 To travel through the air. Replace the last two letters with one letter. Combine with the first word to make one of the creatures in the poem.

9 To run away from something. Change the first two letters.

8 A generally large plant with leaves—can be deciduous or coniferous. Replace the last two letters with one letter.

7 At Halloween, children say "Trick or ____." Replace the first letter with two letters.

6 To win. Or to strike something (such as a drum) repeatedly. Change one letter.

5 A plant whose leaves and fleshy, dark-red root can be eaten. Add one letter.

4 To make a wager or gamble. Change one letter.

3 A club made of wood or metal used to hit a ball in baseball. Or a small mammal that flies, normally at night. Take away three letters.

2 A baseball player who tries to hit a pitched ball. Or a thick mixture of liquid, flour, and eggs to bake into cake. Change one letter.

1 A food that is often spread on toast.

butter

Thinking Challenge

The word ladder starts with *butter* and ends with *fly*. In your notebook, explain how the work of butterflies is similar to what bees do. Then, explain how the survival of humans depends on butterflies.

Drawing Conclusions: "What the Bumblebee Doesn't Know"

Directions: Read the poem and complete the activities.

What the Bumblebee Doesn't Know
by David L. Harrison

1	This bumblebee,
2	this small insect,
3	sipping sweet nectar
4	from this flower
5	on this bright sunny day, doesn't know
6	that the first bumblebees lived
7	thirty million years ago.
8	It doesn't know
9	that humans build buildings
10	that cover clover,
11	grow crops
12	that bumblebees can't use.
13	This bumblebee,
14	this small insect,
15	sipping sweet nectar on this sunny day,
16	doesn't know
17	that all of its kind
18	one day may be gone
19	from the face of the earth.

Name: _____ Date: _____

Thinking about "What the Bumblebee Doesn't Know"

Directions: Complete these activities. For each activity, label a page in your notebook with the date, the title of the poem, and which activity you are completing.

Activity 1: Practice Drawing Conclusions

1. Review "Reading and Enjoying Poems." Use the tips to read "What the Bumblebee Doesn't Know."

2. Circle the stanza that tells the reader this bumblebee is endangered. Using information in the poem, draw conclusions about why this bumblebee is endangered. Write the conclusions in your notebook.

3. Learn more about bumblebees using text or video resources. Use what you learn to draw more conclusions about why bumblebees are endangered.

4. Discuss with your partner: What can be done to stop the bumblebee in the poem and others from becoming extinct?

5. Write your ideas about what people can do to help save bumblebees. Share and discuss your ideas with other students reading the same poem. Add any new ideas you learned to your list.

Activity 2: Word Work: Multiple Forms of Words and Word Families

1. Think about *multiple forms of words*. Refresh your memory by reviewing your teacher's notebook.

2. Choose two of these words from the poem: *sipping, build, use, know.* Write the words in your notebook.

3. With your partner, discuss the multiple forms of the words you chose. Write the different forms in your notebook. Use each one in its own sentence that shows you understand the word's meaning. Underline the word in each sentence.

4. Think about *word families*. Refresh your memory by reviewing your teacher's notebook.

5. Create a T-chart. Choose two of these words from the poem: *bright, kind, sweet, day.* On the left side of the T-chart, write one of the words. On the right side, write the other word. Under each word, list words in the same word family.

6. Share your words with your partner. Help each other add more words. Then, share your words with another pair of students.

Name: _____ Date: _____

"What the Bumblebee Doesn't Know" Word Ladder

Directions: Start at the bottom. Read the clues and write the words.

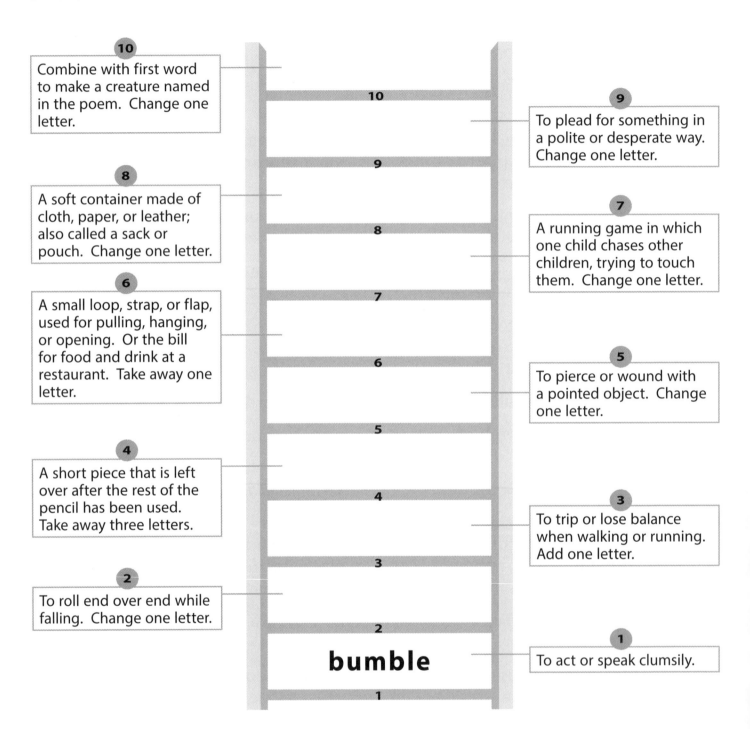

10 Combine with first word to make a creature named in the poem. Change one letter.

9 To plead for something in a polite or desperate way. Change one letter.

8 A soft container made of cloth, paper, or leather; also called a sack or pouch. Change one letter.

7 A running game in which one child chases other children, trying to touch them. Change one letter.

6 A small loop, strap, or flap, used for pulling, hanging, or opening. Or the bill for food and drink at a restaurant. Take away one letter.

5 To pierce or wound with a pointed object. Change one letter.

4 A short piece that is left over after the rest of the pencil has been used. Take away three letters.

3 To trip or lose balance when walking or running. Add one letter.

2 To roll end over end while falling. Change one letter.

1 To act or speak clumsily.

bumble

Thinking Challenge

The word ladder starts with *bumble* and ends with *bee*. In your notebook, explain why the survival of bumblebees will affect the survival of people around the world.

Name: _____   Date: _____

Drawing Conclusions: "The Grass and the Butterfly"

Directions: Read the poem and complete the activities.

The Grass and the Butterfly
by David L. Harrison

1   In Australia, down the coast,
2   down the coast to New South Wales.
3   In New South Wales you'll find some spots,
4   the only spots where Floyd's Grass grows.

5   Floyd's Grass grows close to the sea,
6   close to the sea in swampy land,
7   land where lives the Black Grass-dart Butterfly
8   whose caterpillar lives on Floyd's Grass.

9   Floyd's Grass is in trouble now,
10 in trouble now from too many fires
11 burning the swamps, too many weeds
12 crowding it out, too many cows

13 grazing it down, too many floods
14 from global warming, global warming
15 raising the salty sea, killing Floyd's Grass,
16 killing caterpillars, killing butterflies.

17 In Australia, down the coast,
18 down the coast to New South Wales.
19 In New South Wales you'll find some spots,
20 the only spots, where Floyd's Grass grows,

21 where, when it's gone,
22 will be gone, will be gone,
23 forever.

Name: _____ Date: _____

Thinking About "The Grass and the Butterfly"

Directions: Complete these activities. For each activity, label a page in your notebook with the date, the title of the poem, and which activity you are completing.

Activity 1: Practice Drawing Conclusions

1. Review "Reading and Enjoying Poems." Use the tips to read "The Grass and the Butterfly."

2. Circle the stanzas that explain why Floyd's Grass is in trouble. Reread them.

3. Draw conclusions from the information in the stanzas. Write the conclusions in your notebook. Your conclusions should explain why the Black Grass-dart Butterfly has become endangered.

4. Learn more about butterflies from text or video resources. Use what you learn to draw more conclusions about why butterflies are endangered. Write your conclusions.

5. Discuss with your partner: What can scientists do to save the Black Grass-dart Butterfly? Write your ideas.

6. Reread the last stanza. Why do you think it is so much shorter than the other stanzas? What do you think and feel when you read the word "forever"? Write your answers. Discuss your ideas with other pairs of students reading the same poem.

Activity 2: Word Work: Multiple Forms of Words and Word Families

1. Think about *multiple forms of words*. Refresh your memory by reviewing your teacher's notebook.

2. Choose two of these words from the poem: *grows, burning, grazing, find*. Write the words in your notebook.

3. With your partner, discuss the multiple forms of the words you chose. Write the different forms. Use each word in its own sentence that shows you understand the meaning. Underline the word in each sentence.

4. Think about *word families*. Review *word families* in your teacher's notebook.

5. Create a T-chart. Choose two of these words from the poem: *spots, land, weeds, now*. On the left side of the T-chart, write one of the words. On the right side, write the other word. Under each word, list words in the same word family.

6. Share your words with your partner. Help each other add more words. Then, share your words with another pair of students.

Name: _____   Date: _____

"The Grass and the Butterfly" Word Ladder

Directions: Start at the bottom. Read the clues and write the words.

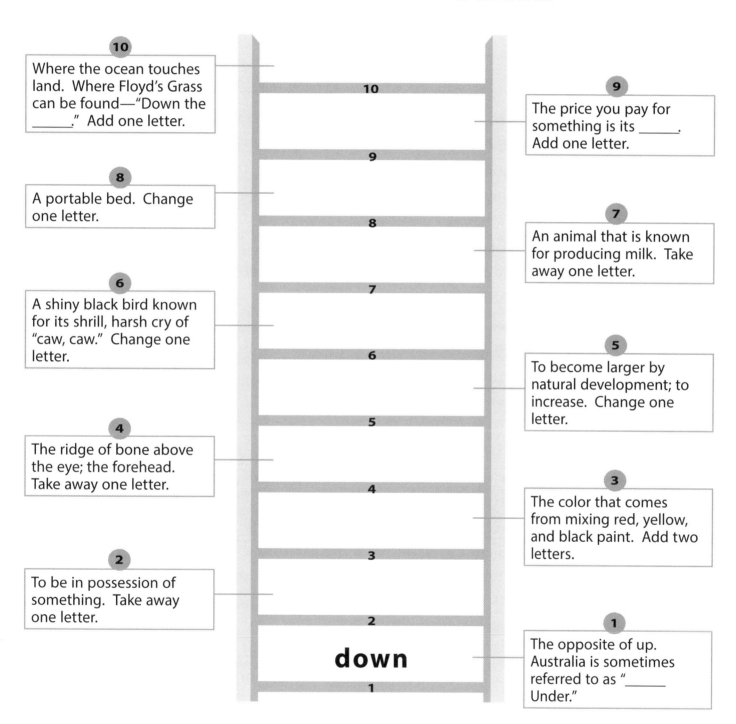

10 Where the ocean touches land. Where Floyd's Grass can be found—"Down the _____." Add one letter.

9 The price you pay for something is its _____. Add one letter.

8 A portable bed. Change one letter.

7 An animal that is known for producing milk. Take away one letter.

6 A shiny black bird known for its shrill, harsh cry of "caw, caw." Change one letter.

5 To become larger by natural development; to increase. Change one letter.

4 The ridge of bone above the eye; the forehead. Take away one letter.

3 The color that comes from mixing red, yellow, and black paint. Add two letters.

2 To be in possession of something. Take away one letter.

1 The opposite of up. Australia is sometimes referred to as "_____ Under."

down

Thinking Challenge

The word ladder starts with *down* and ends with *coast*. In your notebook, explain what the words *down* and *coast* have to do with the survival of the Black Grass-dart Butterfly.

Name: _____   Date: _____

Drawing Conclusions: "Don't Forget"

Directions: Read the poem and complete the activities.

Don't Forget

by David L. Harrison

1 The Giant East Usambara Blade-horned Chameleon
2 lives in the forest.
3 The forest is in the mountains.
4 The mountains are in Tanzania.
5 Tanzania is in Africa.

6 The Giant East Usambara Blade-horned Chameleon
7 doesn't like to leave the forest, and people
8 are cutting down trees—
9   the trees in the forest
10   on the mountains
11   in Tanzania, Africa—
12 to make more room for farming.

13 That is why
14 the Giant East Usambara Blade-horned Chameleon
15 is in trouble.
16 That is why
17 the Giant East Usambara Blade-horned Chameleon
18 may not be around much longer.

19 People like to catch
20 the Giant East Usambara Blade-horned Chameleon
21 and sell it to other people to make money.

TANZANIA

(continued)

Promote Reading Gains with Differentiated Instruction—133013

Drawing Conclusions: "Don't Forget" *(continued)*

Directions: Read the poem and complete the activities.

22   That is why

23   the Giant East Usambara Blade-horned Chameleon

24   is in trouble.

25   That is why

26   the Giant East Usambara Blade-horned Chameleon

27   may not be around much longer.

28   Do not forget the name of

29   the Giant East Usambara Blade-horned Chameleon.

Thinking about "Don't Forget"

Directions: Complete these activities. For each activity, label a page in your notebook with the date, the title of the poem, and which activity you are completing.

Activity 1: Practice Drawing Conclusions

1. Review "Reading and Enjoying Poems." Use the tips to read "Don't Forget."

2. Circle the stanzas that tell you about threats to this chameleon. Using information in the poem, draw conclusions about why it is endangered. Write the conclusions.

3. Learn more about the endangered chameleon using text or video resources. Use what you learn to draw more conclusions about why the chameleon is endangered.

4. Reread the fourth stanza. Write about why this practice affects the numbers of this chameleon.

5. Discuss with your partner the impact of people on this endangered chameleon. What conclusions can you draw about the survival of this chameleon? Write two conclusions in your notebook.

6. Discuss with your partner: Why is it important to save rain forests around the world? How do you think rain forests can be saved? Write your ideas. Discuss your ideas with other students reading the same poem. Add any new ideas to your notebook.

Activity 2: Word Work: Multiple Forms of Words and Word Families

1. Think about *multiple forms of words*. Refresh your memory by reviewing your teacher's notebook.

2. Choose two of these words from the poem: *cutting, catch, leave, forget*. Write the words in your notebook.

3. With your partner, discuss the multiple forms of the words you chose. Write the different forms. Use each word in its own sentence that shows you understand the meaning. Underline the word in each sentence.

4. Think about *word families*. Review *word families* in your teacher's notebook.

5. Create a T-chart. Choose two of these words from the poem: *like, room, make, name*. On the left side of the T-chart, write one of the words. On the right side, write the other word. Under each word, list words in the same word family.

6. Share your words with your partner. Help each other add more words. Then, share your words with another pair of students.

Name: _____ Date: _____

"Don't Forget" Word Ladder

Directions: Start at the bottom. Read the clues and write the words.

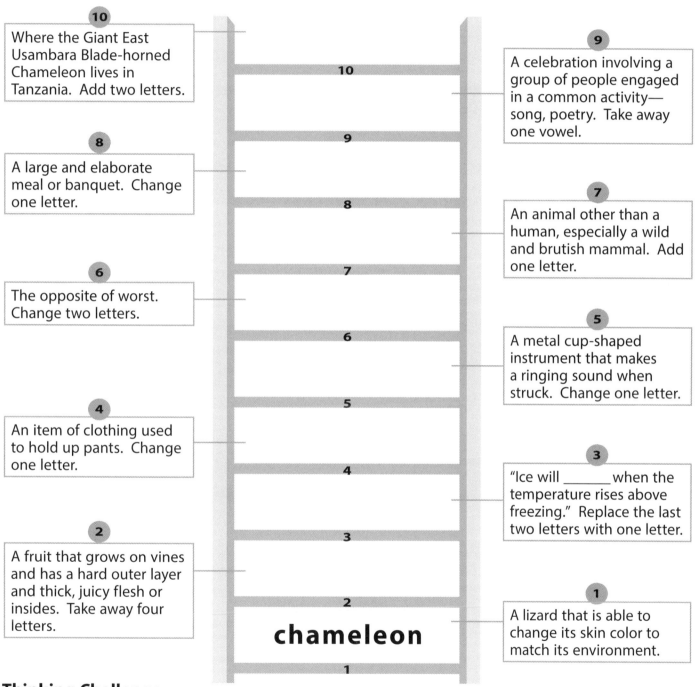

10 Where the Giant East Usambara Blade-horned Chameleon lives in Tanzania. Add two letters.

9 A celebration involving a group of people engaged in a common activity—song, poetry. Take away one vowel.

8 A large and elaborate meal or banquet. Change one letter.

7 An animal other than a human, especially a wild and brutish mammal. Add one letter.

6 The opposite of worst. Change two letters.

5 A metal cup-shaped instrument that makes a ringing sound when struck. Change one letter.

4 An item of clothing used to hold up pants. Change one letter.

3 "Ice will _____ when the temperature rises above freezing." Replace the last two letters with one letter.

2 A fruit that grows on vines and has a hard outer layer and thick, juicy flesh or insides. Take away four letters.

1 A lizard that is able to change its skin color to match its environment.

chameleon

Thinking Challenge

The word ladder starts with *chameleon* and ends with *forest*. Reread the poem. In your notebook, explain why the forest is important to the chameleon's survival. Use information from the poem and from any videos you watched.

Drawing Conclusions: "Down the Fence Row"

Directions: Read the poem and complete the activities.

Down the Fence Row

by David L. Harrison

1	Down
2	the
3	fence
4	row
5	thistles
6	grow,
7	ragweed,
8	dandelions,
9	milkweed,
10	clover,
11	poison oak
12	flowers,
13	vines…
14	Down
15	the
16	fence
17	row
18	creatures
19	thrive,
20	weave nests,
21	hunt,
22	hide,
23	sip nectar,
24	pluck berries;
25	a busy
26	city
27	brimming
28	with life.

(continued)

Promote Reading Gains with Differentiated Instruction—133013   © Shell Education

Name: _____ Date: _____

Drawing Conclusions: "Down the Fence Row" *(continued)*

Directions: Read the poem and complete the activities.

29	Down
30	the
31	fence
32	row
33	tractors
34	chug,
35	blades
36	chew,
37	vines fly,
38	thistles vanish,
39	berries burst;
40	nothing
41	left
42	the
43	way
44	it
45	was.
46	Motors
47	fade,
48	job
49	done.
50	Down
51	the
52	fence
53	row
54	looking
55	good.
56	Homeless
57	creatures
58	wander.

Name: _____   Date: _____

Thinking about "Down the Fence Row"

Directions: Complete this activity. Label a page in your notebook with the date, the name of the poem, and "Activity 1."

Activity 1: Practice Drawing Conclusions

1. Review "Reading and Enjoying Poems." Use the tips to read "Down the Fence Row."

2. Look carefully at "Down the Fence Row" with your partner. Discuss what the poet helps you imagine by using one to two words to a line. Write your conclusion in your notebook.

3. Reread the second stanza with your partner. Find clues about the kinds of plants and creatures living near the fence. List your ideas.

4. Reflect on the last four lines of the second stanza. Discuss with your partner: Why do you think the poet compares life around the fence to a busy city? Write your ideas.

5. Reread stanzas three, four, and five. Draw two conclusions that explain why the plants and creatures are in danger and write them in your notebook.

6. With your partner, discuss how the fence is home to so many plants and creatures. Discuss how scientists and people can save the habitat around the fence. List your ideas.

7. Reread the last three lines of the poem. With your partner, draw conclusions about the survival of these "homeless creatures" that wander. Write your conclusions in your notebook.

8. Share and discuss your conclusions with other students reading the same poem. Add any new ideas to your notebook.

(continued)

Promote Reading Gains with Differentiated Instruction—133013

Name: _____ Date: _____

Thinking about "Down the Fence Row" *(continued)*

Directions: Complete this activity. Label a page in your notebook with the date, the title of the poem, and "Activity 2."

Activity 2: Word Work: Multiple Forms of Words and Word Families

1. Think about *multiple forms of words*. Refresh your memory by reviewing your teacher's notebook.

2. Choose two of these words from the poem: *grow, hunt, hide, wander*. Write the words in your notebook.

3. With your partner, discuss the multiple forms of the words you chose. Write the different forms. Use each word in its own sentence that shows you understand the meaning. Underline the word in each sentence.

4. Think about *word families*. Refresh your memory by reviewing your teacher's notebook.

5. Create a T-chart. Choose two of these words from the poem: *row, pluck, chug, blade*. On the left side of the T-chart, write one of the words. On the right side, write the other word. Under each word, list words in the same word family.

6. Share your words with your partner. Help each other add more words. Then, share your words with another pair of students.

Name: _____   Date: _____

"Down the Fence Row" Word Ladder

Directions: Start at the bottom. Read the clues and write the words.

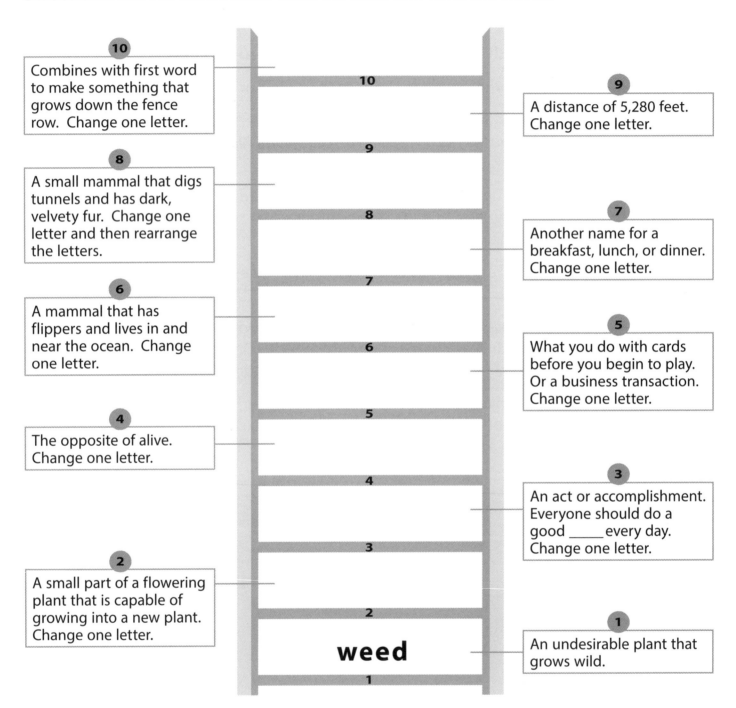

10 Combines with first word to make something that grows down the fence row. Change one letter.

9 A distance of 5,280 feet. Change one letter.

8 A small mammal that digs tunnels and has dark, velvety fur. Change one letter and then rearrange the letters.

7 Another name for a breakfast, lunch, or dinner. Change one letter.

6 A mammal that has flippers and lives in and near the ocean. Change one letter.

5 What you do with cards before you begin to play. Or a business transaction. Change one letter.

4 The opposite of alive. Change one letter.

3 An act or accomplishment. Everyone should do a good _____ every day. Change one letter.

2 A small part of a flowering plant that is capable of growing into a new plant. Change one letter.

1 An undesirable plant that grows wild.

weed

Thinking Challenge

The word ladder starts with *weed* and ends with *milk*. Use text or video resources to learn why milkweed is an important plant. Write what you learn in your notebook.

Name: _____   Date: _____

Drawing Conclusions: "Rolling"

Directions: Read the poem and complete the activities.

Rolling
by David L. Harrison

1   Rolling down the rolly hill,
2   The greeny, giggly, cushiony hill,
3   The tumbly, bumbly, stumbly hill,
4   With tickly grass against my face,
5   Laughing like I'm in a race,
6   Laughing like I'm in first place,
7   Laughing in the morning sun,
8   Laughing because I'm having fun,
9   Laughing down until I'm done,
10   And when I reach the end of it,
11   I know I never want to quit.
12   I run back up, lickety-split,
13   To roll back down again.

14   In wintertime it's where I go,
15   When the hill is bundled up with snow,
16   And I am, too, from head to toe,
17   To tumble down the frosty hill,
18   The snowy, blowy, showy hill,
19   The crusty, crunchy, crispy hill,
20   Filling the air with happy cries,
21   Red-nosed under frosty skies,
22   A rolling hill that's just my size,
23   And at the bottom, with a flop,
24   I know I never want to stop.
25   I climb back up and from the top,
26   Roll back down again.

Thinking about "Rolling"

Directions: Complete these activities. For each activity, label a page in your notebook with the date, the title of the poem, and which activity you are completing.

Activity 1: Practice Drawing Conclusions

1. Review "Reading and Enjoying Poems." Use the tips to read "Rolling."

2. Reread the first stanza. Discuss with your partner the conclusions you draw, and list them in your notebook.

3. Reread the second stanza. Discuss with your partner the conclusions you draw, and list them.

4. Reread the first four lines of the first stanza. Find words that show the fun of rolling down the hill. Share your words with your partner. Write the words.

5. Discuss this question with your partner: How does this poem make you feel about rolling down hills? Discuss the words that raise these feelings. Write the words you discussed.

Activity 2: Word Work: Multiple Forms of Words and Word Families

1. Think about *multiple forms of words*. Refresh your memory by reviewing your teacher's notebook.

2. Choose two of these words from the poem: *rolling, race, climb, run*. Write the words in your notebook.

3. With your partner, discuss the multiple forms of the words you chose. Write the different forms. Use each word in its own sentence that shows you understand the meaning. Underline the word in each sentence.

4. Think about *word families*. Refresh your memory by reviewing your teacher's notebook.

5. Create a T-chart. Choose two of these words from the poem: *hill, face, stop, fun*. On the left side of the T-chart, write one of the words. On the right side, write the other word. Under each word, list words in the same word family.

6. Share your words with your partner. Help each other add more words. Then, share your words with another pair of students.

Name: _____ Date: _____

"Rolling" Word Ladder

Directions: Start at the bottom. Read the clues and write the words.

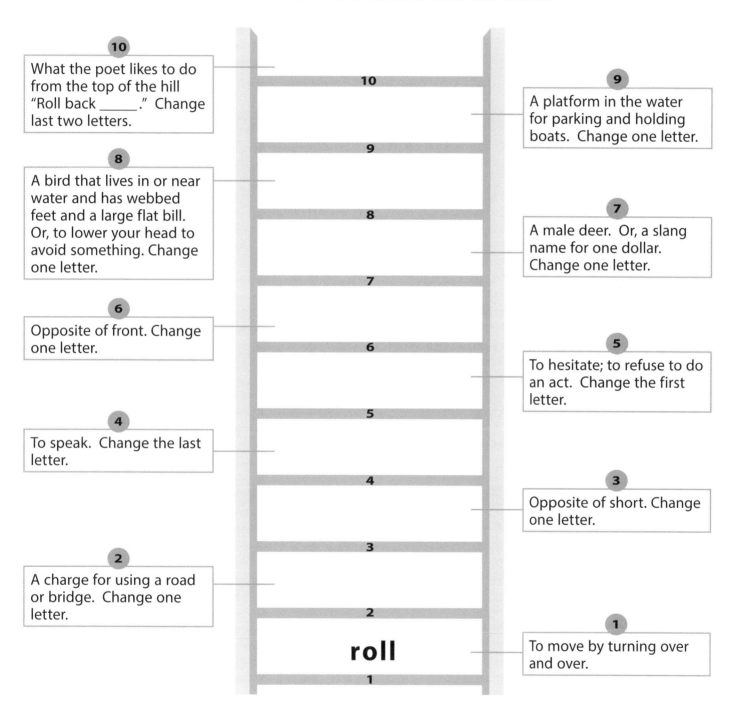

10 What the poet likes to do from the top of the hill "Roll back _____." Change last two letters.

9 A platform in the water for parking and holding boats. Change one letter.

8 A bird that lives in or near water and has webbed feet and a large flat bill. Or, to lower your head to avoid something. Change one letter.

7 A male deer. Or, a slang name for one dollar. Change one letter.

6 Opposite of front. Change one letter.

5 To hesitate; to refuse to do an act. Change the first letter.

4 To speak. Change the last letter.

3 Opposite of short. Change one letter.

2 A charge for using a road or bridge. Change one letter.

1 To move by turning over and over.

roll

Thinking Challenge

The word ladder starts with *roll* and ends with *down*. Reread the poem and reflect on how *roll* and *down* connect to the poem's meaning. In your notebook, explain how each word connects to the poem's meaning.

Name: _____ Date: _____

Drawing Conclusions: "The Stream"

Directions: Read the poem and complete the activities.

The Stream
by David L. Harrison

1	On a mountain
2	like a purple line
3	far away,
4	rain trickles down
5	a steep meadow,
6	a tiny stream
7	hardly deep enough
8	to float a leaf.
9	The water nibbles
10	the bottom deeper,
11	the sides wider,
12	joins gurgles and stirrings
13	from other meadows.
14	The stream
15	grows stronger,
16	leaps over rocks,
17	adds fish and frogs.
18	Clear, cold water
19	running clean and pure—
20	like a gift of the mountain.

(continued)

Promote Reading Gains with Differentiated Instruction—133013

Drawing Conclusions: "The Stream" (continued)

Directions: Read the poem and complete the activities.

21	At the bottom
22	of the slope,
23	the stream offers itself
24	to a passing river
25	running off
26	to join the sea.
27	If the river passes
28	where careless humans live,
29	it may pick up some sunken tires
30	and other debris,
31	as it flows and empties
32	into the sea.

Name: _____   Date: _____

Thinking about "The Stream"

Directions: Complete these activities. For each activity, label a page in your notebook with the date, the title of the poem, and which activity you are completing.

Activity 1: Practice Drawing Conclusions

1. Review "Reading and Enjoying Poems." Use the tips to read "The Stream."

2. Reread the first four stanzas. Think about the images the poet creates.

3. Draw conclusions about the stream as it grows and makes its way down the mountain. Write your conclusions in your notebook. Explain why the poet says, "a gift of the mountain." Give reasons from the first four stanzas.

4. Reread stanzas one, two, and three. Discuss this question with your partner: How does the stream change? Write about the changes in the stream.

5. Discuss ways people and scientists can reverse the pollution of rivers. Explain why this is important. Write your ideas.

6. Share and discuss your ideas with other students reading the same poem. Add any new ideas to your notebook.

Activity 2: Word Work: Multiple Forms of Words and Word Families

1. Think about *multiple forms of words*. Refresh your memory by reviewing your teacher's notebook.

2. Choose two of these words from the poem: *nibbles, empties, gurgles, join*. Write the words in your notebook.

3. With your partner, discuss the multiple forms of the words you chose. Write the different forms. Use each word in its own sentence that shows you understand the meaning. Underline the word in each sentence.

4. Think about *word families*. Refresh your memory by reviewing your teacher's notebook.

5. Create a T-chart. Choose two of these words from the poem: *deep, line, rocks, cold*. On the left side of the T-chart, write one of the words. On the right side, write the other word. Under each word, list words in the same word family.

6. Share your words with your partner. Help each other add more words. Then, share your words with another pair of students.

Name: _____ Date: _____

"The Stream" Word Ladder

Directions: Start at the bottom. Read the clues and write the words.

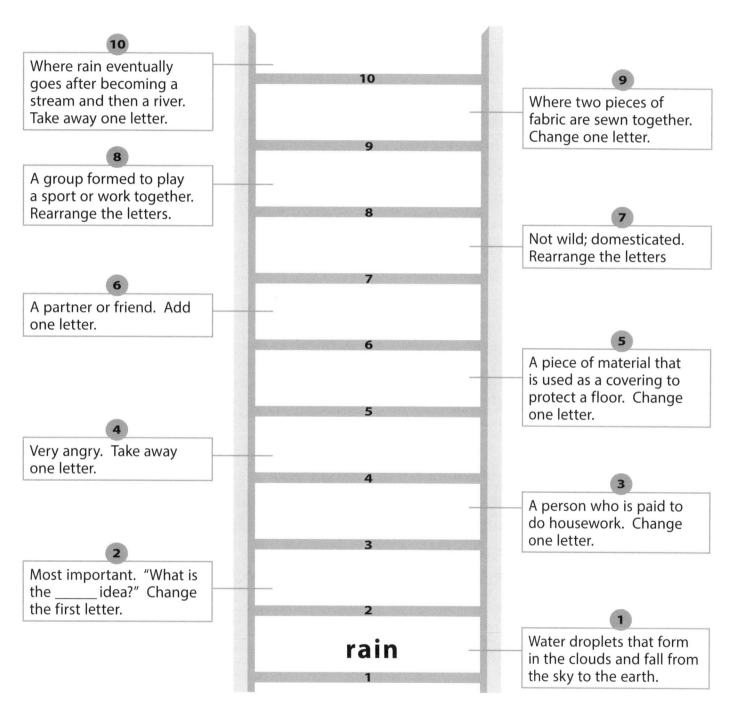

10 Where rain eventually goes after becoming a stream and then a river. Take away one letter.

9 Where two pieces of fabric are sewn together. Change one letter.

8 A group formed to play a sport or work together. Rearrange the letters.

7 Not wild; domesticated. Rearrange the letters

6 A partner or friend. Add one letter.

5 A piece of material that is used as a covering to protect a floor. Change one letter.

4 Very angry. Take away one letter.

3 A person who is paid to do housework. Change one letter.

2 Most important. "What is the _____ idea?" Change the first letter.

1 Water droplets that form in the clouds and fall from the sky to the earth.

rain

Thinking Challenge

The word ladder starts with *rain* and ends with *sea*. Reread the last stanza. Discuss how the poet makes a connection between the rain and the sea. Share your ideas with your partner. Write your ideas in your notebook.

Drawing Conclusions: "Tiger"

Directions: Read the poem and complete the activities.

Tiger
by David L. Harrison

1 One hundred years ago,
2 one hundred thousand tigers roamed,
3 lived their tiger ways in tall-grass,
4 raised their tiger cubs in leafy forests,
5 hunted pigs in piney woods,
6 deer in forests where mangroves grow,
7 one hundred years ago.

8 But tigers have other uses,
9 like adding a wild look to floors and walls.
10 And forests need broad roads
11 so when trees are cut down,
12 lumber trucks can haul them away.

13 Last of one hundred thousand
14 will soon be gone, gone from the forest
15 with their tiger ways, gone from raising
16 their tiger cubs in tall grasses,
17 gone from hunting pigs in piney woods.

18 The only use they'll have left
19 will be staring out at us
20 from human-made zoos.

Name: _____   Date: _____

Thinking about "Tiger"

Directions: Complete these activities. For each activity, label a page in your notebook with the date, the title of the poem, and which activity you are completing.

Activity 1: Practice Drawing Conclusions

1. Review "Reading and Enjoying Poems." Use the tips to read "Tiger."

2. Circle the stanza with information that explains why tigers are endangered.

3. Learn more about tigers using text or video resources.

4. Draw conclusions about why tigers have become endangered. Write your conclusions in your notebook.

5. With your partner, discuss ways you think scientists and other people can save the tigers. List your ideas.

6. Now think of what you and your classmates could do to help save tigers. Discuss these ideas with your partner and write them in your notebook.

7. Share and discuss your ideas with other students reading the same poem. Add any new ideas to your notebook.

Activity 2: Word Work: Multiple Forms of Words and Word Families

1. Think about *multiple forms of words*. Refresh your memory by reviewing your teacher's notebook.

2. Choose two of these words from the poem: *roamed, raised, hunted, staring*. Write the words in your notebook.

3. With your partner, discuss the multiple forms of the words you chose. Write the different forms. Use each word in its own sentence that shows you understand the meaning. Underline the word in each sentence.

4. Think about *word families*. Refresh your memory by reviewing your teacher's notebook.

5. Create a T-chart. Choose two of these words from the poem: *ways, woods, walls, look*. On the left side of the T-chart, write one of the words. On the right side, write the other word. Under each word, list words in the same word family.

6. Share your words with your partner. Help each other add more words. Then, share your words with another pair of students.

Name: _____   Date: _____

"Tiger" Word Ladder

Directions: Start at the bottom. Read the clues and write the words.

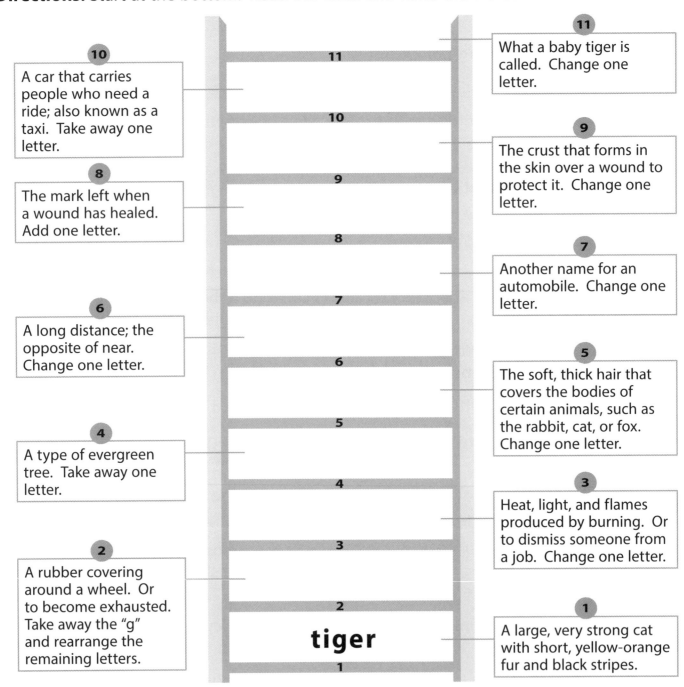

10 A car that carries people who need a ride; also known as a taxi. Take away one letter.

8 The mark left when a wound has healed. Add one letter.

6 A long distance; the opposite of near. Change one letter.

4 A type of evergreen tree. Take away one letter.

2 A rubber covering around a wheel. Or to become exhausted. Take away the "g" and rearrange the remaining letters.

11 What a baby tiger is called. Change one letter.

9 The crust that forms in the skin over a wound to protect it. Change one letter.

7 Another name for an automobile. Change one letter.

5 The soft, thick hair that covers the bodies of certain animals, such as the rabbit, cat, or fox. Change one letter.

3 Heat, light, and flames produced by burning. Or to dismiss someone from a job. Change one letter.

1 A large, very strong cat with short, yellow-orange fur and black stripes.

tiger

Thinking Challenge

The word ladder starts with *tiger* and ends with *cub*. Discuss with your partner why tiger cubs are more important than ever. Write your ideas in your notebook.

Drawing Conclusions: "Milkweed and Monarchs"

Directions: Read the poem and complete the activities.

Milkweed and Monarchs
by David L. Harrison

1   Some farmers say, "The milkweed has to go.
2   That weed's no good for grazing cows.
3   Don't want poison in my cows."
4   "The milkweed," say some farmers, "has to go."

5   Black and yellow Monarch caterpillar,
6   loves that milky milkweed plant,
7   has to have that milkweed plant.
8   No milkweed plant, no Monarch butterfly.

9   "The milkweed," say some farmers, "has to go."

10   Monarch migrates three thousand miles,
11   to trees on mountains far away,
12   on sunny slopes it's never seen.
13   Lays its eggs and perishes heading home.

14   "The milkweed," say some farmers, "has to go."

15   There used to be more Monarch caterpillars,
16   more milkweeds growing in the fields,
17   Monarchs pollinating blossoms,
18   flying off to sun in a distant land.

19   "The milkweed," say some farmers, "has to go."

Thinking about "Milkweed and Monarchs"

Directions: Complete this activity. Label a page in your notebook with the date, the title of the poem, and "Activity 1."

Activity 1: Practice Drawing Conclusions

1. Review "Reading and Enjoying Poems." Use the tips to read "Milkweed and Monarchs."

2. Circle the stanzas that explain why the monarch butterfly is in trouble. Reread them.

3. Using information in the poem, draw conclusions about why monarch butterflies are endangered. Write the conclusions in your notebook.

4. Learn more about threats to butterflies using text or video resources. Use what you learn to draw more conclusions that explain how the disappearance of this butterfly, or any butterfly, can affect the lives of humans. Write these conclusions in your notebook.

5. Discuss with your partner: What can scientists do to save the monarch butterfly? Write your ideas in your notebook.

6. Reread the poem. Think about the line that's repeated. Discuss with your partner how the repeated line made you feel. Why do you think the author ended the poem with the repeated line? Write your ideas.

7. Discuss these questions with your partner: What can be done to keep growing milkweed? How can farmers keep their cows safe? List your ideas in your notebook.

8. Share and discuss your ideas with other pairs reading the same poem. In your notebook, add any new ideas you learned.

(continued)

Thinking about "Milkweed and Monarchs" (continued)

Directions: Complete this activity. Label a page in your notebook with the date, the title of the poem, and "Activity 2."

Activity 2: Word Work: Multiple Forms of Words and Word Families

1. Think about *multiple forms of words*. Refresh your memory by reviewing your teacher's notebook.

2. Choose two of these words from the poem: *grazing, migrates, perishes, pollinating*. Write the words in your notebook.

3. With your partner, discuss the multiple forms of the words you chose. Write the different forms. Use each word in its own sentence that shows you understand the meaning. Underline the word in each sentence.

4. Think about *word families*. Refresh your memory by reviewing your teacher's notebook.

5. Create a T-chart. Choose two of these words from the poem: *slopes, black, sun, land*. On the left side of the T-chart, write one of the words. On the right side, write the other word. Under each word, list words in the same word family.

6. Share your words with your partner. Help each other add more words. Then, share your words with another pair of students.

Name: _____ Date: _____

"Milkweed and Monarchs" Word Ladder

Directions: Start at the bottom. Read the clues and write the words.

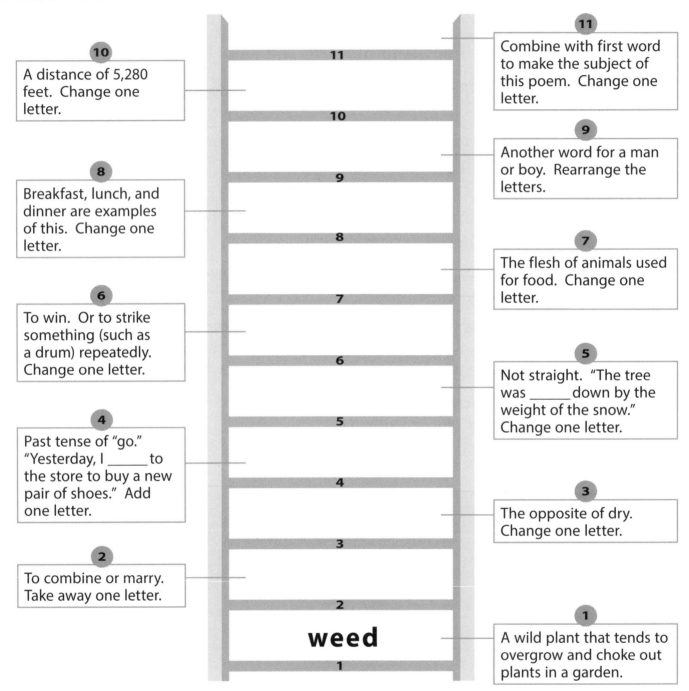

11 Combine with first word to make the subject of this poem. Change one letter.

10 A distance of 5,280 feet. Change one letter.

9 Another word for a man or boy. Rearrange the letters.

8 Breakfast, lunch, and dinner are examples of this. Change one letter.

7 The flesh of animals used for food. Change one letter.

6 To win. Or to strike something (such as a drum) repeatedly. Change one letter.

5 Not straight. "The tree was _____ down by the weight of the snow." Change one letter.

4 Past tense of "go." "Yesterday, I _____ to the store to buy a new pair of shoes." Add one letter.

3 The opposite of dry. Change one letter.

2 To combine or marry. Take away one letter.

weed

1 A wild plant that tends to overgrow and choke out plants in a garden.

Thinking Challenge

The word ladder starts with *weed* and ends with *milk*, referring to the milkweed plant. Discuss with your partner why the milkweed plant is one key to the monarch butterfly's survival. In your notebook, explain why milkweed is key to the butterfly's survival.

Promote Reading Gains with Differentiated Instruction—133013   © Shell Education

Drawing Conclusions: "Your Eyes"

Directions: Read the poem and complete the activities.

Your Eyes
by David L. Harrison

1	Chimpanzee reclining in your tree,
2	gazing solemnly at me
3	through brown eyes, ancient, wise,
4	I wonder what you see.
5	We're not so different, you and I.
6	I imagine, when I try,
7	you in clothes, me in the tree,
8	giving you the eye.
9	I wonder if your soulful gaze
10	is telling me you feel the days
11	are warmer than they used to be,
12	because of human ways.
13	Your forest dwindles year by year,
14	hungry men with guns appear,
15	we give you our diseases too.
16	Can it be your end is near?
17	Somehow things have gone awry.
18	I wonder if chimpanzees cry.
19	Your eyes, so sad, I think you know,
20	your world is passing by.

Name: _____   Date: _____

Thinking about "Your Eyes"

Directions: Complete this activity. Label a page in your notebook with the date, the title of the poem, and "Activity 1."

Activity 1: Practice Drawing Conclusions

1. Review "Reading and Enjoying Poems." Use the tips to read "Your Eyes."

2. How does David L. Harrison build a connection between the narrator ("I") and the chimpanzee? In your notebook, explain the connection. Then, add your opinion about it.

3. Circle the stanza that provides information about why chimpanzees are endangered.

4. Now, draw conclusions. Use the information in the poem to write about why chimpanzees are endangered.

5. Learn more about chimpanzees using text or video resources. Use what you learn to draw more conclusions about endangered chimpanzees. Think of their diet, disease, poaching, and their shrinking habitat.

6. Explain these words in the fourth stanza: "hungry men with guns appear." What are men "hungry" for? Discuss ideas with your partner and write them.

7. Look up the definition of *poaching*. Write it in your notebook. How does poaching relate to stanza four? Discuss with your partner and write your ideas.

8. Read the last stanza. Explain why the narrator wonders if chimpanzees cry.

9. Share and discuss your ideas with other students reading the same poem. Write any new ideas you learned.

(continued)

Thinking about "Your Eyes" *(continued)*

Directions: Complete this activity. Label a page in your notebook with the date, the title of the poem, and "Activity 2."

Activity 2: Word Work: Multiple Forms of Words and Word Families

1. Think about *multiple forms of words*. Refresh your memory by reviewing your teacher's notebook.

2. Choose two of these words from the poem: *gazing, wonder, imagine, reclining*. Write the words in your notebook.

3. With your partner, discuss the multiple forms of the words you chose. Write the different forms. Use each word in its own sentence that shows you understand the meaning. Underline the word in each sentence.

4. Think about *word families*. Refresh your memory by reviewing your teacher's notebook.

5. Create a T-chart. Choose two of these words from the poem: *things, think, know, sad*. On the left side of the T-chart, write one of the words. On the right side, write the other word. Under each word, list words in the same word family.

6. Share your words with your partner. Help each other add more words. Then, share your words with another pair of students.

Name: _____ Date: _____

"Your Eyes" Word Ladder

Directions: Start at the bottom. Read the clues and write the words.

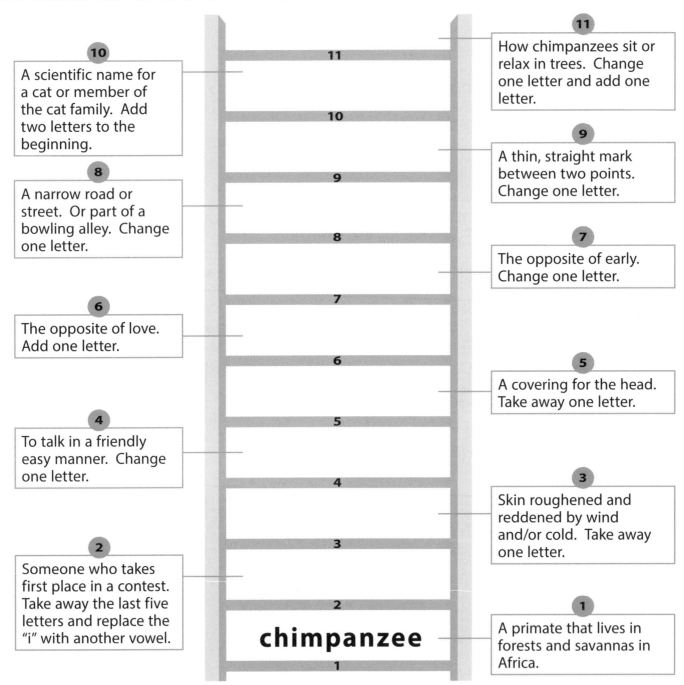

10 A scientific name for a cat or member of the cat family. Add two letters to the beginning.

11 How chimpanzees sit or relax in trees. Change one letter and add one letter.

9 A thin, straight mark between two points. Change one letter.

8 A narrow road or street. Or part of a bowling alley. Change one letter.

7 The opposite of early. Change one letter.

6 The opposite of love. Add one letter.

5 A covering for the head. Take away one letter.

4 To talk in a friendly easy manner. Change one letter.

3 Skin roughened and reddened by wind and/or cold. Take away one letter.

2 Someone who takes first place in a contest. Take away the last five letters and replace the "i" with another vowel.

1 A primate that lives in forests and savannas in Africa.

chimpanzee

Thinking Challenge

The word ladder starts with *chimpanzee* and ends with *recline*. With your partner, discuss the meaning of *recline* and ideas you associate with reclining. In your notebook, explain what humans have in common with chimpanzees. Use the word *recline* and other details from the poem in your explanation.

Chapter 11

Comparing and Contrasting

This chapter provides 11 lessons on comparing and contrasting to develop a deeper understanding of a text. The chapter begins with two interactive focus lessons, during which the teacher demonstrates how to read texts and provides students with a mental model of comparing and contrasting and related word work. The focus lessons ask students to practice what the teacher models, so that they can apply the reading, thinking, and writing processes to their own reading. Following the focus lessons are nine differentiated lessons for students to work through independently or with partners.

When you ask students to compare and contrast, you ask them to reflect on and examine the similarities and differences between two things. Readers can compare and contrast characters, settings, decisions, emotional reactions, events, relationships, themes, authors, personal experiences, concepts, personality traits, strengths, weaknesses, even vacations, storms, habitats, and so forth. Comparing and contrasting is considered a high-level reading strategy, as it develops students' critical and analytical thinking skills by asking them to think about and then identify likenesses and differences. Comparing and contrasting is also a lifelong, practical skill that helps children and adults organize and remember information, as well as use the information to make decisions, such as which backpack, bicycle, or tent is the best one to purchase.

Learn What Students Know about Comparing and Contrasting

Before starting your focus lessons, find out how much experience students have had with comparing and contrasting. Ask students to head a page in their notebooks and write everything they think they know about it. Ask students to explain how they organize their thinking when using this strategy. Tell students that it's okay to write "I don't know anything about comparing and contrasting." If most of the class has had little to no prior experience with the strategy, you may need to repeat parts of the focus lessons or organize a small group to provide additional support and practice. At the end of these lessons, ask students to reread their initial description of comparing and contrasting, then write everything they've learned about the strategy.

Display the following words, which signal to readers that an author is comparing or contrasting. Having these words available supports students while they read and when they write short compare-and-contrast paragraphs.

Compare	Contrast
both	different
alike	but
similar	while
the same	unlike
just like	however
also	on the other hand
too	in contrast
as well as	although

Help students understand that once they identify how things are alike and different, they can use both concepts to move into deeper thinking and draw conclusions, make predictions, or categorize. For example, the fact that the viceroy butterfly looks like the monarch protects the viceroy's population numbers, because birds will avoid eating a viceroy, thinking it's a monarch. In addition, because both types of butterflies taste bad, birds avoid eating both of them, so they also protect one another.

The more practice students have with comparing and contrasting, the easier the process becomes. In addition, the amount of independent reading learners complete at school and at home also supports their abilities to compare and contrast, because as their reading volume increases, they have more opportunities to do this kind of thinking while reading a variety of genres.

Focus Lesson: Comparing and Contrasting

In this focus lesson, you will model how you compare and contrast two types of food—subs and sandwiches. Then you will read aloud the text "Is That Really You?" (page 213) and invite students to compare and contrast monarch and viceroy butterflies.

The Teacher Models: Reading a Text

1. Think aloud and explain to students that comparing and contrasting invites them to consider how two things are alike and how they differ. As an example, in your teacher's notebook, think aloud as you write to show how a sub and a sandwich are alike and different. Create a T-chart. On the left side, write "Sub," and on the right side, write "Sandwich." Invite students to offer similarities and differences between the two. Here's what a group of fourth graders suggested:

A Sub Compared with a Sandwich

Differences	
Sub	**Sandwich**
Long roll	Two slices of bread
Extra fillings: olives, pickles, hot peppers	Extra filling: none
Can serve more than one person	Serves one person

Similarities
Both can have lettuce and tomatoes
Both can have mustard and mayonnaise
Both can be food for any meal
Both can contain meat, fish, or cheese
Conclusion: Both are popular for picnics, packing school lunches, and traveling—easy to pack, carry, and eat.

2. Organize students into partners. Display "Is That Really You?" and read the text aloud. Ask partners to turn-and-talk and discuss what a mimic is, as well as how the title "Is That Really You?" connects to the word *mimic*. Have pairs share ideas.

3. Ask partners to turn-and-talk and discuss some traits animals and people can mimic. Have partners share their ideas to create a class list. As a class, look over the list and draw a conclusion. Here's what a group of third graders suggested:

Ways Animals and People Mimic

Look the same

Sound the same

Have the same markings

Walk alike

Wear the same clothes

Wear the same hairdo

Conclusion: Mimics can confuse other animals and people because they make others think they're the same as something else.

Students Practice

1. Invite partners to discuss why mimics are important, then share their ideas with the class. Here's what a group of fifth graders suggested:

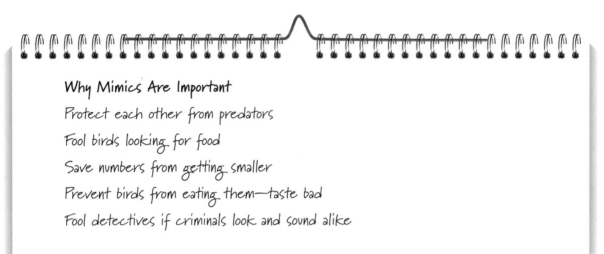

Why Mimics Are Important

Protect each other from predators

Fool birds looking for food

Save numbers from getting smaller

Prevent birds from eating them—taste bad

Fool detectives if criminals look and sound alike

2. Next, reread the third to the sixth paragraphs in "Is That Really You?" and have partners discuss how a monarch and a viceroy are alike and different. Call for volunteers to share their ideas, and point out the part of the text that includes each detail students share. On the board, write how these butterflies are alike and how they differ.

The Teacher Models: Notebook Writing

Demonstrate comparing and contrasting by drawing a Venn diagram or using a template. (See appendix L for a Venn diagram template.) Using the notes on the board that show how the monarch and the viceroy are alike and different, think aloud and complete the Venn diagram. Point out that likenesses go in the part of the circles that overlap. In this area, write how the two types of butterflies are alike. Above the left side of the circles, write the word *monarch*; on the right side of the circles, write the word *viceroy*. Then, write the differences for the monarch and the viceroy in their respective sections (see figure 11.1 for an example).

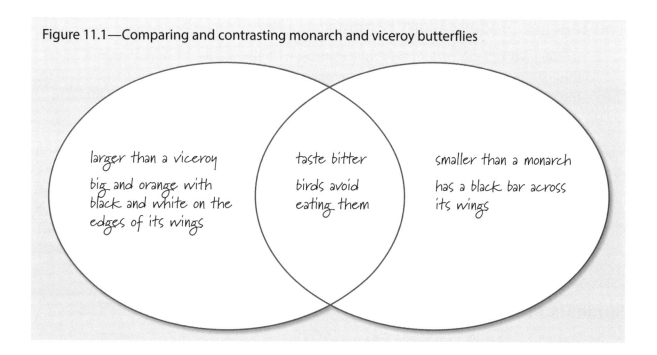

Figure 11.1—Comparing and contrasting monarch and viceroy butterflies

larger than a viceroy
big and orange with black and white on the edges of its wings

taste bitter
birds avoid eating them

smaller than a monarch
has a black bar across its wings

Focus Lesson: Word Families and Using Context Clues to Determine Word Meanings

When students understand and can say one word in a family, such as *grow* (in the *ow* family), they can say other words in that family, such as *blow, crow, mow, know, low, row, slow, stow,* and *tow*. Readers quickly decode by identifying the new onset (e.g., *sl*) and keeping the rime (in this case, *ow*) and therefore can maintain fluency while reading. Having students build sets of words in different word families offers them practice with identifying the onset and rime, as well as analogous thinking—saying other words in a specific family.

Equally important is having students practice using context clues to determine a word's meaning. Students' ability to use context clues to figure out the meanings of unfamiliar words can support their comprehension of a text. When students can't use context clues to determine the meaning of a few words on each page, the text can become confusing, and their comprehension diminishes. It's important for students to know the kinds of context clues that authors leave for them, so that they can quickly understand a word's meaning and avoid disconnecting from the text by stopping to look up words in a dictionary.

In addition to having students practice this skill by using the short texts in the lessons from this book, it's helpful to have them practice during your daily teacher read-alouds and when they read their instructional books. Appendix B includes information for students on using context clues to figure out the meanings of words. Review it with students and have them tape it into their reader's notebooks as a reference to use while practicing this skill.

In this focus lesson, you'll help students understand that building word families can improve their decoding and fluency, and show that using context clues to explain a word's meaning supports their reading comprehension.

The Teacher Models: Word Families

1. Review word families with students, starting with the onset—the initial phonological unit of a word that contains one consonant or a consonant blend. Share these examples: the *gr* in *grow* and the *l* in *low*. Next explain rime—the vowel and consonant(s) that come after the onset. Here's the example for *grow*: *ow*.

2. Display your teacher's notebook and think aloud as you write other words that end in *ow*—*blow, flow, know, low, mow, row, stow, slow, tow*—pointing out that as the opening consonants or onset changes, you're building a new word. Also be sure to point out that the rime *ow* has another sound associated with it, which is found in words such as *cow, chow, clown, how, pow, vow*, and *brown*. In addition, point out that words such as *bow* and *sow* can be pronounced both ways, depending on the context in which the word appears.

Students Practice

1. Ask students to choose two words from this list: *black, wing, shrink, job, plant.*

2. Have them write each word in their notebooks. Next, ask students to build new words for each word they have chosen by changing the opening consonant or consonant blend.

3. Have students share their lists of words with their partners.

The Teacher Models: Using Context Clues to Understand Words' Meanings

1. Reread the first three sentences of "Is That Really You?" Ask volunteers to explain how they understood the meaning of *mimic* or *copycat*.

2. Point out that the first two sentences introduce the terms *mimic* and *copycat*, and the third sentence provides the definition. Explain that a word's definition doesn't always occur in the sentence that includes the word.

Students Practice

1. Display "Is That Really You?" on the board, and reread the first paragraph. Ask students to find the two sentences that use the word *pollen* (toward the end of the paragraph) and reread them silently. Next, ask students to identify the sentence that explains the meaning of *pollen*, and have a volunteer read it out loud. Point out that the explanation comes in a separate sentence close to the first time the author uses it.

2. Have students head a clean page in their reader's notebooks, and ask them to write the word *mimic* and define it in their own words, as well as give examples of what animals can mimic. Then ask students to write the word *pollen*, explain what it means in their own words, and note why pollen is important to butterflies.

Completing the Word Ladder

1. Distribute copies of *"Is That Really You?" Word Ladder* (page 215) to students.

2. Start at the bottom of the ladder. Say the word "copy," and have students pair-share to discuss what they know about the word. In addition to its meaning, point out that the word has two syllables and is a verb.

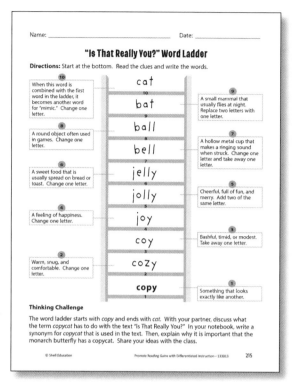

3. Guide students by helping them work their way up the ladder. Model how you use the clues to identify "cozy." Again, have pairs discuss the word.

4. Continue supporting students. However, when you see that they can complete the ladder without your assistance, have them work with partners or independently, completing one word at a time.

5. The Thinking Challenge: The word ladder starts with *copy* and ends with *cat*. Reread the first three sentences of the text. Next, in your teacher's notebook, think aloud and write what the term *copycat* has to do with the text "Is That Really You?"

Turning the Differentiated Lessons over to Students

If students' responses to the interactive focus lessons indicate that all students or a group would benefit from review and/or re-teaching, take time to boost their understanding. Pausing to do this will enable students to complete their work independently or with partners while using the resources you display from your teacher's notebook and the reminders you give to support students (see page 212).

The Differentiated Lessons

The content of the differentiated lessons always follows what you've modeled and what students practiced during the interactive focus lessons. Each differentiated lesson has three parts: 1) the text; 2) directions for students to engage in comparing and contrasting and word work; and 3) a word ladder that connects to the text.

Comparing and Contrasting Lessons			
	Below Grade Level	*At Grade Level*	*Above Grade Level*
Grade 3	Spring, Summer, Fall, Winter (p. 216)	More Bees, Please (p. 220)	There Are Dogs, and There Are Dogs (p. 225)
Grade 4	It All Depends on Who You Are (p. 229)	I'm Thinking about It (p. 234)	Climbing Back (p. 238)
Grade 5	A Nation's Symbol (p. 242)	The Nature of Zoos (p. 247)	What Does an Eel Have for Breakfast? (p. 252)

Reminders to Support Students

To prepare students for working through the differentiated lessons independently or with partners:

- Remind students of the writing on comparing and contrasting and the word work in your teacher's notebook, and display the notebook so students can refer to it as needed. Tell them they can use your notebook as a resource while they work.

- Write these terms on the board: *defining words with context clues* and *word families*. Define these terms and offer examples. Review the types of context clue words and provide examples (see appendix B).

- Write these terms on the board: *comparing* and *contrasting*. Review what they mean, giving examples from the focus lesson.

- Remind students to use quiet voices when talking with their partners.

Focus on Comparing and Contrasting

Directions: Read the text and follow your teacher's directions.

Is That Really You?

by David L. Harrison

1   Do you know what a mimic is? It's a copycat. It's when one person or animal tries to look like another—or sound like another, walk like another, wear hair the same way as another, or buy the same clothes as another. Sometimes mimics are copycats on purpose. But not all mimics choose to be mimics.

2   The monarch butterfly is big and orange, with black and white along the edges of its wings. All summer, it visits gardens to drink nectar, the sweet liquid flowers make to invite insects to land on them. It's like giving away free drinks to draw a crowd. The more bees, wasps, and butterflies that come, the better. While they are busy helping themselves to their treats, their feet and wings scatter the flowers' pollen onto other flowers nearby. Pollen is a fine powder that causes plants to form seeds. In other words, the monarch on the flower is not only pretty; it is also doing a big job.

3   But life is not easy for a butterfly. It seems like there is a bird everywhere you look, and lots of birds think butterflies make a good meal. If you are a big orange, black, and white monarch, birds will see you. But here is a strange thing. Birds leave monarchs alone. Why? What is the monarch's secret weapon? It tastes bad. It may look pretty, but birds know that it tastes bitter.

4   The caterpillar of the monarch is even worse for birds. It feeds only on the milkweed plant, and the milkweed plant is poisonous. A bird that eats a monarch caterpillar (or even a monarch butterfly) will become very sick. The bird might not die, but it will not forget to leave this type of butterfly and its caterpillar alone.

(continued)

Focus on Comparing and Contrasting *(continued)*

Directions: Read the text and follow your teacher's directions.

5   You may have seen another butterfly, called the viceroy, and not known it. That's because it is a mimic of the monarch. If you watch the two butterflies side by side, you can see that they are not the same. The viceroy is a little smaller than the monarch, and it has a black bar across its back wings. But if you don't see two of the insects together, you might not notice the difference. Neither can a bird, and that is important. A bird that has tasted a monarch and gotten sick may leave a viceroy alone, because it thinks it's another monarch. It pays for the viceroy to mimic the monarch.

6   What the bird doesn't know is that the viceroy tastes bad, too! No bird that has eaten a viceroy wants to try another. That protects the monarch, too. Each butterfly protects the other, because they both taste bad.

7   There are other cases in nature where an animal mimics something else. The bumblebee moth looks like a bumblebee. The walking stick looks like a twig. The harmless milk snake looks like a poisonous coral snake. A spider mimics the flower it hunts on. Can you think of other mimics? They're out there.

Name: _____   Date: _____

"Is That Really You?" Word Ladder

Directions: Start at the bottom. Read the clues and write the words.

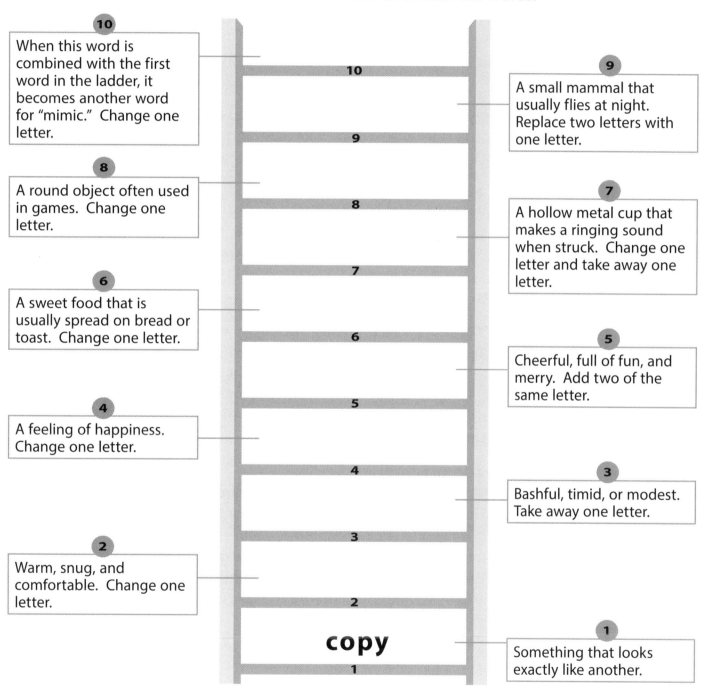

10 When this word is combined with the first word in the ladder, it becomes another word for "mimic." Change one letter.

9 A small mammal that usually flies at night. Replace two letters with one letter.

8 A round object often used in games. Change one letter.

7 A hollow metal cup that makes a ringing sound when struck. Change one letter and take away one letter.

6 A sweet food that is usually spread on bread or toast. Change one letter.

5 Cheerful, full of fun, and merry. Add two of the same letter.

4 A feeling of happiness. Change one letter.

3 Bashful, timid, or modest. Take away one letter.

2 Warm, snug, and comfortable. Change one letter.

1 copy — Something that looks exactly like another.

Thinking Challenge

The word ladder starts with *copy* and ends with *cat*. With your partner, discuss what the term *copycat* has to do with the text "Is That Really You?" In your notebook, write a synonym for *copycat* that is used in the text. Then, explain why it is important that the monarch butterfly has a copycat. Share your ideas with the class.

Name: _____ Date: _____

Comparing and Contrasting: "Spring, Summer, Fall, Winter"

Directions: Read the text and complete the activities.

Spring, Summer, Fall, Winter

by David L. Harrison

1   If you live where you have all four seasons—spring, summer, fall, and winter—there may be some things you like about each season, and some things you don't like as much. Here is a list to get you started. You may think of other things to add.

2   **Things I Like about Spring**
    Days are warmer. Early flowers bloom. Trees sprout buds. Grass turns green. Warm-weather birds return. Robins sing loudly from treetops. Geese and ducks find their mates and look for places to nest. Time to weed the garden and plant seeds. Spring peeper frogs start calling. First strawberries.

3   **Things I Don't Like as Much about Spring**
    You think it won't snow any more, but then it does. Nights turn frosty again and kill the buds on trees. The wind blows every day for weeks. It rains all the time, and you can't go out when you want to. Seems like warm weather is never going to come. Weeds grow quicker than grass.

4   **Things I Like about Summer**
    It finally gets warm. Grass grows at last. Birds have babies in their nests. Baby geese and ducks go out for their first swims. Trees have new, green leaves. Ice cream. Swimming. Barefooted. Shorts. Ballgames. Fishing. Hiking. Insects singing in the dark. Rolling in the grass. Drinking cold water on a hot day. Stars on a clear night. Fireflies twinkling in the evening. Corn on the cob. Blackberries.

(continued)

Promote Reading Gains with Differentiated Instruction—133013

Comparing and Contrasting: "Spring, Summer, Fall, Winter"

(continued)

Directions: Read the text and complete the activities.

5 **Things I Don't Like as Much about Summer**

Mosquitoes. Sweat. Pulling weeds. Sunburn. Having to go to bed before you are ready. Poison ivy. Skunk smell in the air. The sky when a storm is coming. When your friends are gone on vacation. When the library is out of the book you want. When your game is rained out.

6 **Things I Like about Fall**

Trees change colors. You don't sweat as much. Jumping in piles of leaves. Apples. Cider. Halloween. Pumpkin pies. Cookies. Drawing cats and bats and moons at school. Thanksgiving. Late Fall days as hot as Summer.

7 **Things I Don't Like as Much about Fall**

Leaves fall off the trees. Raking leaves. Nights start turning cool. Knowing grass is going to stop growing. Knowing flowers are going to stop blooming. Knowing bees and butterflies will soon be gone. Wearing shoes again. Swimming pools close.

8 **Things I Like about Winter**

First snow. Making snowmen. Seeing your breath in the air. Singing songs. Secrets. School programs. Throwing snowballs. Seeing animal tracks in the snow. Flocks of birds in the sky. Ice on ponds. Fire in fireplaces. Holidays. Special stories. Pecan pie. Hot soups. Snow days. No more bug bites.

9 **Things I Don't Like as Much about Winter**

Gets dark too early. Nothing is growing outside. Summer birds have gone. Dirty snow is ugly. House pets that don't want to go in the snow. Having to stay indoors too much. Tired of the cold. Tired of waiting for Spring. Tired of soup.

Thinking about "Spring, Summer, Fall, Winter"

Directions: Complete these activities. For each activity, label a page in your notebook with the date, the title of the text, and which activity you are completing.

Activity 1: Comparing and Contrasting

1. Work with your partner. Take turns reading the paragraphs of "Spring, Summer, Fall, Winter" out loud. Choose a season. Discuss what you learn about it.

2. Reread "Spring, Summer, Fall, Winter."

3. Choose a different season. Compare and contrast your likes to David L. Harrison's likes. Use a Venn diagram or a T-chart that you draw.

   - To use a Venn diagram: Write your name above the left circle and "David L. Harrison" above the right circle. Write things you both like where the circles overlap. Write the differences under your names.

   - To use a T-chart: On the left side, write your name. On the right side, write "David L. Harrison." List the differences under your names. Then write "What We Both Like," and list those things.

4. Choose your favorite season. Think of all that you like about the season. Next, think of all that you dislike. Discuss your thoughts with your partner.

5. In your notebook write the name of the season. Below it on the left side, write "Like." On the right side, write "Dislike." Then list your likes and dislikes.

Activity 2: Word Work: Word Families and Compound Words

1. Write the term *word families*. Explain everything you know about them.

2. Create a T-chart in your notebook. Choose two of these words from the text: *smell*, *day*, *cold*, *book*. On the left side of the T-chart, write one of the words. On the right side, write the other word. Under each word, list words in the same word family. Share your words with your partner.

3. Discuss compound words with your partner. Define compound words in your notebook.

4. Reread "Spring, Summer, Fall, Winter," and find compound words.

5. Write the compound words in your notebook. Share with your partner.

Name: _____   Date: _____

"Spring, Summer, Fall, Winter" Word Ladder

Directions: Start at the bottom. Read the clues and write the words.

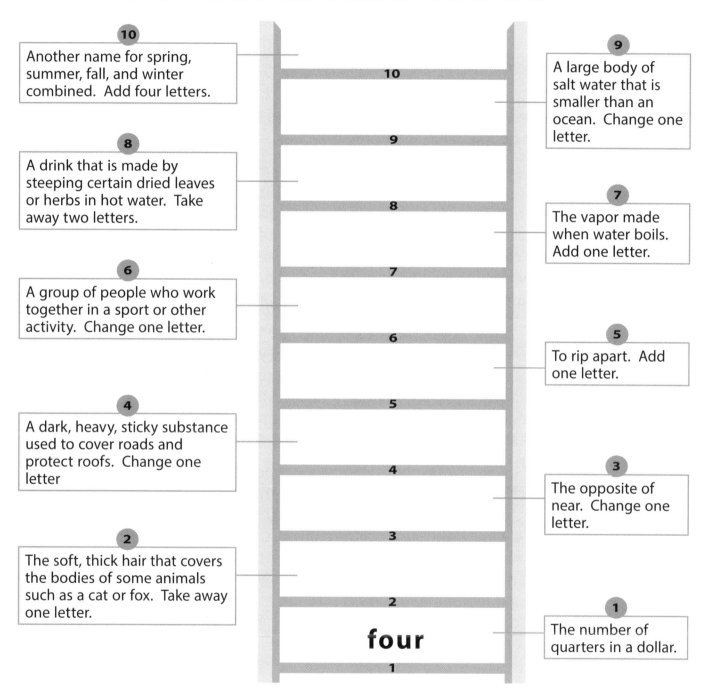

10 Another name for spring, summer, fall, and winter combined. Add four letters.

9 A large body of salt water that is smaller than an ocean. Change one letter.

8 A drink that is made by steeping certain dried leaves or herbs in hot water. Take away two letters.

7 The vapor made when water boils. Add one letter.

6 A group of people who work together in a sport or other activity. Change one letter.

5 To rip apart. Add one letter.

4 A dark, heavy, sticky substance used to cover roads and protect roofs. Change one letter

3 The opposite of near. Change one letter.

2 The soft, thick hair that covers the bodies of some animals such as a cat or fox. Take away one letter.

1 The number of quarters in a dollar.

four

Thinking Challenge

The word ladder starts with *four* and ends with *seasons*. Choose your least favorite season. In your notebook, list reasons you dislike this season. Next, try to find reasons for liking this season. Write those in your notebook. Share and discuss your ideas with your partner.

Name: _____   Date: _____

Comparing and Contrasting: "More Bees, Please"

Directions: Read the text and complete the activities.

More Bees, Please

by David L. Harrison

1   In a nest of honeybees, there are three kinds of bees—the queen bee, the drones, and the workers. Most people have seen only one.

2   When flowers are in bloom, there may be fifty thousand bees in a big hive, or nest, but there will be only one queen bee. She is the only one that lays eggs to make more bees. There is no time off for her. Other bees clean her, feed her, and protect her. She spends her whole life inside the hive, doing her job. In one year, the queen can lay two hundred thousand eggs!

3   A drone is a male bee. Drones are the queen's sons, and she usually makes only a few. They have the same mother, so they are brothers. Drones don't gather food. They don't make anything or help around the hive. They don't clean up after themselves, and they eat three times more than anyone else.

4   The queen bee has one job, but she does it over and over. The drone has one job, too, but he does it only once. When a new queen bee is ready, she flies out and mates with drones from different hives so that she can start making bees. After drones mate, they die. The rest hang out around the nest. Late in the year, when the flowers are gone and food is running low, the rest of the bees drive the drones out of the hive. They don't last long on their own.

(continued)

Promote Reading Gains with Differentiated Instruction—133013   © Shell Education

Comparing and Contrasting: "More Bees, Please" *(continued)*

Directions: Read the text and complete the activities.

5   All the other bees in the hive are female. Because they have the same mother, they are sisters. While the queen is laying eggs and their brothers are mostly goofing off, the sisters do all the work, which is why they are called workers. A busy nest of bees can get messy. The workers clean it. The hive needs a place to keep its honey and its young bees, called larvae, after they hatch. The workers make wax inside their bodies and mold it into honeycomb. Each small part of a honeycomb is a tiny wax cup. Each side of the comb may hold three thousand cups.

6   The workers place new eggs in cups and care for them while they grow up. The workers go after water, pollen, and nectar. Pollen is a fine powder that plants need to make new plants, but bees need it for food. Nectar is a sweet liquid made inside blossoms. Bees make honey with it. Guess who does the work? They store it in the honeycomb.

7   A queen bee may live for years. A drone may last one season. A worker lives a few weeks. For a while, she works inside. After that, she makes thousands of trips to bring water, pollen, and nectar for the queen bee, brothers, and sisters. This is why every busy bee you see is female. She will fly and work until she wears out and dies. Thanks to the queen bee, there are always new workers to take her place.

Name: _____ Date: _____

Thinking about "More Bees, Please"

Directions: Complete this activity. Label a page in your notebook with the date, the title of the text, and "Activity 1."

Activity 1: Comparing and Contrasting

1. Work with your partner. Take turns reading the paragraphs of "More Bees, Please" out loud. Discuss why you think the author calls this piece "More Bees, Please." Find details in the text to support your thinking.

2. Reread "More Bees, Please." Discuss what you learn about the queen bee, drones, and worker bees.

3. Write the term *queen bee*. List everything you have learned about the queen bee.

4. Compare and contrast drones and worker bees. You can use a Venn diagram or a T-chart that you draw.

   ■ To use a Venn diagram: Write "drones" above the left circle and "workers" above the right circle. Write how drones and workers are alike where the circles overlap. Write the differences under each type of bee.

   ■ To use a T-chart: On the left side, write "drones." On the right side, write "workers." List the differences under each type of bee. Then write "How They're Alike," and list ways they are alike.

5. Review your work. Use details to draw a conclusion about drones and workers. Or make a prediction about both types of bees.

6. Discuss your conclusion or prediction with your partner. Write what you discussed in your notebook.

(continued)

Promote Reading Gains with Differentiated Instruction—133013   © Shell Education

Name: _____ Date: _____

Thinking about "More Bees, Please" (continued)

Directions: Complete this activity. Label a page in your notebook with the date, the title of the text, and "Activity 2."

Activity 2: Word Work: Word Families and Using Context Clues

1. Write the term *word families.* Explain everything you know about them.

2. Create a T-chart. Choose two of these words from the text: *hive, nest, late, make.* On the left side of the T-chart, write one of the words. On the right side, write the other word. Under each word, list words in the same word family. Share your words with your partner.

3. Reread the first six paragraphs of the text. Focus on how the author defines the queen bee, drones, and workers. Discuss what you have learned with your partner.

4. In your notebook, explain each type of bee's main job in building and maintaining the hive.

5. With your partner, discuss: What are the differences in length of life among the queen bee, drone, and workers? Write about these differences and explain why you think these differences exist.

6. Skim the fifth and sixth paragraphs. Review how workers make honeycomb. Draw a honeycomb or use words to describe it. Explain the two uses of a honeycomb's cups.

7. Write the words *larvae, pollen,* and *nectar.* Skim the fifth and sixth paragraphs again. Use context clues to define each word. Choose one of the words. Use the word in its own sentence that shows you understand its meaning.

Name: _____   Date: _____

"More Bees, Please" Word Ladder

Directions: Start at the bottom. Read the clues and write the words.

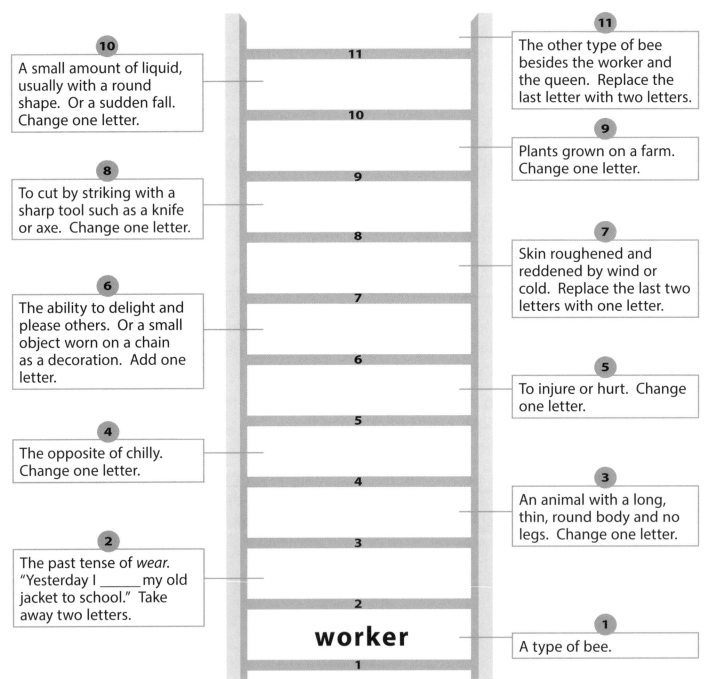

11 The other type of bee besides the worker and the queen. Replace the last letter with two letters.

10 A small amount of liquid, usually with a round shape. Or a sudden fall. Change one letter.

9 Plants grown on a farm. Change one letter.

8 To cut by striking with a sharp tool such as a knife or axe. Change one letter.

7 Skin roughened and reddened by wind or cold. Replace the last two letters with one letter.

6 The ability to delight and please others. Or a small object worn on a chain as a decoration. Add one letter.

5 To injure or hurt. Change one letter.

4 The opposite of chilly. Change one letter.

3 An animal with a long, thin, round body and no legs. Change one letter.

2 The past tense of *wear*. "Yesterday I _____ my old jacket to school." Take away two letters.

worker

1 A type of bee.

Thinking Challenge

The word ladder starts with *worker* and ends with *drone*. With your partner, discuss what each type of bee—worker and drone—contributes to the hive. Then identify the bee that ensures that the hive stays healthy and strong. Explain why people who love honey should thank this type of bee.

Comparing and Contrasting: "There Are Dogs, and There Are Dogs"

Directions: Read the text and complete the activities.

There Are Dogs, and There Are Dogs

by David L. Harrison

1   There are millions of dogs in the world—perhaps as many as nine hundred million! This is what that number looks like: 900,000,000. If you add all the people in the United States, Canada, Great Britain, Germany, Italy, France, Brazil, and Mexico together, that's how many nine hundred million is. There are wild dogs, lost dogs, and dogs in animal shelters, but most dogs live with people. We love our dogs, and our dogs love us.

2   There are over 450 dog breeds in many shapes and sizes. The smallest breed, the Chihuahua (chuh-WAA-wuh), may stand only six inches tall and weigh just three pounds. The biggest breed, the mastiff, may stand 35 inches tall and weigh 230 pounds.

3   Where did so many kinds of dogs come from? The first dogs branched off from an ancient kind of wolf that died long ago. It may have happened as far back as thirty-two thousand (32,000) years ago. Dogs may have already been dogs when they first met humans, or they might have become dogs later.

4   Some people think that somewhere a pack of wolves began to like the food scraps that human hunters threw for them to eat. As time passed, the wild beasts began to trust the hunters. They liked how warm it was around the campfires on cold nights. The hunters liked having the animals around to guard them when they slept. Maybe wolf cubs liked to have their ears scratched and their bellies rubbed and became pets.

5   No matter how it happened, dogs are our pets now. Some of them even work for us. People breed and train dogs to be good at doing things we need. Want a heavy sled pulled across the ice? There are strong dogs for that.

(continued)

Comparing and Contrasting:
"There Are Dogs, and There Are Dogs" *(continued)*

Directions: Read the text and complete the activities.

6   When a duck hunter shoots a duck and needs to get it out of cold water, there are dogs that do that. There are fierce dogs to guard us, dogs with keen noses to track down a missing person, and bossy dogs to herd our sheep. There are dogs trained to guide us if we can't see, and dogs that know how to make us feel better when we need it.

7   But no matter whether a dog is six inches tall or weighs 230 pounds, it is still a dog. It will sniff other dogs' butts to say "Hi." It will use its tail to tell others that it is happy, worried, or ready to fight. It may use its voice to let us know that it is hungry or needs to go out—now! It may perk up its ears to tell us something is up or melt our hearts with its trusting eyes.

8   We take our dogs for walks on leashes, give them treats when they're good, and feed them from sacks or cans. They don't know it, but a long time ago, they likely came from wolves.

Name: _____   Date: _____

Thinking about "There Are Dogs, and There Are Dogs"

Directions: Complete these activities. For each activity, label a page in your notebook with the date, the title of the text, and which activity you are completing.

Activity 1: Comparing and Contrasting

1. Work with your partner. Take turns reading the paragraphs of "There Are Dogs, and There Are Dogs" out loud. Discuss why you think the author calls this piece "There Are Dogs, and There Are Dogs." Find details in the text to support your thinking.

2. Reread "There Are Dogs, and There Are Dogs." Discuss where dogs came from.

3. Reread the fourth paragraph. In your notebook, list what you learned about wolves.

4. Learn more about wolves using text or video resources. Write notes, and discuss what you learned with your partner.

5. Compare and contrast wolves and dogs. You can use a Venn diagram or a T-chart that you draw.

   - To use a Venn diagram: Write "wolves" above the left circle and "dogs" above the right circle. Write how wolves and dogs are alike where the circles overlap. Write ways they are different under each type of animal.

   - To use a T-chart: On the left side, write "wolves." On the right side, write "dogs." List the differences under each type of animal. Then write "How They're Alike," and list ways they are alike.

6. Review your work. Use details to draw a conclusion about wolves and dogs. Or make a prediction about both types of animals. Discuss your conclusion or prediction with your partner. Write about what you discussed in your notebook.

Activity 2: Word Work: Word Families and Using Context Clues

1. Write the term *word families*. Explain everything you know about them.

2. Create a T-chart. Choose two of these words from the text: *pets, breed, tall, take*. On the left side of the T-chart, write one of the words. On the right side, write the other word. Under each word, list words in the same word family. Share your words with your partner.

3. Reread the first paragraph of the text. Explain in your notebook how the context clues help you understand the idea of *nine hundred million*.

4. Use examples from the text to explain this sentence to your partner: "Some of them [dogs] even work for us." Write your ideas in your notebook.

Name: _____ Date: _____

"There Are Dogs, and There Are Dogs" Word Ladder

Directions: Start at the bottom. Read the clues and write the words.

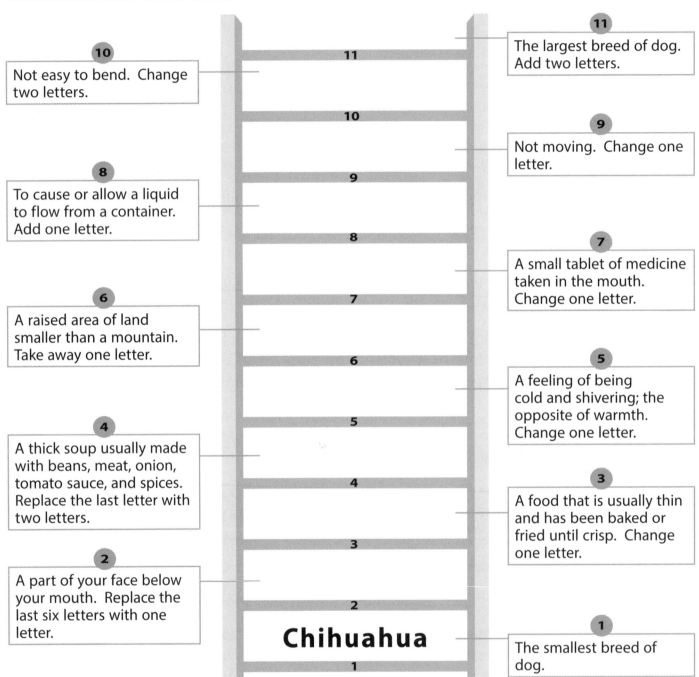

11 The largest breed of dog. Add two letters.

10 Not easy to bend. Change two letters.

9 Not moving. Change one letter.

8 To cause or allow a liquid to flow from a container. Add one letter.

7 A small tablet of medicine taken in the mouth. Change one letter.

6 A raised area of land smaller than a mountain. Take away one letter.

5 A feeling of being cold and shivering; the opposite of warmth. Change one letter.

4 A thick soup usually made with beans, meat, onion, tomato sauce, and spices. Replace the last letter with two letters.

3 A food that is usually thin and has been baked or fried until crisp. Change one letter.

2 A part of your face below your mouth. Replace the last six letters with one letter.

1 The smallest breed of dog.

Chihuahua

Thinking Challenge

The word ladder starts with *Chihuahua* and ends with *mastiff*. With your partner, compare and contrast the Chihuahua and the mastiff. Show how they are alike and different. Think about how both of these dogs connect to a big idea in "There Are Dogs, and There Are Dogs." Write your thoughts in your notebook.

Comparing and Contrasting: "It All Depends on Who You Are"

Directions: Read the text and complete the activities.

It All Depends on Who You Are

by David L. Harrison

1   To a mouse, the great horned owl is bad news, but to a great horned owl, the mouse is food. How you see a thing depends on who you are. If you were a great horned owl, you might have to get past the idea of eating mice for a living, but otherwise, being an owl isn't so bad. For one thing, you could fly, and let's face it, who hasn't wished that they could fly?

2   But if you were a mouse, the good news is that you don't have to go around eating mice! Ha-ha. Mostly, you are a vegetarian, so you eat a lot of seeds and grains. That's not all bad, but there's always that chance of getting caught by a great horned owl with talons that grab and a beak that cuts like a knife.

3   But back to the owl. The giant bird, with wings that spread out nearly five feet wide, didn't set out to eat mice any more than spiders chose to eat flies. It's the way nature made it. If you are a great horned owl, it takes a lot of food to fill you. Snapping up insects is one way to do it, but it may be quicker to eat one mouse than to round up a bellyful of bugs.

4   But back to the mouse. It takes only six weeks for a baby mouse to grow up and start having offspring—babies of her own. Then her babies grow up and start having babies, and then their children start having babies, and their children start having babies. If the great horned owl didn't keep eating mice, we would soon be overrun by huge numbers of mice.

(continued)

Comparing and Contrasting:
"It All Depends on Who You Are" (continued)

Directions: Read the text and complete the activities.

5   But back to the owl. The female great horned owl usually only lays two or three eggs annually, which means every year. Most young owls die before their first birthday, so there are many more mice than owls, and owls eat many other small creatures besides mice. It looks like the mice are winning!

6   But back to the mouse. Besides having to worry about the great horned owl, the mouse must keep an eye out for other animals that like to eat it: hawks, eagles, herons, crows, blue jays, cats, bobcats, wild dogs, foxes, coyotes, wolves, skunks, snakes, and other kinds of owls.

7   But back to the owl. It's a good thing it has such soft feathers, so that it can fly without a sound. And it's a good thing it has such huge eyes that can see well in the dark.

8   It's a good thing for mice that they are quiet and good at hiding and quick as a . . . well . . . a mouse. It's a good thing that mice are so good at making more mice.

9   To a mouse, the great horned owl is bad news. To a great horned owl, the mouse is food. It all depends on who you are.

Name: _____   Date: _____

Thinking about "It All Depends on Who You Are"

Directions: Complete this activity. Label a page in your notebook with the date, the title of the text, and "Activity 1."

Activity 1: Comparing and Contrasting

1. Work with your partner. Take turns reading the paragraphs of "It All Depends on Who You Are" out loud. Discuss how the title connects to what you just read.

2. Reread "It All Depends on Who You Are." Discuss why the owl is bad news for mice. In your notebook, write your reason.

3. With your partner, discuss how the mouse and the owl are alike and the ways the mouse and the owl are different.

4. Compare and contrast owls and mice. You can use a Venn diagram or a T-chart that you draw.

   ■ To use a Venn diagram: Write "owls" above the left circle and "mice" above the right circle. Write how owls and mice are alike where the circles overlap. Write ways they are different under each type of animal.

   ■ To use a T-chart: On the left side, write "owls." On the right side, write "mice." List the differences under each type of animal. Then write "How They're Alike" and list ways they are alike.

5. Review your work. Use details to draw a conclusion about owls and mice. Or make a prediction about both types of animals.

6. Discuss your conclusion or prediction with your partner. Write what you discussed in your notebook.

(continued)

Thinking about "It All Depends on Who You Are" *(continued)*

Directions: Complete this activity. Label a page in your notebook with the date, the title of the text, and "Activity 2."

Activity 2: Word Work: Word Families and Using Context Clues

1. Write the term *word families*. Explain everything you know about them.

2. Create a T-chart. Choose two of these words from the text: *bad, snakes, get, fill*. On the left side of the T-chart, write one of the words. On the right side, write the other word. Under each word, list words in the same word family. Share your words with your partner.

3. Reread the second paragraph. With your partner, discuss what you learn about the word *vegetarian*.

4. Reread the fourth paragraph and use context clues to figure out the meaning of the word *offspring*.

5. Reread the fifth paragraph to understand the meaning of the word *annually*.

6. In your notebook, write the words *vegetarian, offspring*, and *annually*. Use context clues to explain the meaning of each word. Choose one of the words. Use the word in its own sentence that shows you understand its meaning.

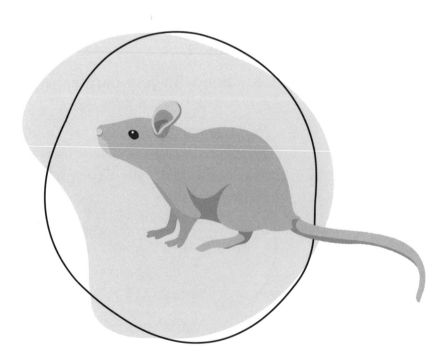

Name: _____ Date: _____

"It All Depends on Who You Are" Word Ladder

Directions: Start at the bottom. Read the clues and write the words.

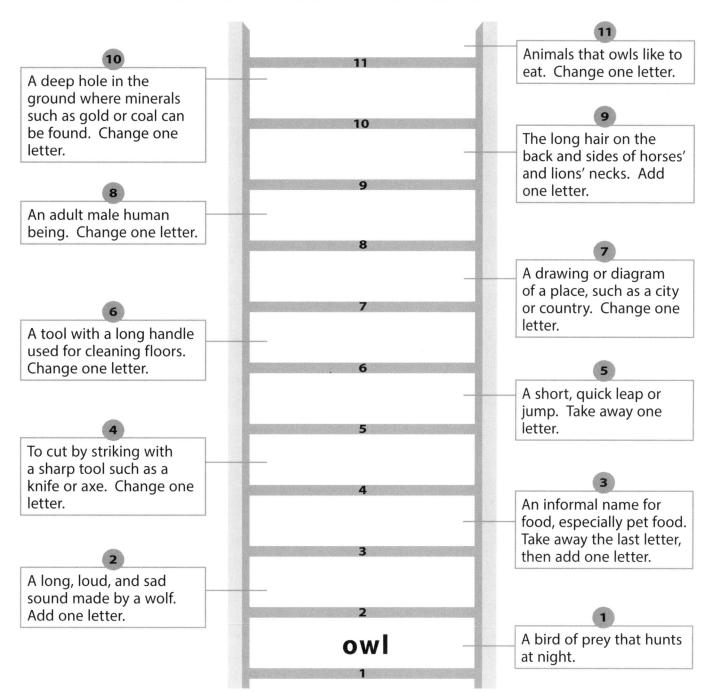

11 Animals that owls like to eat. Change one letter.

10 A deep hole in the ground where minerals such as gold or coal can be found. Change one letter.

9 The long hair on the back and sides of horses' and lions' necks. Add one letter.

8 An adult male human being. Change one letter.

7 A drawing or diagram of a place, such as a city or country. Change one letter.

6 A tool with a long handle used for cleaning floors. Change one letter.

5 A short, quick leap or jump. Take away one letter.

4 To cut by striking with a sharp tool such as a knife or axe. Change one letter.

3 An informal name for food, especially pet food. Take away the last letter, then add one letter.

2 A long, loud, and sad sound made by a wolf. Add one letter.

1 A bird of prey that hunts at night.

owl

Thinking Challenge

The word ladder starts with *owl* and ends with *mice*. With your partner, discuss the link between owls and mice in "It All Depends on Who You Are." In your notebook, explain the link.

Name: _____   Date: _____

Comparing and Contrasting: "I'm Thinking about It"

Directions: Read the text and complete the activities.

I'm Thinking about It
by David L. Harrison

First Voice (Kid 1)

Got your paper done yet?

It was fun. The teacher said to choose a word that describes ourselves and write a paragraph to show an example of why we picked our word.

I chose *learner*. My paragraph is about how I like to read and find out about things that interest me.

So, what word do you think describes you best?

Our paper is due today!
How can you procrastinate so long?

Questions? Like what?
You already know yourself!

Second Voice (Kid 2)

I'm thinking about it.

What word did you pick?

Good word. I like to read and find out about interesting things too.

I'm thinking about it.

Well, there's a lot to know before I can start. I have a lot of questions.

Sure, but how well do I know me? How well can anybody know anybody? I try to think about what I was like as a baby, but I can only remember back to being three. What happened before then? What was I like before I could talk?

(continued)

Comparing and Contrasting: "I'm Thinking about It" (continued)

Directions: Read the text and complete the activities.

First Voice (Kid 1)	**Second Voice (Kid 2)**
What difference does it make? You're supposed to write about what you're like now!	
	I know, but what if something happened before I was three that made me like I am today? What about that? I need to know. Was I afraid of anything? The cat? Shadows? The sound of loud trucks?
I think you're just putting your paper off.	
	That's what my mom says, too, but I just want to get it right.
I know the word that describes you perfectly!	
	What?
Procrastinator.	
	Procrastinator? Why do you say that? Everybody asks questions. You do. You've been asking me questions about when I'm going to write my paper. Right?
Right. So, when are you?	
	I'm thinking about it.

Thinking about "I'm Thinking about It"

Directions: Complete these activities. For each activity, label a page in your notebook with the date, the title of the text, and which activity you are completing.

Activity 1: Comparing and Contrasting

1. Work with your partner. Take turns reading "I'm Thinking about It" out loud. Discuss how the title connects to what you read.

2. Reread the text. Discuss how the two kids are different. Then discuss how both kids are alike.

3. Compare and contrast the two kids using a Venn diagram or a T-chart that you draw.

   - To use a Venn diagram: Write "Kid 1" above the left circle and "Kid 2" above the right circle. Write how the kids are alike where the circles overlap. Write ways they are different under each kid.

   - To use a T-chart: On the left side, write "Kid 1." On the right side, write "Kid 2." List the differences under each kid. Then write "How They're Alike." List ways they are alike.

4. Review your work. Use the details to draw a conclusion about the two kids. Or make a prediction about both kids.

5. Discuss your conclusion or prediction with your partner. Write what you discussed in your notebook.

Activity 2: Word Work: Word Families and Using Context Clues

1. Write the term *word families*. Explain everything you know about them.

2. Create a T-chart. Choose two of these words from the text: *yet, like, fun, cat*. On the left side of the T-chart, write one of the words. On the right side, write the other word. Under each word, list words in the same word family. Share your words with your partner.

3. Reread the text. Think about when Kid 1 says they are a *learner*. Next think about when Kid 1 describes Kid 2 as a *procrastinator*. Discuss the meaning of both words with your partner.

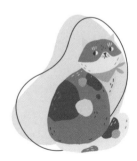

4. In your notebook, write the words *learner* and *procrastinator*. Use context clues to explain the meaning of each word. Choose one of the words. Use the word in its own sentence that shows you understand its meaning.

Name: _____ Date: _____

"I'm Thinking about It" Word Ladder

Directions: Start at the bottom. Read the clues and write the words.

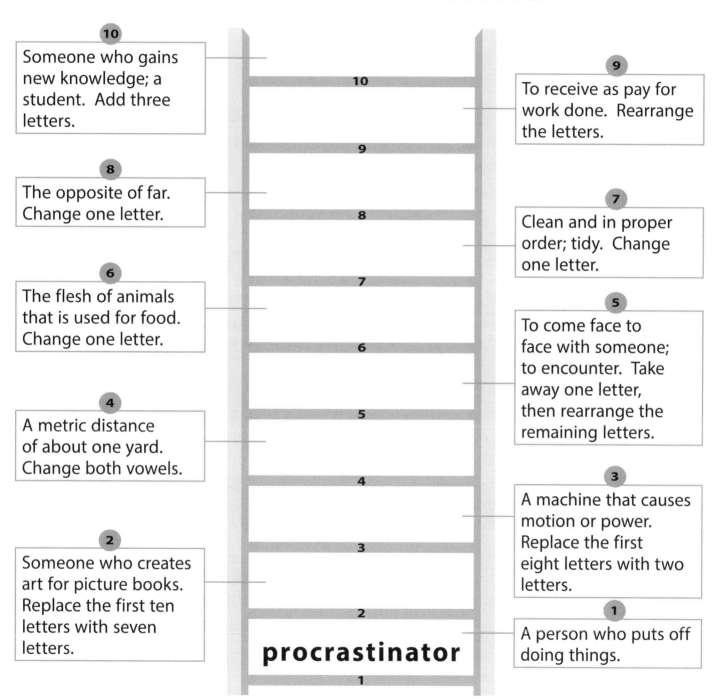

10 Someone who gains new knowledge; a student. Add three letters.

9 To receive as pay for work done. Rearrange the letters.

8 The opposite of far. Change one letter.

7 Clean and in proper order; tidy. Change one letter.

6 The flesh of animals that is used for food. Change one letter.

5 To come face to face with someone; to encounter. Take away one letter, then rearrange the remaining letters.

4 A metric distance of about one yard. Change both vowels.

3 A machine that causes motion or power. Replace the first eight letters with two letters.

2 Someone who creates art for picture books. Replace the first ten letters with seven letters.

1 A person who puts off doing things.

procrastinator

Thinking Challenge

The word ladder starts with *procrastinator* and ends with *learner*. Think about a time when you procrastinated. Discuss what happened with your partner. Then write about the procrastinator in the poem. Support your ideas with text evidence.

Comparing and Contrasting: "Climbing Back"

Directions: Read the text and complete the activities.

Climbing Back

by David L. Harrison

1 One of the rarest animals on Earth is called the Amur (ah-MOOR) leopard. It is found in parts of Russia, China, and North Korea near the Sea of Japan. The Amur leopard comes from an ancient family.

2 The Amur leopard is fast and strong. A male can weigh more than 150 pounds. These big cats are good swimmers and climbers that can come down a tree headfirst. They can leap 10 feet into the air, dash at 37 miles per hour, and jump 20 feet when running down a meal. They are meat eaters (carnivores) that hunt mostly at night. They feed on deer, wild pigs, and even moose. In a pinch, they will take a rabbit, a raccoon, or even a mouse. Amur leopards need a lot of room to roam. Their home-base area can range from 20 to 120 square miles.

3 Life has changed for the Amur leopard, but it doesn't understand what is causing this change. An animal doesn't "get" things the way we humans do. When more and more of the forest where an animal lives gets cut down or burned off, its home base grows smaller. The Amur leopard doesn't understand what the distant growling of saws has to do with it. It doesn't know what the nose-pinching odor of smoke among the trees means.

4 Poachers kill leopards for their beautiful spotted fur and sell the pelts. Hunters illegally take large numbers of the animals the leopards eat. The harder it is to find food, the fewer Amur leopards there will be. The fewer the leopards, the harder it becomes to find mates and reproduce.

5 After hundreds of thousands of years of living on Earth, by the year 2000, only about 30 Amur leopards remained. That made them one of the rarest animals on Earth. Unless something amazing happened, the last of their kind would soon disappear into history.

(continued)

Comparing and Contrasting: "Climbing Back" *(continued)*

Directions: Read the text and complete the activities.

6   Almost at the last minute, something amazing did happen. An organization called the World Wildlife Fund (WWF) worked with governments, zoos, and other organizations to create a plan to save the leopard. A huge area was set aside as protected land for the endangered creature. Strict new rules were created about how and where trees could be cut down.

7   Deer, boars, and other animals that Amur leopards live on were also protected. This helped their numbers increase and support more leopards. Zoos began breeding programs to raise Amur leopards and return some of their young into the wild.

8   Will the plan work? It will take a long time to find out, but good signs already exist. By 2021, the number of Amur leopards in the wild had grown from 30 to around 100. That's a change in the right direction. Around 180 more Amur leopards live in zoos. It may be early to celebrate, but it isn't too soon to hope.

Name: _____ Date: _____

Thinking about "Climbing Back"

Directions: Complete these activities. For each activity, label a page in your notebook with the date, the title of the text, and which activity you are completing.

Activity 1: Comparing and Contrasting

1. Work with your partner. Take turns reading the paragraphs of "Climbing Back" out loud. Discuss how the title connects to the Amur leopard.

2. Reread "Climbing Back." Discuss with your partner: Why is the Amur leopard one of the rarest animals on Earth?

3. Reread paragraphs 3 to 7. Discuss how the situation for Amur leopards has improved because of the efforts of the World Wildlife Fund (WWF).

4. Compare and contrast the situation for Amur leopards. Use a Venn diagram or a T-chart that you draw.

   - To use a Venn diagram: Write "before the WWF" above the left circle and "after the WWF" above the right circle. Under "before" and "after," write the differences. Where the circles overlap, write one way the situation for Amur leopards has stayed the same.

   - To use a T-chart: On the left side, write "before the WWF." On the right side, write "after the WWF." List the differences on each side. Then write "How They're Alike," and list one way the situation for Amur leopards has stayed the same.

5. Review your work. Use details to draw a conclusion about the Amur leopard. Or make a prediction about it. Discuss your conclusion or prediction with your partner. Write what you discussed in your notebook.

Activity 2: Word Work: Word Families and Using Context Clues

1. Write the term *word families*. Explain everything you know about them.

2. Create a T-chart. Choose two of these words from the text: *found*, *dash*, *find*, *mate*. On the left side of the T-chart, write one of the words. On the right side, write the other word. Under each word, list words in the same word family.

3. Reread paragraphs 2 and 4. Use context clues to figure out the meanings of the words *carnivores*, *roam*, and *poachers*.

4. Write each word and explain its meaning. Use each word in its own sentence that shows you understand the word's meaning. Underline the word in its sentence.

Name: _____   Date: _____

"Climbing Back" Word Ladder

Directions: Start at the bottom. Read the clues and write the words.

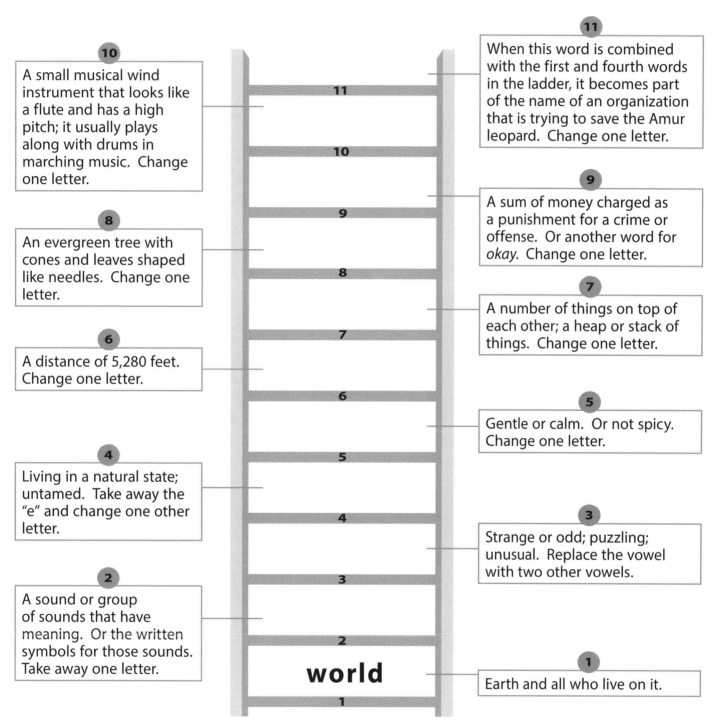

10 A small musical wind instrument that looks like a flute and has a high pitch; it usually plays along with drums in marching music. Change one letter.

11 When this word is combined with the first and fourth words in the ladder, it becomes part of the name of an organization that is trying to save the Amur leopard. Change one letter.

8 An evergreen tree with cones and leaves shaped like needles. Change one letter.

9 A sum of money charged as a punishment for a crime or offense. Or another word for *okay*. Change one letter.

6 A distance of 5,280 feet. Change one letter.

7 A number of things on top of each other; a heap or stack of things. Change one letter.

4 Living in a natural state; untamed. Take away the "e" and change one other letter.

5 Gentle or calm. Or not spicy. Change one letter.

2 A sound or group of sounds that have meaning. Or the written symbols for those sounds. Take away one letter.

3 Strange or odd; puzzling; unusual. Replace the vowel with two other vowels.

world

1 Earth and all who live on it.

Thinking Challenge

The word ladder starts with *world* and ends with *life*. Reflect on how each word connects to "Climbing Back." In your notebook, write the connection each word has to this text.

Name: _____ Date: _____

Comparing and Contrasting: "A Nation's Symbol"

Directions: Read the text and complete the activities.

A Nation's Symbol

by David L. Harrison

1   When the United States became a nation in 1776, the Continental Congress wanted a seal. A seal would stand for who the people were as a country, so a good design was important. Three great leaders—Benjamin Franklin, Thomas Jefferson, and John Adams—were given the task. They tried, but in the end, their idea was turned down.

2   A second committee was formed in 1780, but its idea struck out, too. In 1782, a third committee tried to design a seal. When it also failed, the secretary of the Continental Congress, a man named Charles Thompson, was asked to finish the job. Charles pulled together ideas from the committees and added his own, and the United States of America at last had its seal, six years after the effort began.

3   The main thing you see on the front of the nation's seal is an eagle. This is not just any eagle; it is the bald eagle, the grandest-looking bird in the land. The bald eagle was not the only bird that had been discussed. The dove was another.

4   One story is that Benjamin Franklin thought the turkey should be chosen for the seal. That's not true, but he did like the turkey and called it a "bird of high character." The turkey does have some things going for it. It sleeps in trees, it can be hard to spot, and it flies in short bursts up to 60 miles per hour. It may be handsome to other turkeys, but it is not bald-eagle-handsome.

(continued)

Promote Reading Gains with Differentiated Instruction—133013

Comparing and Contrasting: "A Nation's Symbol" *(continued)*

Directions: Read the text and complete the activities.

5   The mourning dove has a pretty voice—a soft, cooing sound. It's a calm bird, and some people see it as a sign of peace, love, and faith—all good traits. But neither the dove nor the turkey had what the Continental Congress was looking for. The bald eagle stands out from the crowd. It looks you in the eye. It is watchful, strong, and unafraid. It soars on mighty wings. In the end, it was clear that no other bird was right for the nation's seal.

6   There were 13 original colonies that became states, so on the seal, above the eagle's head, are 13 stars. In its beak, the eagle holds a banner with 13 bars—six red ones and seven white ones. White stands for purity. Red is for bravery. Together the bars represent (stand for) the 13 colonies that came together to form the union.

7   One of the eagle's claws holds 13 arrows to show that the United States stands ready to defend itself if it needs to. The other claw holds an olive branch of peace. The eagle is looking that way, toward peace. The seal also needed a motto to briefly state the nation's beliefs. The one chosen for the new country was spelled out in Latin—*e pluribus unum*—which means "out of many, one."

8   Six years of hard work went into the process of designing a seal that the Continental Congress would accept. It was that important.

Thinking about "A Nation's Symbol"

Directions: Complete this activity. Label a page in your notebook with the date, the title of the text, and "Activity 1."

Activity 1: Comparing and Contrasting

1. Work with your partner. Take turns reading the paragraphs of "A Nation's Symbol" out loud. Discuss the meaning of the word *symbol*. Find examples of symbols in the sixth and seventh paragraphs.

2. Write the word *symbol* in your notebook. Explain what it means and give two examples from the text.

3. With your partner, discuss this question: Why did some people want the mourning dove to be the nation's symbol?

4. With your partner, discuss this question: Why did the bald eagle beat the turkey and the mourning dove?

5. Compare and contrast the bald eagle and the turkey. You can use a Venn diagram or a T-chart that you draw.

   ■ To use a Venn diagram: Write "bald eagle" above the left circle and "turkey" above the right circle. Write how bald eagles and turkeys are alike where the circles overlap. Write ways they are different under each type of bird.

   ■ To use a T-chart: On the left side, write "bald eagle." On the right side, write "turkey." List the differences under each type of bird. Then write "How They're Alike," and list ways they are alike.

6. Review your work. Use the details to draw a conclusion about why the bald eagle is on the national seal of the United States.

7. Discuss your conclusion with your partner. Write what you discussed in your notebook.

(continued)

Name: _____   Date: _____

Thinking about "A Nation's Symbol" (continued)

Directions: Complete this activity. Label a page in your notebook with the date, the title of the text, and "Activity 2."

Activity 2: Word Work: Word Families and Using Context Clues

1. Write the term *word families*. Explain everything you know about them.

2. Create a T-chart. Choose two of these words from the text: *love, that, land, not*. On the left side of the T-chart, write one of the words. On the right side, write the other word. Under each word, list words in the same word family. Share your words with your partner.

3. Reread the fifth paragraph. In your notebook, use context clues to explain what the word *soars* means. Then explain how the bald eagle's wings link to the word *soars*.

4. Reread the sixth and seventh paragraphs. In your notebook, write the motto of the United States. Next, write what it means. Then explain the reason the seal needed a motto.

5. Symbols stand for or represent other ideas. In your notebook, write what the 13 arrows in the seal stand for. Then write what the olive branch represents.

Name: _____ Date: _____

"A Nation's Symbol" Word Ladder

Directions: Start at the bottom. Read the clues and write the words.

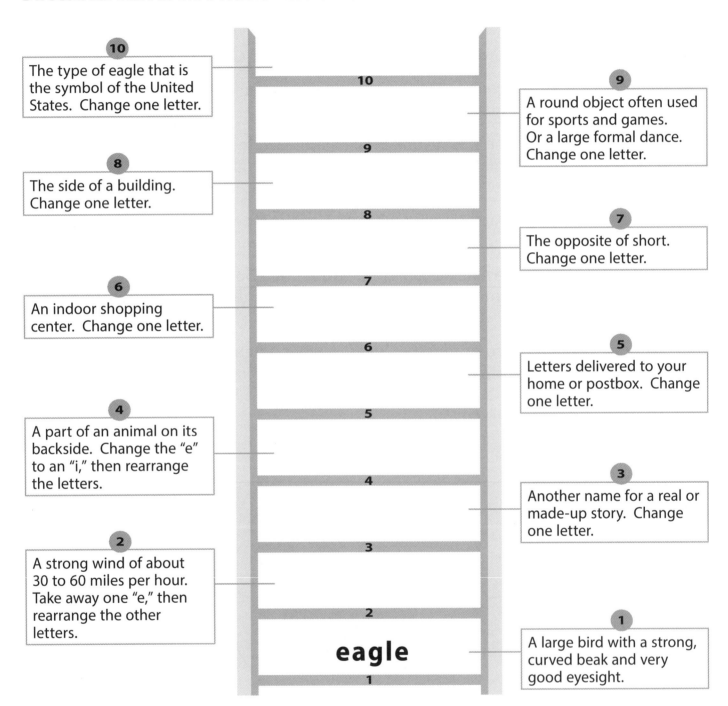

10 The type of eagle that is the symbol of the United States. Change one letter.

9 A round object often used for sports and games. Or a large formal dance. Change one letter.

8 The side of a building. Change one letter.

7 The opposite of short. Change one letter.

6 An indoor shopping center. Change one letter.

5 Letters delivered to your home or postbox. Change one letter.

4 A part of an animal on its backside. Change the "e" to an "i," then rearrange the letters.

3 Another name for a real or made-up story. Change one letter.

2 A strong wind of about 30 to 60 miles per hour. Take away one "e," then rearrange the other letters.

1 A large bird with a strong, curved beak and very good eyesight.

eagle

Thinking Challenge

The word ladder starts with *eagle* and ends with *bald*. Discuss with your partner what the bald eagle symbolizes, and write your ideas in your notebook.

Comparing and Contrasting: "The Nature of Zoos"

Directions: Read the text and complete the activities.

The Nature of Zoos

by David L. Harrison

1   More than ten thousand zoos are scattered around the world. Zoos range from enormous to small. At the small end, a zoo can be a tourist attraction along the highway. You can see a few animals, use the restroom, buy a soft drink, and be on your way. At the enormous end, the Bronx Zoo in New York is as big as two hundred football fields. It is home to more than four thousand animals.

2   Most zoos started as collections of wild animals for people to see. Cages were plain and sometimes so small that large animals hardly had space to move around. Zoos were more about pleasing customers than taking care of animals' needs.

3   Private owners of some zoos knew very little about the animals in their collections. Sometimes bringing wild creatures and people so close together resulted in unpleasant surprises. Visitors who wandered too close to the lion's cage learned that a bored lion might squirt vile-smelling urine through the bars. Imagine the yelling from a rudely showered crowd.

4   You can argue in favor of zoos or against them. You can say it's unethical (wrong and unfair) to take animals from their natural habitats and pen them up for the rest of their lives. In the wild, creatures such as the tiger roam over large territories. Each species (kind) of animal has a role to play in its natural habitat.

ELEPHANT

(continued)

Comparing and Contrasting: "The Nature of Zoos" (continued)

Directions: Read the text and complete the activities.

5   Something else to think about is that wild creatures live in a kill-or-be-killed world. Many die young in battles for mates. Others perish in squabbles over territory. Disease takes others, and so do wounds from prey that fights back. Food can be hard to find or catch.

6   Modern zoos are held to high standards based on how they treat their animals. Many zoos today work to meet these standards. They are designed to help animals feel more at home. Animals are fed the kinds of food they need at regular times. Their health is checked.

7   Most animals in today's zoos live longer than those in the wild. Animals born and raised in zoos may not have the skills to survive in the wild, but they will never need them. Zoos play an important role in educating the public about the animals on display. They teach people how to take better care of the natural habitats where animals live.

8   Zoos play another important role. A growing number of species worldwide are becoming extinct, or disappearing forever at a rapid rate. To save some of these animals, zoos have programs that raise their young so that they can survive when returned to the wild. Gone are the days when zoos collected animals only so people could look at them. The world changes. Needs change. Zoos change, too.

PANDA

Name: _____ Date: _____

Thinking about "The Nature of Zoos"

Directions: Complete this activity. Label a page in your notebook with the date, the title of the text, and "Activity 1."

Activity 1: Comparing and Contrasting

1. Work with your partner. Take turns reading the paragraphs of "The Nature of Zoos" out loud. Discuss how the title links to the kinds of zoos in the world.

2. Reread "The Nature of Zoos." Think about the purpose of zoos. Discuss with your partner: Why are some people in favor of zoos and others against zoos? Give reasons from the text that support being for or against zoos.

3. Reread paragraphs 5, 6, and 7. With your partner, discuss the benefits of modern zoos for animals.

4. Compare and contrast early zoos and modern zoos. You can use a Venn diagram or a T-chart that you draw.

   ■ To use a Venn diagram: Write "early zoos" above the left circle and "modern zoos" above the right circle. Write how early zoos and modern zoos are alike where the circles overlap. Write ways they are different under each type of zoo.

   ■ To use a T-chart: On the left side, write "early zoos." On the right side, write "modern zoos." List the differences under each type of zoo. Then write "How They're Alike," and list ways they are alike.

5. Review your work. Use the details to make a prediction about why modern zoos will be important to animals in the future.

6. Discuss your prediction with your partner. Write what you discussed in your notebook.

(continued)

Thinking about "The Nature of Zoos" *(continued)*

Directions: Complete this activity. Label a page in your notebook with the date, the title of the text, and "Activity 2."

Activity 2: Word Work: Word Families and Using Context Clues

1. Write the term *word families*. Explain everything you know about them.

2. Create a T-chart. Choose two of these words from the text: *small, can, back, play*. On the left side of the T-chart, write one of the words. On the right side, write the other word. Under each word, list words in the same word family. Share your words with your partner.

3. Reread the third paragraph. Use context clues to explain what the word *rudely* means. Write its meaning in your notebook.

4. Reread the fourth paragraph. Then think about the meanings of *unethical* and *natural habitats*. Write each term and use context clues to explain its meaning.

5. Skim the last paragraph to learn about the meaning of the word *extinct*. In your notebook, explain what *extinct* means. Include a reason why the extinction of animals is a serious problem.

Name: _____   Date: _____

"The Nature of Zoos" Word Ladder

Directions: Start at the bottom. Read the clues and write the words.

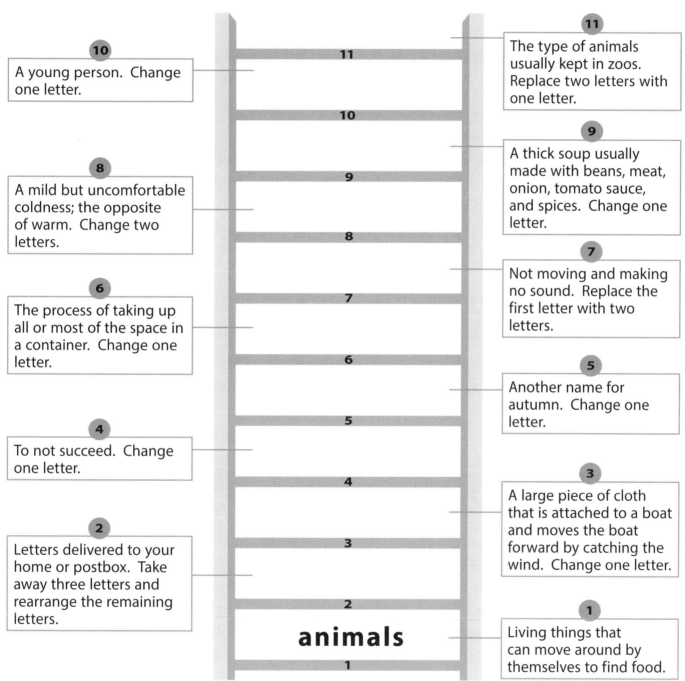

10 A young person. Change one letter.

11 The type of animals usually kept in zoos. Replace two letters with one letter.

8 A mild but uncomfortable coldness; the opposite of warm. Change two letters.

9 A thick soup usually made with beans, meat, onion, tomato sauce, and spices. Change one letter.

6 The process of taking up all or most of the space in a container. Change one letter.

7 Not moving and making no sound. Replace the first letter with two letters.

5 Another name for autumn. Change one letter.

4 To not succeed. Change one letter.

3 A large piece of cloth that is attached to a boat and moves the boat forward by catching the wind. Change one letter.

2 Letters delivered to your home or postbox. Take away three letters and rearrange the remaining letters.

animals

1 Living things that can move around by themselves to find food.

Thinking Challenge

The word ladder starts with *animals* and ends with *wild*. How does the word *wild* connect to how the habitats in zoos have changed in modern times? In your notebook, explain why it's important for zoos to include animals' natural habitats. Share your ideas with your partner.

Comparing and Contrasting:
"What Does an Eel Have for Breakfast?"

Directions: Read the text and complete the activities.

What Does an Eel Have for Breakfast?

by David L. Harrison

1   What did the freshwater eel, swimming in the Delaware River in Pennsylvania, have for breakfast this morning? Trick question: it didn't have breakfast. People are the only ones who have breakfast or lunch or dinner. Other creatures don't set aside times to eat or name their meals. If you were a hungry freshwater eel in the Delaware River in Pennsylvania this morning, and found a worm, you would eat it. Simple as that.

2   Eels may frighten some people because they look like snakes, but they're really a kind of fish, so they like things that most fish like—water insects, crayfish, frogs, other fish, and worms. If you could ask an eel about its motto (the belief that guides its actions), and the eel could talk, it might say, "Hunt. Find. Eat."

3   Mostly, what animals eat depends on when they are hungry, what they can find or catch, and what time of year it is. During the growing season, robins peck around for worms, but if the weather turns cold and the ground freezes, many of them migrate south for the winter and pig out (make that "bird out") on berries. Bullfrogs croak their way through warm months, swallowing whole anything they can stuff into their mouths, but if winter turns frosty, they may claw down into a pond's muddy bottom and hibernate till spring. Honeybees buzz through a lot of pollen and honey during the blooming season, but they make enough extra honey to see them through the winter nibbling leftovers.

(continued)

Comparing and Contrasting:
"What Does an Eel Have for Breakfast?" *(continued)*

Directions: Read the text and complete the activities.

4   In the animal world there are herbivores (plant-eaters), carnivores (meat-eaters), and omnivores (plant-and-meat-eaters), and they come in all sizes. Elephants become enormous on bark and leaves. Koalas stick to the hard-to-digest leaves of the eucalyptus tree. The lizard's lightning-quick tongue helps it capture bugs. Anteaters have a nose that probes down tunnels after ants and termites and a long, sticky tongue that means death to the tiny insects that don't escape. The vulture thrives on foul-smelling, putrid, disease-ridden carcasses that would kill most other creatures.

5   We humans eat more kinds of food than other animals do. We are the only ones who cook our food and season it, the only ones who stand at a grill, waiting for our hamburgers to finish. We are the only ones to mix foods together to make different foods. A cow may graze enough grass and weeds in a day to qualify as a salad, but we're the only ones to add a salad dressing.

6   We like to change our menu for every meal and decide what sorts of food are "proper" for each one. For breakfast we might eat cereal, eggs, a burrito, or rice. Bagels, pancakes, and yogurt are favorites, too. Don't waste your time asking a freshwater eel in the Delaware River in Pennsylvania what it had for breakfast. What did *you* have for breakfast?

Thinking about "What Does an Eel Have for Breakfast?"

Directions: Complete this activity. Label a page in your notebook with the date, the title of the text, and "Activity 1."

Activity 1: Comparing and Contrasting

1. Work with your partner. Take turns reading the paragraphs of "What Does an Eel Have for Breakfast?" out loud. Discuss how the title connects to what you learned about the eating habits of eels.

2. Reread "What Does an Eel Have for Breakfast?" Discuss what you learned about the eating habits of other animals.

3. Reread the fifth and sixth paragraphs. Discuss how the eating habits of humans differ from the eel and other animals.

4. Compare and contrast eating habits of animals and humans. You can use a Venn diagram or a T-chart that you draw.

   - To use a Venn diagram: Write "eating habits of animals" above the left circle and "eating habits of humans" above the right circle. Write ways eating habits of animals and humans are alike where the circles overlap. Write the differences under each heading.

   - To use a T-chart: On the left side, write "eating habits of animals." On the right side, write "eating habits of humans." List the differences under each heading. Then write "How They're Alike," and list ways they are alike.

5. Review your work. Use the details to draw a conclusion about the eating habits of animals and humans.

6. Discuss your conclusion with your partner. Write what you discussed in your notebook.

(continued)

Thinking about "What Does an Eel Have for Breakfast?" (continued)

Directions: Complete this activity. Label a page in your notebook with the date, the title of the text, and "Activity 2."

Activity 2: Word Work: Word Families and Using Context Clues

1. Write the term *word families*. Explain everything you know about them.

2. Create a T-chart. Choose two of these words from the text: *trick, grow, might, catch*. On the left side of the T-chart, write one of the words. On the right side, write the other word. Under each word, list words in the same word family. Share your words with your partner.

3. Reread the second paragraph. Think about the meaning of the word *motto*. In your notebook, write the word *motto* and its meaning.

4. Reread the fourth paragraph. Write the words *herbivores*, *carnivores*, and *omnivores*. Define each of the words by using context clues.

5. Choose two of the words from step 4. Use each one in its own sentence that shows you understand the word's meaning.

6. Write the word *putrid* in your notebook. Use context clues to explain its meaning.

"What Does an Eel Have for Breakfast?" Word Ladder

Directions: Start at the bottom. Read the clues and write the words.

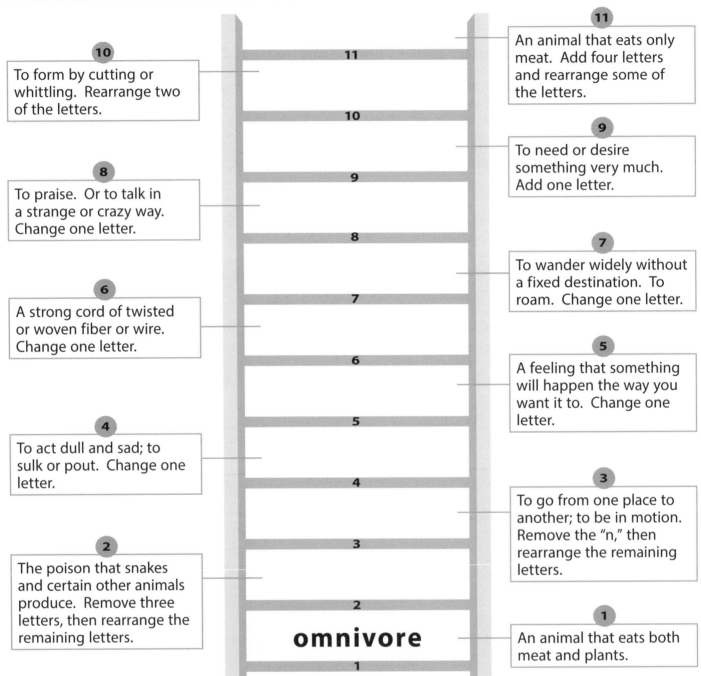

10 To form by cutting or whittling. Rearrange two of the letters.

8 To praise. Or to talk in a strange or crazy way. Change one letter.

6 A strong cord of twisted or woven fiber or wire. Change one letter.

4 To act dull and sad; to sulk or pout. Change one letter.

2 The poison that snakes and certain other animals produce. Remove three letters, then rearrange the remaining letters.

11 An animal that eats only meat. Add four letters and rearrange some of the letters.

9 To need or desire something very much. Add one letter.

7 To wander widely without a fixed destination. To roam. Change one letter.

5 A feeling that something will happen the way you want it to. Change one letter.

3 To go from one place to another; to be in motion. Remove the "n," then rearrange the remaining letters.

1 An animal that eats both meat and plants.

omnivore

Thinking Challenge

The word ladder starts with *omnivore* and ends with *carnivore*. In your notebook, explain how these terms connect to "What Does an Eel Have for Breakfast?" Share your ideas with your partner.

Helping Students Choose Good-Fit Books

Here we present guidelines for you to use when modeling how to choose a good-fit book, along with tips you can give students about how to choose books for themselves. Self-selecting good-fit books is a lifelong skill—one that is worth the time it takes to learn. The learning time line differs for every child. The key is to continue modeling, thinking aloud, and listening to students' comments and body language, as doing so can support your decisions about whether to confer with a student to offer extra support. Avoid the temptation to select books for students, even if you offer two or three and then let them choose from those options.

Modeling How to Choose a Good-Fit Book

Before sending students off to choose their own books, model and think aloud the process of choosing good-fit books, using different texts as examples. Keep in mind that it will take weeks or even months for developing readers to feel safe enough to choose a book they can read.

- Think aloud to show what happens when you choose a book that's too difficult: you can't say many words, you don't know many word meanings, and you can't recall details.
- Then invite students to turn-and-talk and decide what you should do, explaining why.
- Think aloud to show what happens when you find a good-fit book: it's easy to read, it's enjoyable for you, and you can retell the story or information.
- Then invite students to turn-and-talk and explain whether you should read the book.
- Keep modeling, emphasizing that independent reading should be enjoyable and easy.
- Reassure students that they are safe in your class when they select a book that looks easy. Explain that the more they read, the faster they'll improve.

Choosing a Good-Fit Book: Tips for Students

Share these tips with students as you model the process.

- Look for books on topics and genres that interest you.
- Study the front cover illustration, and read the information on the back cover or the inside cover flap.
- Think of books you've read and enjoyed before. Is the topic, genre, or author similar?
- Review and enjoy the illustrations or photographs.
- Read the chapter titles in the table of contents, and ask, "Does this interest me?"

- Take a test drive and read two or three pages or the first chapter. Can you retell key points?
- Ask a friend to recommend a book.
- Ask your teacher to recommend a book.

Responding When a Student Wants to Abandon a Book

It's okay for students to abandon books, because having them finish books they dislike can reinforce negative attitudes toward reading. First, let students know there are times they may want to abandon a book, and that in those instances you'll talk about why they don't want to finish it. Explain that this will help you understand why they disliked the book and enable you to help them select books that are a good fit.

Name: _____   Date: _____

Be a Word-Meaning Detective by Using Context Clues

Context clues are words and phrases provided by authors that allow you to quickly figure out the meaning of an unfamiliar word while you read. You'll find clues in these places:

- The sentence that the word is in

- The paragraph that comes before the word

- The paragraph that comes after the word

Here are examples of context clues that author David L. Harrison provides.

Definitions	The author offers a definition immediately after or close to the unfamiliar word or in the sentence that comes after the word.
Example (from "Is That Really You?"):	
Do you know what a **mimic** is? It's a copycat. It's when one person or animal tries to look like another—or sound like another, walk like another, wear hair the same way as another, or buy the same clothes as another.	

Synonyms	A synonym is a similar word or phrase that can be substituted for another word. It can follow a comma, follow a dash, be in parentheses, or come after these words: *such as, is called, that is, in other words*. The similar word can also be in the next sentence.
Example (from "The Nature of Zoos"):	
You can say it's **unethical** (wrong and unfair) to take animals from their natural habitats and pen them up for the rest of their lives.	

Comparisons	The author helps you create a mental picture or understand an unfamiliar word by linking the word or phrase to an example you might know. Look for these words: *like, as,* and *similar to*.
Example (from "The Sea Bear"):	
Like a good **topcoat**, over the fat and the black skin, the bear wears a heavy layer of fur, thicker than any other kind of bear's fur.	

Be a Word-Meaning Detective by Using Context Clues (continued)

Concrete examples	These clues help you figure out the unfamiliar word's meaning with an example that you'll understand. Examples can be in the sentence with the new word, or they can follow these phrases: *for example*, *such as*, and *an example is*.

Example (from "Rain Forest"):

> The rain forest, where **monsoons** roar
> their wild-thing songs on jungle floor.
> Sodden soil where droplets seep.
> Rivers twist swift and deep.
> Night and day it pounds and pours.
> The rain forest, where monsoon roars.

Conjunctions	These words link ideas and help you explain unknown words by connecting them to words and ideas you know. Look for these coordinating conjunctions: *and*, *but*, *or*, *for*, *so*, and *yet*. Common subordinating conjunctions—such as *when*, *if*, *since*, *whenever*, and *because*—include details that can help you understand an unfamiliar word.

Example (from "It All Depends on Who You Are"):

Mostly, you are a **vegetarian,** so you eat a lot of seeds and grains.

Words or phrases that modify	Adjectives and adverbs can provide clues to a word's meaning.

Example (from "Octopus"):

> Octopus, octopus,
> escape-artist octopus,
> ink-squirting octopus,
> **magician** of the sea.

Making the Rounds: Conferring on the Go

As students work on the differentiated lessons, circulate among them, carrying a pencil and a clipboard with dated sticky notes, which you will use to make reminders for students. Look for behaviors indicating that students need your support. Observe, listen, make "I notice" statements, and ask students questions while they read and write about reading with partners or independently. Such daily interactions enable you to check on students' abilities to apply focus lessons to accessible texts.

Giving Reminders to Students

It's helpful for students to have notes of your conversations that include key points that can act as reminders and support them as they work. Place these sticky notes in students' notebooks, so that they can refer to them as they continue on their own. Ask students to keep each sticky note on the page you discussed, so that you can observe their edits or revisions and improvement.

Allowing Students to Benefit from Wait Time

When you ask a question and students don't respond immediately, allow wait time rather than rushing to fill the silence with talk and solutions. Students should talk most of the time, and your questions should develop thinking that enables them to solve problems. Once you pose a question or state an observation, give students enough time to think about a response. If students don't respond, you can repeat the question or statement and ask, "Do you need more time to think?"

Being a Good Listener

Listen carefully and jot down questions you have; ask these once the student has finished talking. Avoid interrupting a student—at all costs. Use your sense of the student to make further comments and ask questions that will boost confidence and encourage the student to speak. Close the brief meeting with a positive comment that lets the student know that they are moving forward and have a clearer understanding of the strategy they're practicing. Be positive, even if a student requires more support. If the student does not need additional support, say something like "You've made an excellent start; now you and your partner can complete the task together [or now you're ready to work independently]." If the student does require extra support, you might say, "Excellent start. You can complete this section, and when you're finished, I'll help you with the next part." The point is to sustain students' belief that they can move from their frustration zone to their independent learning zone.

Quick Coaching and Cheerleading

Two- or three-minute conversations enable you to stop and support five to seven students each time the class meets during 20 minutes of instructional reading. Promote a positive growth mindset, and gradually release more and more responsibility for completing the work to the students, until they can do it independently.

Responding to Negative Statements

When students make negative comments about reading such as, *I hate reading. It's boring. You'll never get me to like reading,* respond by honoring their feelings. Use comments like: *I'm glad you could be honest* or *Your words help me understand your feelings.* Such responses let students know you accept and value their feelings. Changing students' negative feelings toward reading takes time, careful listening, and observing. As you notice small changes in students' attitudes toward reading, share them so students gain an awareness of their growth and progress. Jot what you notice on dated sticky notes and invite students to put these on a separate page in their notebooks so they can reread them and see their progress. For example, *I noticed you didn't want to stop reading your book today. You checked out two books to read at home. You and your partner are enjoying discussing your poem.* Always point out positives and build on what students are doing well.

Summarizing Texts

Often, students find summarizing texts to be a challenge because summaries are short and require that students select a few key ideas. To help students move from retelling an entire text to summarizing, think aloud and model how you take notes using a read-aloud text or a text from one of the focus lessons in this book. Then have students turn their notes for Somebody Wanted But So Then (SWBST) or the Five Ws Plus How (both shown below) into a few sentences for their summaries.

Summarizing Fiction and Narrative Biographies

Use SWBST to support students in summarizing fiction and narrative biographies. Explain that students should avoid giving the ending away in their summaries, as this spoils the text for others who want to read it.

- **Somebody:** The main character, or protagonist
- **Wanted:** What the main character wants, or their goal
- **But:** The problem that keeps the main character from achieving their goal
- **So:** The character's solution to the problem of reaching their goal
- **Then:** Tell more about what happens without giving away the ending

Sample Notes and Summary for "Cinderella"

- **Somebody:** Cinderella
- **Wanted:** To have a beautiful gown and a carriage to take her to the ball to meet the prince
- **But:** Cinderella's stepmother wouldn't let her go.
- **So:** Cinderella's fairy godmother dressed her in a stunning gown and glass slippers and provided a carriage. When the prince danced with Cinderella, he fell in love with her.
- **Then:** She lost a slipper leaving the ball before midnight. The prince found her glass slipper and used it to search for his true love.

Summary created by turning notes into sentences:

In the fairy tale "Cinderella," a young girl named Cinderella lived with her stepmother, who wouldn't let her go to the ball. Cinderella's fairy godmother heard her wish to attend the ball and dressed Cinderella in a stunning gown and glass slippers. She told Cinderella that she had to leave the ball before midnight. As Cinderella ran from the ball, a glass slipper fell off her foot. The prince found the slipper and used it to search for his true love.

Summarizing Informational Texts

Informational texts can be short texts such as those in this book, articles from magazines, news articles, or nonfiction books. The Five Ws Plus How can support students as they select information from a text and write a short summary.

- **Who:** Who is the person (or event) the text is about?
- **What:** What happened?
- **When:** When did it happen?
- **Where:** Where did it happen?
- **Why:** What was the cause of this?
- **How:** Explain how the event took place.

Sample Notes and Summary for "Climate Strike"
(Note: See page 148 for the text of this story.)

- **Who:** Greta Thunberg, a Swedish high school student
- **What:** Greta decided to have a school strike to call her government's attention to the need for action to stop climate change.
- **When:** She was in high school.
- **Where:** She skipped school and stood outside the Government Building in Sweden and held a sign she had painted that said "School Strike for Climate!"
- **Why:** The effects of climate change—global warming, caused by fossil fuels that humans burn—and government inaction caused Greta to take action.
- **How:** Other students, politicians, and adults noticed what Greta was doing. In 13 months, she had so many fans that four million people joined a climate strike around the globe.

Summary created by turning notes into sentences:

In "Climate Strike" by David L. Harrison, a Swedish high school student, Greta Thunberg, decided to call her government's attention to global warming with a climate strike. She skipped school and stood outside the Government Building holding a sign she had painted that read "School Strike for Climate!" The effects of global warming resulting from the fossil fuels that humans burn, combined with governments not taking action, caused Greta to skip school and take action. Other students, politicians, and adults noticed what Greta was doing. Thirteen months later, she had so many fans that four million people joined her in a climate strike around the world.

Thinking Aloud and Modeling

- Display your teacher's notebook on the board as you write in it to show students how you take notes.
- Include the title and author in the first sentence of the summary.
- Turn the notes into sentences.
- Reread the summary out loud to ensure that it makes sense.

Written Conversations

Written conversations between two students or between a teacher and a student can be about vocabulary, specific literary elements, open-ended questions, or emotional reactions to a text (Daniels and Daniels 2013). Here are some guidelines for written conversations:

- **Determine the participants:** The conversation can take place between pairs of students or a student and the teacher.

- **Start with open-ended questions:** The teacher or students pose a question that does not have a yes/no answer or only one correct answer (e.g., "How did events or people in the text change the character?" "List all the connotations for the word *changemaker*," or "Explain why you believe the character reversed a decision").

- **Complete a written conversation:** There are two ways to have a written conversation.

    a. A student (or the teacher) writes the heading on the paper and writes the question or prompt on the left-hand side. On the right-hand side, the other student writes their first name and a response or poses another question. After two to four exchanges, students can share their written conversations under a document camera, and their classmates can comment or pose questions.

    b. Students write their ideas and thoughts that respond to the open-ended question or prompt on paper. After the teacher notices that most students have stopped writing, they invite partners to exchange papers and read each other's responses. Each student skips a line after their partner's thoughts and writes their name and their thoughts, reactions to what their partner has written, or questions. Students can share their notes and questions with their partner or use these written conversations in a small-group or whole-class discussion.

Here's an excerpt of a written conversation between Laura Robb and a fifth-grade student who was practicing including text details to support their thinking:

Robb:	Why should you include text details to support your idea?
Student:	I guess it's to show that my idea works.
Robb:	You understand that the evidence can show others that your thinking is on target.
Student:	I know. But I don't do it in my notebook.
Robb:	Can you help me understand why?
Student:	[after long pause] If I don't remember the stuff, I don't look back—it takes too much time.

Often, these conversations reveal an issue a student is wrestling with and give the teacher a chance to work through it. In this case, Laura modeled and then had the student practice skimming to find the details needed for support.

Sketchnoting

When students sketchnote, they create a visual story about their interpretation of a poem or text that can include their emotional reactions, themes, inferences about characters, settings, and so on. Students mix words with sketches. They don't have to be artists to create sketchnotes; the goal of sketchnoting is to create visual images of thinking. The ability to visualize and draw shows comprehension, and it supports the retention and recall of information and ideas (McGregor 2018). The more students practice sketchnoting, the easier it is for them to organize thoughts and ideas.

There are no strict rules; students' sketchnotes will reflect their unique learning styles.

It's helpful to watch a short YouTube video on sketchnoting with students to illustrate the concept for them. Here's a video to investigate:

- "My Pencil Made Me Do It: A Beginner's Guide to Sketchnoting in the Classroom" (3:47) Carrie Baughcum

You might also want to read a book about sketchnoting. Here are two to explore:

- *Sketchnoting in the Classroom: A Practical Guide to Deepen Student Learning* (Carter 2019)

- *Ink and Ideas: Sketchnotes for Engagement, Comprehension, and Thinking* (McGregor 2018)

Scheduled Conference Form

Name:	Date:

Topic to be discussed:

Points to be discussed:

Student's reactions and responses to practicing with teacher:

Goal negotiated by teacher and student:

Additional comments:

Date of follow-up conference (if needed):

Planning and Writing Analytical Paragraphs

Modeling the Process

You can present this lesson to the whole class or a small group of students. At times pairs will work together. We suggest that you start with the whole class and then support small groups as needed.

- Develop a writing plan that includes the thesis or position statement, notes for text evidence that supports the thesis, and notes for a conclusion that keeps readers thinking.
- Show students how you look back in the text and take notes that support the thesis.
- Think aloud about your closing: it should add something extra that grows out of the paragraph and keeps readers thinking.
- Give the paragraph a title that links to its topic, and use your plan to write a paragraph.
- Create a wrap-up sentence: think of a sentence related to the topic that encourages readers to continue thinking about it.
- Write in front of students, so that they can view your process.

Sharing the Pen: Students Collaborate with You

Invite students to share the pen with you and collaborate to better understand the process.

- **Planning:** Provide students with the thesis or position statement and have them offer two or three pieces of supporting text evidence. Write the plan on chart paper.
- **Drafting:** Prepare another piece of chart paper with the paragraph's title and the first sentence, which contains a position or thesis statement. Ask students to turn each piece of evidence in the plan into a sentence, and add their sentences to the paragraph. Students may benefit from doing this with partners.
- **Wrap-up:** Invite students to think of a closing sentence that relates to the topic but also asks readers to continue thinking about it.

Differentiating for Students Who Need Support

Adjust the amount of text evidence students need to support a claim. For example, a developing reader and writer or an English learner might work on successfully integrating one piece of text evidence in an essay. Once that student experiences success with one piece of evidence, ask them to try including two, then three.

Inviting Students to Work through the Planning Process

Circulate among students as they work during every part of the process, offering support and modeling rewrites on sticky notes. The list that follows provides suggestions of what to look for as you move among students.

- Compose a few thesis or position statements; let students choose the one they will defend.
- Have students list text evidence in their own words that defends the opening statement they have chosen.
- For the conclusion, support students in determining what to include that will keep readers thinking.
- Check students' plans as they work and offer feedback.
- Have students use their plans to compose a first draft.
- Repeat the collaboration process until you feel that students can work independently.

Assessing Content

- Create a single-point rubric for assessment (see chapter 7, page 71, for more information on this type of rubric).
- First, ask students to evaluate their own work and revise it for clarity of content.
- Next, ask peer partners to assess and discuss each other's work; each student writes suggestions for their partner on a sticky note, then the other student considers these suggestions and rewrites.
- After students have done a self-evaluation and assessed their peer partner's work, provide them with teacher feedback: state positives first, then frame one or two suggestions as questions.

Grammar and Punctuation

- Observe students' needs for grammar instruction and use them for writing lessons.
- Add grammar and punctuation standards to the analytical paragraphs after students are comfortable with the process for writing the paragraphs.
- Editing for grammar and punctuation is separate from content assessment but should follow the same process: self, peer, then teacher.

Using Literary Elements

Literary elements can be turned into prompts and questions for discussing fictional texts. Introduce literary elements using an interactive read-aloud, and have students practice identifying them with narrative texts.

- **Antagonists:** These are forces that work against the protagonist and create tension in narrative texts. There are two kinds of antagonists:
  - **External:** Nature, other characters, decisions, actions taken, and interactions
  - **Internal:** The character's thoughts and emotions
- **Climax:** This is the moment or point of greatest intensity in the plot. Short stories usually have one climax, but novels can have small climaxes as the plot unfolds. The major climax is near the end. The climax, the highest point of the action, can deepen comprehension of plot details and also offer insights into themes.
- **Denouement or return to normalcy:** Events that resolve the climax in a novel, short story, drama, or narrative poem are often referred to as the outcome. Understanding the outcomes of a narrative can lead to figuring out smaller themes and central themes and deepen readers' understanding of how the plot brought them back to a feeling of normalcy.
- **Other characters:** Observing how other characters relate to, dialogue with, and interact with the protagonist can deepen readers' knowledge of all the characters' personalities, as well as the themes in a story.
- **Plot:** The plot consists of the events that occur and enable readers to observe characters in diverse situations. Plot supports an understanding of theme, conflicts, setting, and characters' personalities. Often referred to as *rising action*, the plot builds from the opening of the story to a high point of interest called the climax.
- **Point of view:** This refers to who's narrating the story:
  - A first-person narrator is often the protagonist. In this point of view, the narration uses first-person pronouns: *I, me, mine, we, us, our, ours* as well as third-person pronouns: *he, him, his, she, her, hers, it, its, they, them, their, theirs.*
  - An objective narrator acts like an outside or external observer who sees and records information and events from a *neutral perspective*. In this point of view, the narration uses third-person pronouns: *he, him, his, she, her, hers, it, its, they, them, their, theirs.*
  - An omniscient narrator is also an outside observer but knows everything about the characters—their conflicts and problems, decisions and motivation, thoughts and feelings. Told from the third-person point of view, the narration uses these pronouns: *he, him, his, she, her, hers, it, its, they, them, their, theirs.*

- **Problem:** This is something that gets in the way of a character's desire or goal and requires an action or decision to overcome, such as whether to risk diving from the high board as required by the PE teacher when you're a weak swimmer or lying to your parents about where you've been to avoid punishment. Problems require characters to figure out solutions, such as what to do when they have no money for food or how to cope after a hurricane's wind and rain destroyed part of their town. How characters tackle problems and deal with their inability to resolve certain problems can provide readers with deep insights into personality and decision-making processes.

- **Protagonist:** This is the main character in the narrative, who has problems to solve. Observing how the protagonist interacts with others, makes decisions, and tries to solve problems offers insight into this character's personality and motivations.

- **Setting:** This is the time and place of the narrative. A short text can focus on one setting, while longer texts usually have multiple settings. How characters function in and react to a setting can deepen readers' understanding of characters' motivation and personality traits.

- **Symbolism:** A symbol is something that represents an idea, emotion, or concept. For example, the U.S. flag symbolizes patriotism and love of country. To many people, blue symbolizes peace or justice, and red symbolizes hardiness, courage, or love. Red also symbolizes the blood of those who fought for freedom. Narrative authors sometimes select objects to symbolize or represent an emotion or idea they're trying to help the reader understand.

- **Theme:** This is a statement about people and life that the author makes with the narrative. In folktales and fairy tales, the theme is frequently stated as a moral or lesson at the end of the story.

Name: _____ Date: _____

Checklist: Partner or Small-Group Discussions

Directions: Read each statement, and write "Always," "Sometimes," or "Never."

Type of discussion: _____

_____ I share my ideas with my partner or group.

_____ I give evidence from the poem or short text to support my ideas.

_____ I listen to others without interrupting.

_____ I ask questions to better understand my classmates' thinking.

_____ I disagree politely if I have a different point of view.

_____ I respond to what others say and respect their ideas.

_____ I try to keep the discussion going by asking questions.

How I can improve during discussions:

Additional comments:

Teacher's Assessment: Discussions

Place a check next to items you observed the student doing during partner or small-group discussions. Place a dash next to items that need additional practice or teacher support.

Name _____ **Date** _____

Preparation

_____ Brought book or materials

_____ Brought notebook

Participation

_____ Contributes to discussion

_____ Listens without interrupting

_____ Values diverse ideas

_____ Uses text evidence as support

_____ Uses prior knowledge as support

_____ Points to details in the text to support thinking

_____ Asks meaningful questions

_____ Helps keep the discussion moving forward

_____ Disagrees politely

Interpretation

_____ Makes logical predictions by using information in the text

_____ Draws logical conclusions supported by text evidence

_____ Makes inferences and supports them with text evidence

_____ Compares and contrasts by showing likenesses and differences

_____ Can explore alternate interpretations

Additional comments: _____

_____

_____

_____

Name: _____   Date: _____

Venn Diagram

Directions: Compare how two things are alike and different.

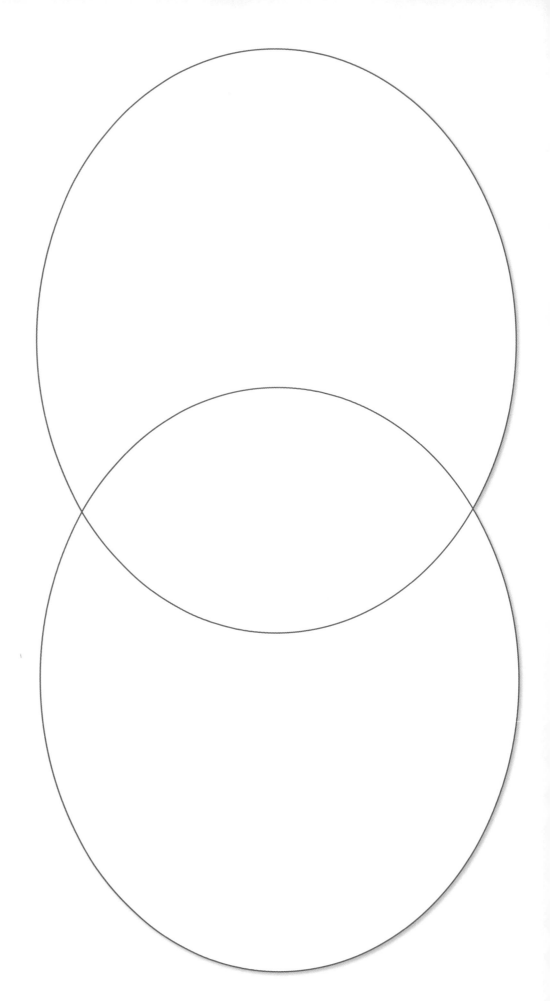

Name: _____   Date: _____

Prompts That Keep a Discussion Moving Forward

Directions: Tape this list of prompts inside your reader's notebook.

These prompts and questions can help your group continue the conversation when there is a pause.

- So, we're supposed to [restate prompt].
- Does anyone have a different idea?
- Can you find evidence in the text that supports that?
- Is there more than one way to think about that?
- Can you explain that term?
- What points in the text support that claim?
- I'm unsure of your point. Can you clarify it?
- What made you say that? Can you give text evidence?
- Tell me more about that idea.
- Here's how I see that idea.
- Let's check the directions (or rubric).
- I agree with _____ but disagree with _____.

References

Afflerbach, Peter. 2022. *Teaching Readers (Not Reading): Moving Beyond Skills and Strategies to Reader-Focused Instruction.* New York: Guilford Press.

Alexander, Kwame. 2021. *Out of Wonder.* New York: Scholastic.

Allington, Richard L. 1977. "If They Don't Read Much, How They Ever Gonna Get Good?" *Journal of Adult and Adolescent Literacy* 21 (1): 57–61.

Allington, Richard L. 2007. "Intervention All Day Long." *Voices from the Middle* 14 (4): 7–14.

Allington, Richard L. 2012. *What Really Matters for Struggling Readers: Designing Research-Based Programs.* Boston: Pearson.

Allington, Richard L. 2014. "How Reading Volume Affects Both Reading Fluency and Reading Achievement." *International Electronic Journal of Elementary Education* 7 (1): 13–26.

Allington, Richard L., and Anne M. McGill-Frazen. 2021. "Reading Volume and Reading Achievement: A Review of Recent Research." *Reading Research Quarterly* 56 (S1): S231–S238.

Anderson, Richard C., Paul T. Wilson, and Linda G. Fielding. 1988. "Growth in Reading and How Children Spend Their Time Outside of School." *Reading Research Quarterly* 3 (23): 285–303.

Baughcum, Carrie. 2017. "My Pencil Made Me Do It: A Beginner's Guide to Sketchnoting in the Classroom." July 21, 2017. YouTube. youtube.com/watch?v=zNJyuJl5LKk.

Bear, Donald R., Marcia R. Invernizzi, Shane R. Templeton, and Francine Johnston. 2011. *Words Their Way: Word Study for Phonics, Vocabulary, and Spelling Instruction,* 5th edition. New York: Pearson.

Beck, Isabel L., Margaret G. McKeown, and Linda Kucan. 2013. *Bringing Words to Life: Robust Vocabulary Instruction.* New York: Guilford Press.

Bishop, Rudine Sims. 1990. "Windows, Mirrors, and Sliding Glass Doors." *Perspectives: Choosing and Using Books for the Classroom* 6 (3): ix–xi.

Bray, Barbara, and Kathleen McClaskey. 2016. *How to Personalize Learning: A Practical Guide for Getting Started and Going Deeper.* Thousand Oaks, CA: Corwin.

Brozo, William G., Gerry Shiel, and Keith Topping. 2007. "Engagement in Reading: Lessons from Three PISA Countries." *Journal of Adolescent and Adult Literacy* 51 (14): 304–315.

Carter, Nicole. 2019. *Sketchnoting in the Classroom: A Practical Guide to Deepen Students' Learning.* Eugene, OR: International Society for Technology in Education.

Crowder, S. Travis. 2020. *Reflective Readers: The Power of Reader's Notebooks.* New Rochelle, NY: Benchmark Education.

Daniels, Harvey. 2002. *Literature Circles: Voice and Choice in Book Clubs and Reading Groups*. Portland, ME: Stenhouse.

Daniels, Harvey, and Elaine Daniels. 2013. *The Best-Kept Teaching Secret: How Written Conversations Engage Kids, Activate Learning, Grow Fluent Writers, K–12*. Thousand Oaks, CA: Corwin.

Davis, Cathy M. 2010. *Reader's Theater Scripts, Grade 3*. Huntington Beach, CA: Shell Education.

Duke, Nell K., Annie Ward, and P. David Pearson. 2021. "The Science of Reading Comprehension Instruction." *The Reading Teacher* 74 (6):1–31.

Fisher, Douglas, William G. Brozo, Nancy Frey, and Gay Ivey. 2007. *50 Content Area Strategies for Adolescent Literacy*. Upper Saddle River, NY: Merrill/Prentice Hall.

France, Paul E. 2019. *Reclaiming Personalized Learning: A Pedagogy for Restoring Equity and Humanity to Our Classrooms*. Thousand Oaks, CA: Corwin.

Graham, Steve, Katherine R. Harris, and Tonya Santangelo. 2015. "Research-Based Writing Practices and the Common Core: Meta-Analysis and Meta-Synthesis." *Elementary School Journal* 115 (4): 498–522.

Graham, Steve, and Michael Hebert. 2010. *Writing to Read: Evidence for How Writing Can Improve Reading*. New York: Carnegie Corporation of New York.

Grimes, Nikki. 2018. *A Pocketful of Poems*. New York: Clarion Books.

Harvey, Stephanie, and Annie Ward. 2017. *From Striving to Thriving: How to Grow Capable, Confident Readers*. New York: Scholastic.

Harvey, Stephanie, Annie Ward, Maggie Hoddinott, and Suzanne Carroll. 2021. *Intervention Reinvention: A Volume-Based Approach to Reading Instruction*. New York: Scholastic.

Howard, Mary. 2009. *RTI From All Sides: What Every Teacher Needs to Know*. Portsmouth, NH: Heinemann.

Krashen, Stephen D. 2004. *The Power of Reading: Insights from the Research*. Portsmouth, NH: Heinemann.

LaBerge, David, and S. Jay Samuels. 1974. "Toward a Theory of Automatic Information Processing in Reading." *Cognitive Psychology* 6: 293–323. doi.org/10.1016/0010-0285(74)90015-2.

Marzano, Robert, J. 2010. "Teaching Inference." In *Educational Leadership*, (67) 80–81.

McGee, Brenda, and Debbie Keiser Triska. 2010. *Reader's Theater . . . and So Much More! (Grades 5–6)*. Philadelphia: Routledge.

McGregor, Tanny. 2018. *Ink and Ideas: Sketchnotes for Engagement, Comprehension, and Thinking*. Portsmouth, NH: Heinemann.

Miller, Donalyn. 2009. *The Book Whisperer: Awakening the Inner Reader in Every Child*. San Francisco: Jossey-Bass.

Miller, Donalyn, and Colby Sharp. 2018. *Game Changer! Book Access for All Kids.* New York: Scholastic.

National Reading Panel. 2000. *Teaching Children to Read: An Evidence-Based Assessment of the Scientific Research Literature on Reading and Its Implications for Reading Instruction.* Washington, DC: National Institute of Child Health and Human Development and U.S. Department of Education.

O'Brien Mackey, Sarah. 2005. "Reading and Writing for Understanding." *Usable Knowledge,* July 21, 2005. Harvard Graduate School of Education. gse.harvard.edu/news/ uk/05/07/reading-and-writing-understanding.

Owocki, Gretchen. 2010. *The RTI Daily Planning Book, K–6.* Portsmouth, NH: Heinemann.

Owocki, Gretchen, and Yetta Goodman. 2002. *Kidwatching: Documenting Children's Literacy Development.* Portsmouth, NH: Heinemann.

Pearson, P. David, and Margaret C. Gallagher. 1983. "The Instruction of Reading Comprehension." *Contemporary Educational Psychology* 8 (3): 317–344.

Prelutsky, Jack, ed. 2007. *The Random House Book of Poetry for Children.* New York: Random House.

Raphael, Taffy E. 2006. *QAR Now: A Powerful and Practical Framework That Develops Comprehension and Higher-Level Thinking in All Students.* New York: Scholastic.

Rasinski, Timothy. 2010. *The Fluent Reader.* 2nd ed. New York: Scholastic.

Rasinski, Timothy, and Chase Young. 2024. *Build Reading Fluency: Practice and Performance with Reader's Theater and More,* 2nd edition. Huntington Beach, CA: Shell Education.

Rasinski, Timothy V., and Nancy Padak. 2005. *3-Minute Reading Assessments: Word Recognition, Fluency, and Comprehension, Grades 1–4.* New York: Scholastic.

Rasinski, Timothy V., D. Ray Reutzel, David Chard, and Sylvia Linan-Thompson. 2011. "Reading Fluency." In *Handbook of Reading Research, Vol. 4.,* edited by Michael L. Kamil, P. David Pearson, Elizabeth B. Moje, and Peter Afflerbach, 286–319. New York: Routledge.

Robb, Laura. 2010. *Teaching Reading in Middle School: A Strategic Approach to Teaching Reading That Improves Comprehension and Thinking.* New York: Scholastic.

Robb, Laura. 2014. *Vocabulary Is Comprehension: Getting to the Root of Text Complexity.* Thousand Oaks, CA: Corwin.

Robb, Laura. 2016. *The Reading Intervention Toolkit.* Huntington Beach, CA: Shell Education.

Robb, Laura. 2017. *Read, Talk, Write: 35 Lessons That Teach Students to Analyze Fiction and Nonfiction.* Thousand Oaks, CA: Corwin.

Robb, Laura. 2022. *Increase Reading Volume: Practical Strategies That Boost Students' Achievement and Passion for Reading.* Champaign, IL: NCTE.

Robb, Laura, and Evan Robb. 2020. *Schools Full of Readers: Tools for Teachers, Coaches, and Leaders to Support Students.* New Rochelle, NY: Benchmark Education.

Rosenblatt, Louise. 1978. *The Reader, the Text, the Poem: The Transactional Theory of the Literary Work.* Carbondale: Southern Illinois University Press.

Rothstein, Dan, and Luz Santana. 2011. "Teaching Students to Ask Their Own Questions." *Harvard Education Letter* 27 (5): 1–2.

Samuels, S. Jay, and Yi-Chen Wu. 2004. "How the Amount of Time Spent on Independent Reading Affects Reading Achievement: A Response to the National Reading Panel." citeseerx.ist.psu.edu/viewdoc/summary?doi=10.1.1.539.9906.

Saskia, Lacey. 2016. *Foods for the Future.* Huntington Beach, CA: Teacher Created Materials.

Shanahan, Timothy. 2019. "How Would You Schedule the Reading Instruction?" *Shanahan on Literacy* (blog), January 26, 2019. shanahanonliteracy.com/blog/how-would-you-schedule-the-reading-instruction.

Shanahan, Timothy. 2021. "What is the Science of Reading?" *Shanahan on Literacy* (blog), November 6, 2021. shanahanonliteracy.com/blog/what-is-the-science-of-reading-1.

Schreiber, Peter A. 1980. "On the Acquisition of Reading Fluency." *Journal of Reading Behavior* 12: 177–186.

Schreiber, Peter A. 1991. "Understanding Prosody's Role in Reading Acquisition." *Theory into Practice* 30: 158–164.

Shepard, Aaron. 2017. *Folktales on Stage: Children's Plays for Reader's Theater with 16 Scripts from World Folk and Fairy Tales and Legends, Including Asian, African, and Native American.* New York: Shepard Publications.

Smith, Charles R. 2007. *Hoop Kings.* Cambridge, MA: Candlewick Press.

Sparks, Sarah D. 2021. "Is the Bottom Falling Out for Readers Who Struggle the Most?" *Education Week,* June 15, 2021. edweek.org/teaching-learning/is-the-bottom-falling-out-for-readers-who-struggle-the-most/2021/06.

Stevens, E. A., M. A. Walker, and S. Vaughn. 2017. "The Effects of Reading Fluency Interventions on the Reading Fluency and Reading Comprehension Performance of Elementary Students with Learning Disabilities: A Synthesis of the Research from 2001 to 2014." *Journal of Learning Disabilities* 50 (5): 576–590. doi.org/10.1177/0022219416638028.

Terada, Youki. 2019. "The Science of Drawing and Memory." *Edutopia,* March 14, 2019. edutopia.org/article/science-drawing-and-memory.

Vygotsky, L. S. 1978. *Mind in Society: The Development of Higher Psychological Processes.* Cambridge, MA: Harvard University Press.

Wilkinson, Ian A. G., and Kristin Bourdage. 2021. *Quality Talk about Text: Discussion Practices for Talking and Thinking about Text.* Portsmouth, NH: Heinemann.

Young, Chase, Patricia Durham, Melinda Miller, Timothy V. Rasinski, and Forrest Lane. 2019. "Improving Reading Comprehension with Readers Theater." *Journal of Educational Research* 112 (5): 615–626. doi.org/10.1080/00220671.2019.1649240.

Young, Chase, David Paige, and Timothy V. Rasinski. 2022. *Artfully Teaching the Science of Reading.* New York: Routledge.

Zimmerman, Susan, and Ellin O. Keene. 2007. *Mosaic of Thought.* Portsmouth, NH: Heinemann.

Zutell, Jerry, and Timothy V. Rasinski. 1991. "Training Teachers to Attend to Their Students' Oral Reading Fluency." *Theory into Practice* 30 (3): 211–217.

Word Ladders Answer Key

"The Nature of Nature"
(page 84)

1. listen
2. glisten
3. list
4. last
5. laser
6. lace
7. lack
8. luck
9. lock
10. look

"The Blue Whale" (page 87)

1. whale
2. whole
3. hole
4. home
5. hope
6. hoe
7. hue
8. true
9. clue
10. blue

"Hummingbird" (page 90)

1. hardly
2. hard
3. hare
4. hear
5. heap
6. reap
7. rear
8. bear
9. beard
10. heard

"Octopus" (page 93)

1. escape
2. cape
3. care
4. car
5. war
6. wart
7. part
8. tart
9. start
10. artist

"The Book or the Snake"
(page 96)

1. snake
2. stake
3. take
4. lake
5. bake
6. rake
7. brake
8. break
9. brook
10. book

"The Lizard Catcher" (page 99)

1. mother
2. moth
3. math
4. mash
5. mass
6. moss
7. mess
8. miss
9. mission
10. permission

"A Mosquito" (page 102)

1. mosquitoes
2. quit
3. quip
4. ship
5. shape
6. shame
7. shade
8. share
9. hare
10. hate

"Desert" (page 105)

1. desert
2. dessert
3. deer
4. dear
5. fear
6. clear
7. ear
8. hear
9. heart
10. heat

"Rain Forest" (page 108)

1. monsoons
2. soon
3. spoon
4. spool
5. pool
6. cool
7. cost
8. coast
9. roast
10. roar

"Winter in the Mountains"
(page 111)

1. blueberries
2. blue
3. true
4. clue
5. club
6. tub
7. stub
8. sub
9. scrub
10. cubs

"Making the World a Better Place" (page 122)

1. speak
2. peak
3. pea
4. pet
5. pit
6. fit
7. fir
8. fur
9. four
10. our
11. out

"The Crow" (page 127)

1. crow
2. cow
4. row
4. rot
5. rat
6. tar
7. art
8. tart
9. start
10. smart

"There's More to a Worm"
(page 131)

1. worm
2. warm
3. war
4. wear
5. pear
6. bear
7. hear
8. heat
9. heart
10. earth

"The Sea Bear" (page 135)

1. bear
2. bare
3. bale
4. gale
5. tale
6. stale
7. stole
8. sole
9. solar
10. polar

"The Storyteller" (page 139)

1. teller
2. taller
3. tale
4. stale
5. sale
6. sole
7. sore
8. shore
9. store
10. story

"The First Cave Artist"
(page 143)

1. artist
2. start
3. stare
4. spare
5. space
6. race
7. brace
8. brave
9. crave
10. cave

"Was There a Real Alice?"
(page 147)

1. land
2. lad
3. law
4. low
5. glow
6. grow
7. grown
8. crown
9. drown
10. wonder

"Climate Strike" (page 151)

1. global
2. goal
3. foal
4. fowl
5. owl
6. low
7. law
8. raw
9. war
10. warning
11. warming

"How Old Do You Have to Be?" (page 156)

1. change
2. chance
3. chant
4. can't
5. pant
6. want
7. wart
8. ward
9. word
10. world

"Who Wants to Make Life Better?" (page 160)

1. space
2. spice
3. slice
4. lice
5. lace
6. lake
7. lane
8. pane
9. cane
10. came
11. camp

"And What Can We Conclude?" (page 171)

1. butter
2. batter
3. bat
4. bet
5. beet
6. beat
7. treat
8. tree
9. flee
10. fly

"What the Bumblebee Doesn't Know" (page 174)

1. bumble
2. tumble
3. stumble
4. stub
5. stab
6. tab
7. tag
8. bag
9. beg
10. bee

"The Grass and the Butterfly" (page 177)

1. down
2. own
3. brown
4. brow
5. grow
6. crow
7. cow
8. cot
9. cost
10. coast

"Don't Forget" (page 181)

1. chameleon
2. melon
3. melt
4. belt
5. bell
6. best
7. beast
8. feast
9. fest
10. forest

"Down the Fence Row" (page 186)

1. weed
2. seed
3. deed
4. dead
5. deal
6. seal
7. meal
8. mole
9. mile
10. milk

"Rolling" (page 189)

1. roll
2. toll
3. tall
4. talk
5. balk
6. back
7. buck
8. duck
9. dock
10. down

"The Stream" (page 193)

1. rain
2. main
3. maid
4. mad
5. mat
6. mate
7. tame
8. team
9. seam
10. sea

"Tiger" (page 196)

1. tiger
2. tire
3. fire
4. fir
5. fur
6. far
7. car
8. scar
9. scab
10. cab
11. cub

"Milkweed and Monarchs" (page 200)

1. weed
2. wed
3. wet
4. went
5. bent
6. beat
7. meat
8. meal
9. male
10. mile
11. milk

"Your Eyes" (page 204)

1. chimpanzee
2. champ
3. chap
4. chat
5. hat
6. hate
7. late
8. lane
9. line
10. feline
11. recline

"Is That Really You?" (page 215)

1. copy
2. cozy
3. coy
4. joy
5. jolly
6. jelly
7. bell
8. ball
9. bat
10. cat

"Spring, Summer, Fall, Winter" (page 219)

1. four
2. fur
3. far
4. tar
5. tear
6. team
7. steam
8. tea
9. sea
10. seasons

"More Bees, Please" (page 224)

1. worker
2. wore
3. worm
4. warm
5. harm
6. charm
7. chap
8. chop
9. crop
10. drop
11. drone

"There Are Dogs, and There Are Dogs" (page 228)

1. Chihuahua
2. chin
3. chip
4. chili
5. chill
6. hill
7. pill
8. spill
9. still
10. stiff
11. mastiff

"It All Depends on Who You Are" (page 233)

1. owl
2. howl
3. chow
4. chop
5. hop
6. mop
7. map
8. man
9. mane
10. mine
11. mice

"I'm Thinking about It" (page 237)

1. procrastinator
2. illustrator
3. motor
4. meter
5. meet
6. meat
7. neat
8. near
9. earn
10. learner

"Climbing Back" (page 241)

1. world
2. word
3. weird
4. wild
5. mild
6. mile
7. pile
8. pine
9. fine
10. fife
11. life

"A Nation's Symbol"
(page 246)

1. eagle
2. gale
3. tale
4. tail
5. mail
6. mall
7. tall
8. wall
9. ball
10. bald

"The Nature of Zoos"
(page 251)

1. animals
2. mail
3. sail
4. fail
5. fall
6. fill
7. still
8. chill
9. chili
10. child
11. wild

"What Does an Eel Have for Breakfast?" (page 256)

1. omnivore
2. venom
3. move
4. mope
5. hope
6. rope
7. rove
8. rave
9. crave
10. carve
11. carnivore

Index

Digital Resources

Accessing the Digital Resources

The digital resources can be downloaded by following these steps:

1. Go to **www.tcmpub.com/digital**

2. Use the 13-digit ISBN number to redeem the digital resources.

3. Respond to the question using the book.

4. Follow the prompts on the Content Cloud website to sign in or create a new account.

5. The content redeemed will appear on your My Content screen. Click on the product to look through the digital resources. All file resources are available for download. Select files can be previewed, opened, and shared. Any web-based content, such as videos, links, or interactive text, can be viewed and used in the browser but is not available for download.

For questions and assistance, please contact Teacher Created Materials.

email: customerservice@tcmpub.com

phone: 800-858-7339

Contents of the Digital Resources

The digital resources include templates for the student activity pages in this book.